D0927572

INTERPRETING BONHOEFFER

INTERPRETING BONHOEFFER

HISTORICAL PERSPECTIVES, EMERGING ISSUES

CLIFFORD J. GREEN AND GUY C. CARTER, EDITORS

Fortress Press
Minneapolis

INTERPRETING BONHOEFFER

Historical Perspectives, Emerging Issues

Copyright © 2013 Fortress Press. All rights reserved. Except for brief quotations in critical articles or reviews, no part of this book may be reproduced in any manner without prior written permission from the publisher. Visit http://www.augsburgfortress.org/copyrights/ or write to Permissions, Augsburg Fortress, Box 1209, Minneapolis, MN 55440.

Scripture quotations are from the New Revised Standard Version Bible, copyright © 1989 by the Division of Christian Education of the National Council of the Churches of Christ in the USA. Used by permission. All rights reserved.

Cover image: bpk, Berlin / Staatsbibliothek zu Berlin / Art Resource, NY

Cover design: Alisha Lofgren

Library of Congress Cataloging-in-Publication Data

Print ISBN: 978-1-4514-6541-9

eBook ISBN: 978-1-4514-6964-6

The paper used in this publication meets the minimum requirements of American National Standard for Information Sciences — Permanence of Paper for Printed Library Materials, ANSI Z329.48-1984.

Manufactured in the U.S.A.

This book was produced using PressBooks.com, and PDF rendering was done by PrinceXML.

In Memoriam Hans Pfeifer

Hans Pfeifer wrote one of the earliest Bonhoeffer dissertations, and attended the first International Bonhoeffer Congress in Düsseldorf-Kaiserswerth in 1971. There the International Bonhoeffer Society was founded, and Hans became the second Secretary of the German Section of the Society. More recently he served on the German Editorial Board of the Dietrich Bonhoeffer Werke, and was the chief editor of DBW 9, The Young Bonhoeffer. *Especially important was his role as the liaison between the German board and the Editorial Board of the Dietrich Bonhoeffer Works English Edition, to which he made an essential contribution. Together with Christian Gremmels, Hans Pfeifer was a founding editor of the* Dietrich Bonhoeffer Jahrbuch. *This reflected his commitment to research, scholarship, and authentic interpretation, so that Pfeifer's writings are read with worldwide respect. As an ordained minister Hans Pfeifer served as a pastor in congregations and as a high school teacher. Highly respected as a scholar, Hans Pfeifer was equally valued as a colleague and a friend. To truly remember and honor him is to be committed to the high standards of scholarship that he embodied.*

CONTENTS

PART II. EMERGING ISSUES OF INTERPRETATION

D. New Research in Text and Context

E. New Theological Issues and Interpretations

Epilogue

Afterword

Editors' Foreword

Clifford J. Green and Guy C. Carter

The time is ripe for a synoptic assessment of Dietrich Bonhoeffer. As we near the seventieth anniversary of his death in 1945, his popularity has never been greater. Yet one could argue that he is simultaneously the most quoted and the most misinterpreted Christian theologian of the twentieth century. This volume, under the broad rubric *Interpreting Bonhoeffer*, presents leading Bonhoeffer scholars addressing the multifaceted challenge of understanding and conveying to later generations a sophisticated Christian thinker and courageous historical actor from the traumatic mid-twentieth century.

The publication of this volume closely corresponds to the publication of the final volume of the sixteen-volume complete works, the Dietrich Bonhoeffer Works English Edition. That everything is now in English makes it not only possible, but also necessary, that we read Bonhoeffer the man and Bonhoeffer the theologian *whole*. The time is past when one could credibly extrapolate a theology from a few phrases plucked from his provocative *Letters and Papers from Prison*. No longer can one tear a few sentences from their historical and intellectual context to deploy in an argument about a contemporary war or some other contested ethical or political issue. Nor is it legitimate to project the preferences and prejudices of competing religious parties onto Bonhoeffer by interpreting all of his theology through one of his influential books, *Discipleship*, for example, or his prison letters and *Ethics*. Respect for the man, respect for truth, and responsibility to future generations require more patience, more honesty, and more effort to truly understand the legacy of Dietrich Bonhoeffer.

These sentiments informed the conference "Bonhoeffer for the Coming Generations" that was held at Union Theological Seminary, New York City, in November 2011. The international participants were invited to commemorate the Dietrich Bonhoeffer Works English Edition (DBWE) and also the Bonhoeffer Lectures in Public Ethics. Both undertakings date their beginnings to the mid-eighties. The year 1986 saw the publication of the first volume of the German Dietrich Bonhoeffer Werke (DBW), the critical edition on which the English scholarly edition rests. About the same time, thanks to the initiatives of Helmut Reihlen, Berlin, and Donald Shriver, then President of

Union Theological Seminary, the Bonhoeffer Chair in Theology and Ethics was planned and later inaugurated at Union, together with a Scholar Exchange program between Germany and North America, and the annual Bonhoeffer Lectures in Public Ethics. These lectures are held in alternating years in Germany and North America, and are devoted to major public issues addressed in light of Bonhoeffer's legacy. Initially the American Bonhoeffer lectures were held at Union; in the past decade they have also been held in other cities such as Washington, D.C., and Minneapolis. Typical subjects have been: universal human rights; guilt and reconciliation in politics; economic justice; solidarity and women's wisdom; race and reparations; medical ethics and the value of human life; world poverty and moral responsibility; peace; genocide; and state and church.

This rich tradition of over two decades of scholarly work on the Bonhoeffer Works editions, and of engagement with critical issues of ethics and public life, was expressed in the conference "Bonhoeffer for the Coming Generations." Invited speakers represented Asia, Africa, and Latin America, as well as Europe and North America. Papers were presented by younger scholars as well as seasoned veterans. Because of the very intentional focus of the conference planning, an unusual coherence around aspects of interpretation was the outcome, and is evident in the chapters that follow.

While the volume has two main parts, the content of the book is organized under five themes dealing with various aspects of Bonhoeffer interpretation: public ethics in six different countries; the perspective of translators; the work of historians; new research in Bonhoeffer's texts and biography; and new issues and interpretations by theologians. The conference program proceed as follows.

The first day of the conference, and the first part of this book, was inspired by the Bonhoeffer Lectures in Public Ethics. While these lectures have been held to date in Germany and the United States, the influence of Bonhoeffer's legacy of ethical thinking and personal acting can be found in Christian communities worldwide. So, the first chapters begin with examples of how the Bonhoeffer legacy has engaged issues of public life in Germany, Britain, and the United States, and then move to the distinctive challenges faced during the last half-century in the widely different cultural, religious, and political situations of South Africa, Brazil, and Japan.

The second day of the conference commemorated the Dietrich Bonhoeffer Works English Edition, proleptically celebrating its completion in 2013, when the last of the sixteen volumes, *Theological Education at Finkenwalde* (volume 14), will be published. The present book therefore moves the theme of interpretation to focus on the art of translation, with chapters from two of the project's translators. They are introduced, as it were, by a chapter from the person who straddled both languages as the liaison between the German and English editorial boards, Hans Pfeifer.

The language expertise of translators inevitably requires historical sophistication. Historians have naturally been deeply involved in Bonhoeffer scholarship, given the momentous times of his life and the complexity of some of the issues it involved, for example, the conspiracy against Hitler, and the contradictory ways that different parts of the German church responded to the National Socialist regime. One prominent interest of historians has been Bonhoeffer's contested relationship to the Jews, and the pertinence of his theology to Christian-Jewish relations after the Holocaust. All these matters of interpretation appear in the chapters by historians. And readers will find the historians regularly puncturing common tendencies to oversimplify, to mythologize, and to heroize Bonhoeffer and the Confessing Church in popular biographies—even worse, attempts to paint him as the patron saint of their ideological causes.

In Part 2, the latter part of the book, the interpretive work of theologians comes to the fore. It is probably possible to understand, appreciate, and interpret the systems of some theologians relatively independently of their historical circumstances; one thinks of Paul Tillich, for example. Not so with Bonhoeffer, for much of his theology and ethics was forged in engagement with theological antagonists in the church as well as with the doctrines and policies of Nazi politics. Yet Bonhoeffer's theology is not an epiphenomenon of the church struggle and resistance to Nazism. A thinker of the first order, whose often subtle intellectual decisions and distinctions are overlooked by fascination with the drama of his life, his theological and ethical thinking must be examined in its own integrity. Thus the chapters in the section on "New Research in Text and Context" are devoted to close readings of two of his most influential texts, *Discipleship* and *Ethics*; to a detailed reflection on the influence on him of the Harlem Renaissance; and to a comparison of his understanding of the "church for others" with Paul's critique of empire. Each of these brings forth new research, particularly from younger scholars.

The final section of the book addresses three intra-theological topics. Chapter 18 analyzes how Bonhoeffer's Christology is to be interpreted in societies characterized by religious pluralism. Chapter 19 introduces a key aspect of Bonhoeffer's methodology to show how his theological concept of "person" clarifies his agreement and disagreement with Karl Barth. And Chapter 20 proposes that Bonhoeffer's understanding of worldly Christianity, from his dissertation to his prison letters, is a quest for a new Christian paradigm.

The Epilogue actually began the conference as a keynote address. It is chiefly a meditation on the theme of "being with," first articulated by Bonhoeffer as a mark of the church in *Sanctorum Communio*, and here presented as a corrective, perhaps, to the overuse of his theme—also found in the same place—of "being for," as in Jesus "the man for others" and the life of the church as "being for others."

The conference, and its commemoration of the Dietrich Bonhoeffer Works English Edition and the Bonhoeffer Lectures in Public Ethics, was honored by the presence of the German Consul General in New York, Busso von Alvensleben. His speech at the closing banquet is presented as the Afterword.

The Editors wish to express special thanks to Professor Christiane Tietz, President of the International Bonhoeffer Society in the Federal Republic of Germany and Professor of Systematic Theology at the University of Zurich, for her initial encouragement to undertake this book project immediately following the November 2011 Conference "Bonhoeffer for the Coming Generations," as well as for her help in exploring ways and means to realize this project. Sincere thanks go as well to Fortress Press, which continues to be not only a publisher but a friend of the Dietrich Bonhoeffer Works English Edition and of so very many works by and about Dietrich Bonhoeffer in English translation. To the learned contributors in whom the international impact of Dietrich Bonhoeffer's life and thought is mirrored, we extend our greetings of thanks and congratulations for their part in this effort.

Abbreviations

DARB *Dictionary of American Religious Biography*, ed. Henry Warner Bowden. Westport, CT: Greenwood, 1977.

DB-ER Eberhard Bethge, *Dietrich Bonhoeffer: A Biography*. Revised edition, edited by Victoria J. Barnett. Minneapolis: Fortress Press, 1999.

DBW *Dietrich Bonhoeffer Werke*. Gütersloh: Chr. Kaiser / Gütersloher Verlagshaus, 1986–99.

DBWE *Dietrich Bonhoeffer Works*. Wayne Whitson Floyd Jr., Victoria J. Barnett, Barbara Wojhoski, general editors. 16 vols. Minneapolis: Fortress Press, 1996–2013.

DBWE 1: *Sanctorum Communio: A Theological Study of the Sociology of the Church*. Edited by Clifford J. Green. Translated by Reinhard Krauss and Nancy Lukens. Minneapolis: Fortress Press, 1998.

DBWE 2: *Act and Being: Transcendental Philosophy and Ontology in Systematic Theology*. Edited by Wayne Whitson Floyd Jr. Translated by H. Martin Rumscheidt. Minneapolis: Fortress Press, 1996.

DBWE 3: *Creation and Fall: A Theological Exposition of Genesis 1–3*. Edited by John W. de Gruchy. Translated by Douglas Stephen Bax. Minneapolis: Fortress Press, 1997.

DBWE 4: *Discipleship*. Edited by Geffrey B. Kelly and John D. Godsey. Translated by Barbara Green and Reinhard Krauss. Minneapolis: Fortress Press, 2001.

DBWE 5: *Life Together* and *Prayerbook of the Bible*. Edited by Geffrey B. Kelly. Translated by Daniel W. Bloesch and James H. Burtness. Minneapolis: Fortress Press, 1996.

DBWE 6: *Ethics*. Edited by Clifford J. Green. Translated by Reinhard Krauss and Charles C. West. Minneapolis: Fortress Press, 2005.

DBWE 7: *Fiction from Tegel Prison*. Edited by Clifford J. Green. Translated by Nancy Lukens. Minneapolis: Fortress Press, 2000.

DBWE 8: *Letters and Papers from Prison*. Edited by John W. de Gruchy. Translated by Lisa E. Dahill, Isabel Best, Reinhard Krauss, Nancy Lukens, Barbara Rumscheidt, and Martin Rumscheidt, with Douglas W. Stott. Minneapolis: Fortress Press, 2010.

DBWE 9: *The Young Bonhoeffer 1918–1927.* Edited by Paul Duane Matheny, Clifford J. Green, and Marshall D. Johnson. Translated by Mary C. Nebelsick with assistance of Douglas W. Stott. Minneapolis: Fortress Press, 2002.

DBWE 10: *Barcelona, Berlin, New York: 1928–1931.* Edited by Clifford J. Green. Translated by Douglas W. Stott. Minneapolis: Fortress Press, 2008.

DBWE 11: *Ecumenical, Academic and Pastoral Work: 1931–1932.* Edited by Victoria J. Barnett, Mark S. Brocker, and Michael B. Lukens. Translated by Anne Schmidt-Lange, with Isabel Best, Nicholas Humphrey, and Marion Pauck. Supplementary material translated by Douglas W. Stott. Minneapolis: Fortress Press, 2012.

DBWE 12: *Berlin: 1932–1933.* Edited by Larry L. Rasmussen. Translated by Isabel Best and David Higgins. Supplementary material translated by Douglas W. Stott. Minneapolis: Fortress Press, 2009.

DBWE 13: *London, 1933–1935.* Edited by Keith Clements. Translated by Isabel Best. Supplementary material translated by Douglas W. Stott. Minneapolis: Fortress Press, 2007.

DBWE 14: *Theological Education at Finkenwalde: 1935–1937.* Edited by H. Gaylon Barker and Mark S. Brocker. Translated by Douglas W. Stott. Minneapolis: Fortress Press, 2013.

DBWE 15: *Theological Education Underground: 1937–1940.* Edited by Victoria J. Barnett. Translated by Claudia D. Bergmann, Peter Frick, and Scott A. Moore. Supplementary material translated by Douglas W. Stott. Minneapolis: Fortress Press, 2011.

DBWE 16: *Conspiracy and Imprisonment 1940–1945.* Edited by Mark S. Brocker. Translated by Lisa E. Dahill. Supplementary material translated by Douglas W. Stott. Minneapolis: Fortress Press, 2006.

DEK *Deutsche Evangelische Kirche (Reichskirche)*

EKD *Evangelische Kirche in Deutschland*

RGG *Religion in Geschichte und Gegenwart. Handwörterbuch für Theologie und Religionswissenschaft.* Tübingen: Mohr Siebeck, 1909–2007

1st edition, ed. Friedrich Michael Schiele and Leopold Zscharnack with cooperation of Hermann Gunkel and Otto Scheel, 1909–13.

2nd edition, ed. Hermann Gunkel and Leopold Zscharnack, 1927–32.

3rd edition, ed. Kurt Galling and Hans von Campenhausen, 1957–65.

4th edition, ed. Hans D. Betz, Don S. Browning, Bernd Janowski, and Eberhard Jüngel, 1998–2007.

Editions indicated by superscript in citation.

PART I

Interpretation from Historical Perspectives

A. Bonhoeffer and Public Ethics in Six Nations, 1945–2010

Inspiration, Controversy, Legacy: Responses to Dietrich Bonhoeffer in Three Germanys

Wolfgang Huber

I have been invited to present the German case for the influence of Dietrich Bonhoeffer on public ethics. As a German myself, I may seem an obvious choice to interpret Bonhoeffer's influence from a German perspective. But there is an enormous difference between Bonhoeffer's time, ending in 1945, and the later contexts of the responses to his life and work. It is true that Dietrich Bonhoeffer cannot be read ahistorically, but this is equally true for the reception of his work. The way Bonhoeffer's legacy was used in different contexts depended on the respective social circumstances, political developments, and ecclesial preconditions.

Our reflection on Bonhoeffer's influence on public ethics begins with the German case. But there is not a single German case; there are at least three. The response to Dietrich Bonhoeffer in Germany took place in three different arenas. That is due to the political history of Germany after the end of the Nazi regime and the liberation of Germany as well as Europe from the terror of violence and war that originated in Germany, followed by the division not only of this country but of Europe. There were quite different conditions and ways in which Bonhoeffer's theology was received and interpreted after 1945 in the two parts of Germany, the (old) Federal Republic of Germany in the West and the (former) German Democratic Republic in the East, the one belonging to the political alliance of western democratic countries under the leadership of the United States of America, the other forming a part of the Warsaw Pact under the leadership of the Soviet Union. Now for some twenty years, since 1989/90, we have another Germany—a third Germany—after the opening of the wall on November 9, 1989 and the reunification of the country eleven months later.

But even such a distinction between three Germanys includes many problematic simplifications. The predominant challenge for such an approach consists in the fact that the response to Dietrich Bonhoeffer's life and work took place from the very beginning in an international framework. In the immediate aftermath of his death as a conspirator and martyr his role was interpreted internationally. Those who heard about him in the first years after the end of World War II had to listen to voices like that of the American theologian Reinhold Niebuhr, the Anglican bishop of Chichester George Bell from Great Britain, or the General Secretary of the emerging World Council of Churches, the Dutch theologian Willem Visser 't Hooft. It was in the first instance his personal life story that made Dietrich Bonhoeffer an international figure. His two visits to Union Theological Seminary, in 1930/31 and 1939, played an outstanding role in the international formation of this theologian. But his time as a vicar in Barcelona, his years as a pastor in London, his visits to Sweden or Switzerland, and his participation in many ecumenical conferences in different countries also contributed their part. His plan to visit Mahatma Gandhi in India shows in a nutshell the global perspective in which he understood what we call today public ethics. After 1945 his work therefore found a worldwide resonance and has always had an international dimension. The present discussion will surely give some evidence for that. I shall restrict myself to just one example in this connection, the fact that the very latest piece of research on Bonhoeffer's peace ethics that has come to my attention was written by a theologian from Rwanda who presented his investigation as a doctoral dissertation at a German university.[1]

My first impulse is to say that public ethics in Dietrich Bonhoeffer's sense has to be put in an international perspective and cannot be limited to a national horizon. Or, to quote Carl-Friedrich von Weizsäcker, Bonhoeffer understood *oecumene* "in its original sense as the whole earth populated by human beings," and "as a modern person he could breathe only with difficulty in the provincialism which he found around himself."[2]

However, the following observations concentrate on the impact of Bonhoeffer's theology for public ethics in the three Germanys after 1945. I shall

1. Pascal Bataringaya, "Impulse der Friedensethik Dietrich Bonhoeffers," doctoral dissertation, University of Bochum, 2011.

2. Carl-Friedrich von Weizsäcker, "Thoughts of a Non-Theologian on Dietrich Bonhoeffer's Theological Development," *The Ecumenical Review* 28, no. 2 (April 1976): 156–73.

set aside other vivid debates on his theology, for instance on his Christological concentration, on his ethical concept in general, or on his idea of a nonreligious interpretation of biblical concepts—to name only these three. Some of these issues I addressed on other occasions. I choose only three examples for this specific look at Bonhoeffer and public ethics, namely resistance, peace, and the church for others.

BONHOEFFER'S RECEPTION IN A DIVIDED GERMANY

My retrospective examination of Bonhoeffer's role in public ethics begins with the insight that his influence, from the very beginning, is predominantly not based on his theoretical concepts but on his personal example.[3] His decision to risk his life for a future in peace and justice, and his death as a martyr only a few weeks before the end of Hitler's dictatorship, made him an example of a responsible life in difficult times. His relevance for public ethics relates first of all to his importance as a role model. To trust in God and to act responsibly in the real world are the two basic elements of a way of life that inspired people to follow Bonhoeffer's example under quite different circumstances.

It has to be seen under this perspective that the fragments of *Ethics*, published by Eberhard Bethge already in 1949, and the *Letters and Papers from Prison*, published in 1951, found a completely different resonance. It was the German title "Resistance and Submission" (*Widerstand und Ergebung*) that was formative for the picture of Dietrich Bonhoeffer for at least two decades. Key quotations from this book were characteristic for the public posture of persons who tried to transfer Bonhoeffer's example into their private and public life. "By powers of good so wondrously protected, // we wait with confidence, befall what may. // God is with us at night and in the morning // and oh, most certainly on each new day" became characteristic for the dimension of submission to God's will and of trust in his guidance.[4] "Not always doing and daring what's random, but seeking the right thing, // Hover not over the possible, but boldly reach for the real" can be seen as one of the key sentences for the preparedness to address the real challenges of the present time.[5]

However, the term "resistance" created trouble. For a remarkably long time the step from Christian witness to political resistance was seen by people in positions of political responsibility, and even more by church officials, as highly

3. Cf. Christian Gremmels and Hans Pfeifer, eds., *Theologie und Biographie. Zum Beispiel Dietrich Bonhoeffer* (München: Chr. Kaiser, 1983).

4. *Letters and Papers from Prison*, DBWE 8:550.

5. Ibid., 513.

ambiguous. Although the inner legitimacy of the new democracy on West-German soil depended to a high degree on the courage (and the failure) of the conspirators of July 20, 1944, it took several years until the Federal Republic of Germany officially recognized the conspirators as precursors of this new democracy. And only then could a discussion start on the question whether or not all their convictions really met democratic standards. Disobedience against political authorities, and the decision to break the military oath, were mostly understood as incompatible with the duties of a citizen, and even more with the obligations of a military person. It took therefore a remarkably long time until the judgments against the conspirators were withdrawn or the deserters in World War II were vindicated.

Theology was a little bit quicker than the general public in this regard. As early as 1952 the two Protestant theologians Ernst Wolf and Hans-Joachim Iwand presented a memorandum in the context of the "Remer Trial" on the legitimacy of political resistance, including so-called tyrannicide.[6] These two representatives of Lutheran theology, who were at the same time inspired by the theology of Karl Barth, used the examples of Dietrich Bonhoeffer and the Norwegian Lutheran Bishop Eivind Berggrav to present the duty of every individual Christian to resist, if necessary even including violent means, in cases of an absolute perversion of the state, or in the case of duties based on justice that follow from obligations toward one's neighbor. That statement stood clearly in opposition to the official concept of the Protestant churches in remembering the victims of Nazism. The official politics of commemoration separated Christian martyrdom very clearly from political resistance. Martyrs in this sense were only those persons who did not suffer "because they disagreed with the politics of the Third Reich . . . but only and alone because they were convinced that the confession of the church was attacked."[7] It was therefore unusual and an important breakthrough at the same time, when Wolf and Iwand argued in 1952 for the legitimacy of tyrannicide on theological grounds.

Two years later the President of the Federal Republic of Germany, Theodor Heuss, expressed his respect for the German Resistance on the occasion of the tenth anniversary of July 20, 1944.[8] That was a time in which

6. Hans-Joachim Iwand and Ernst Wolf, "Entwurf eines Gutachtens zur Frage des Widerstandsrechts nach evangelischer Lehre," in *Junge Kirche* 13 (1952): 192–201 (cf. Hans-Richard Reuter, "Widerstands-recht. Ethisch," in RGG⁴ 8:1525–27.

7. Bernhard Heinrich Forck, *Und folget ihrem Glauben nach* (Stuttgart, 1949), 7.

8. Cf. Theodor Heuss, "Dank und Bekenntnis," in *Bekenntnis und Verpflichtung. Reden zur 10-jährigen Wiederkehr des 20. Juli 1944* (Stuttgart: Vorwerk, 1955), 9–21. The preface to this volume ends as follows: "The lectures and essays contained here give an account of the diverse aspects of the 20th

Letters and Papers from Prison were not yet published in East Germany. The book appeared there only in 1957, six years after its publication in the West. The hesitation of the censors was due to the prominent place of resistance already in the title of the book.[9] The East-German theologian Christoph Haufe functioned as an expert for the censors. He warned that the politics of the church in East Germany could also be treated under the heading of "Resistance and Submission" (*Widerstand und Ergebung*). It was exactly the time in which the state attacked young Christians, put them in prison, and tried to discourage them as much as possible. Christoph Haufe feared that people could regard the situation in which Bonhoeffer had written as parallel to the actual situation in the German Democratic Republic. The censors were not as fearful as this theologian. They thought that readers could distinguish between Nazi Germany and the communist regime of those days. From then onwards it was more or less obligatory in the GDR to call Bonhoeffer's resistance "antifascist" and to use the phrase "antifascist resistance" as often as possible in order to underline that there was no comparison possible between the first and the second dictatorship on German soil. The hope was that it would become self-evident that there was no reason to draw connections between Bonhoeffer's attitude toward the Nazi regime and the question of political responsibility in the system of the so-called "really existing socialism" of the GDR.

In West-Germany, Bonhoeffer's example was from time to time used in the context of civil disobedience as a means of political demonstration on moral grounds. That contributed to a perspective that even gained additional importance in the third, the united Germany. Now Bonhoeffer's actual contributions to an ethic of responsibility play the central role in the reception of his public ethics. Not an assumed heroism of our actions, but the question of how a future generation can live, that is decisive. This is shown in our days by the contrast between global poverty on the one hand and the irrationalities of global financial markets on the other, or by the great challenges of climate change, demographic development, and new forms of collective and individual

of July 1944. Their commonality lies in an unrestricted confession concerning the deed and attitude of the 20th of July 1944. Today as well, the position one takes toward this event is the touchstone for discerning the spirits when it comes to the building up of our life in state and society" (translation GCC). The volume includes the text of Eberhard Bethge, "Die deckungslose Tat," [deed without a cover], 121–23. Cf. G. R. Ueberschaer, *Der 20. Juli 1944. Bewertung und Rezeption des deutschen Widerstandes gegen das NS-Regime* (Cologne, 1994).

9. Cf. Wolf Krötke, "Der zensierte Bonhoeffer. Zu einem schwierigen Kapitel der Theologiegeschichte in der DDR," in *Zeitschrift für Theologie und Kirche* 92 (2013): 329–56, esp. 332f.

violence. It is to the credit of the Dietrich Bonhoeffer Lectures on both sides of the Atlantic that they took up many of those new issues and perspectives.

PEACE ETHICS

To speak about Dietrich Bonhoeffer's public ethics under the perspective of resistance, as I have been doing, means to look at these ethics from the end, from his involvement in the conspiracy against Hitler's tyranny. An awareness of public ethics came only later in the young Bonhoeffer. Whereas Bonhoeffer's political ethics can be described as a process from pacifism to resistance, the process of reception went the other way around: from resistance to pacifism.

That was due to the fact that the peace problem gained growing awareness in central Europe in the times of Cold War and the arms race between East and West. Here I cannot describe in detail the stages of peace ethics and peace initiatives within the churches in Germany—East and West—after the end of World War II. In Germany the debates on remilitarization in the early fifties and on nuclear armament in the late fifties, then the debate on conscientious objection in the West, and the situation of the so-called "construction troops"[10] in the East, and from the early seventies onwards the hot debate on the deployment of new nuclear missiles—all these were some phases of this debate.

Bonhoeffer's early peace ethics started with his new awareness of the Sermon on the Mount in 1932 and culminated in his contributions to the Fanø Conference in 1934. During the arms race debate of the seventies and eighties they gained growing importance for the Peace Movement in the East as well as in the West of Germany. Again and again the words from Bonhoeffer's address to the Fanø Conference were quoted: "Who will call us to peace so that the world will hear, will have to hear? . . . Only the one great Ecumenical Council of the Holy Church of Christ over all the world can speak out so that the world, though it gnash its teeth, will have to hear, so that the peoples will rejoice because the Church of Christ in the name of Christ has taken the weapons from the hands of their sons, forbidden war, and proclaimed the peace of Christ against the raging world."[11] In these peace debates Dietrich Bonhoeffer's voice gained growing public importance—and that meant the voice of a theologian whose breakthrough to the biblical word was not related

---

10. Alleged penal battalions of the "German People's Army" (*Deutsche Volksarmee*) into which those who failed to have their petitions as conscientious objectors approved were remanded.

11. Bonhoeffer, *London 1933–1935*, DBWE 13:309.

to the highly intellectual text of St. Paul's letter to the Romans, but had its basis in the "unbearable-gracious simplicity of the Sermon on the Mount."[12]

It was in the spirit of Dietrich Bonhoeffer that young people in the GDR started in the early eighties to wear the sign "swords into plowshares" on their jackets, briefcases, or backpacks. The symbol represented the prophetic saying in Isaiah and Micah: "They shall beat their swords into plowshares, and their spears into pruning hooks: nation shall not lift up sword against nation, neither shall they learn war anymore."[13] The symbol for the prophetic vision of peace that the young people had on their jackets, briefcases, or backpacks was taken from a sculpture of the Soviet artist Yevgeni Vuchetich that is located in front of the United Nations building in New York. The governing party in the East, the Socialist Unity Party of Germany,[14] charged the bearers of the symbol with an "undifferentiated pacifism." The intention of this reproach was easy to understand: The military armament of the Warsaw treaty states had to be described as a service of peace, whereas the military armament of Western states had to be seen as a preparation for war; therefore the only acceptable position was to affirm the nuclear armament of the East and to criticize only and alone the parallel efforts of the West. Again the critical point was whether or not it was permitted to apply the impulses of Dietrich Bonhoeffer to the situation in the GDR itself.

The controversy in the Federal Republic was different as far as freedom of expression was concerned. Big manifestations of the peace movement, partly in combination with large assemblies of the German Protestant Kirchentag, brought the dangers of nuclear armament on both sides to public awareness. The Sermon on the Mount was printed in full-length in the pages of a daily newspaper. The controversy referred in this case to the question, whether a pacifist position based on the Sermon on the Mount reflected only an ethic of conviction that did not take into account the real challenges of the time and was not sufficiently aware of the consequences of its proposals, namely a unilateral or a gradual disarmament instead of a "balance of power," realized in the form of a continuing nuclear arms race. The debate continues today, whether the criticism of the arms race of the seventies and eighties, or whether the decision to counterbalance the military efforts of the other side, contributed more to the end of this kind of military confrontation—an end joyfully reached with the fall of the Berlin Wall in 1989.

12. Von Weizsäcker, "Thoughts of a Non-Theologian," 41.

13. Micah 4:3.

14. *Sozialistische Einheitspartei Deutschlands*, commonly abbreviated as *SED*.

But one point is not controversial. This whole debate, inspired to a high degree by Dietrich Bonhoeffer, especially by his vision of the "great Ecumenical Council," led to the conciliar process for justice, peace, and the integrity of creation that dominated the exchange on public ethics ecumenically and internationally from 1983 until 1989/90. The initiative for this process was due to a great extent to the participants from the GDR at the General Assembly of the World Council of Churches in Vancouver in 1983. But they also brought this initiative back to their own country. There were only few regions on the globe in which this process included as many groups and individuals from the grassroots as in the GDR and—more or less comparably—also in the Federal Republic of Germany. In the GDR this process resulted in the convocations of Magdeburg and Dresden. These assemblies were extremely important precedents for the civil rights groups that had a great impact on the peaceful revolution of 1989. They contributed to an atmosphere in which the Monday prayers in many churches became occasions for free public speech. In different ways the churches created the space for an emerging civil society. Here the democratic transition started around the newly established political parties and round tables. In this way Bonhoeffer's public ethics played a remarkable role in the preparation for the historic change that was witnessed by Europe and the world in 1989 and 1990.

Some optimists thought that the end of the Cold War would also put an end to the big challenges for peace ethics. What an error! Under new circumstances the problem of violence is again on the agenda. Christian peace ethics went through a transformation from an ethics of just war to an ethic of just peace. Bonhoeffer's way from pacifism to resistance included the question for peace ethics after 1990: under which conditions can the use of violence as a last resort be unavoidable to uphold or to restore the rule of law? Whether the "responsibility to protect" can have a place in an ethic of responsibility in Bonhoeffer's sense is one of the great ethical challenges of our times.

CHURCH FOR OTHERS

There is no Christian public ethic without a reflection on the church as the subject of such public ethics. Here again we can observe an inverted process of reception. The church was a major topic of Bonhoeffer's theology from the very beginning. "Christ existing as church-community" was the sign before the brackets right from the time of his first dissertation, his first lectures at the university, and his first reflections on the center of Christian theology, namely the teaching about Jesus Christ himself. But again a broader reception did not start with these early beginnings but with the end, the diagnosis of a religionless time, the program of nonreligious interpretation of biblical concepts and the proclamation of the church for others: "The church is church only when it is there for others."[15]

Albrecht Schönherr, a student of Dietrich Bonhoeffer at Finkenwalde and later my predecessor as Bishop in the Berlin-Brandenburg church, realized very soon the importance of these reflections.[16] For him and many others, Bonhoeffer's anticipation of a religionless time functioned as a kind of model for the situation of the church under the anti-Christian regime of the Socialist Unity Party. What Christians in the GDR experienced in their daily life was for them not a deviation or a wrong track in history but an occasion to live a mature Christian life in the midst of the worldliness of the world. The secular character of the new regime was seen as an anticipation of what would become a general feature of the modern world. Therefore "Resistance and Submission" became a general heading for Christian life in the GDR, and the occasion to live under those conditions could even be seen as a part of God's plan.

But there was an evident ambiguity. The legacy of Dietrich Bonhoeffer encouraged independent criticism as well as it allowed adaptation to given circumstances. State officials could use Dietrich Bonhoeffer symbolically to express their expectation that the church would function as a cultic association that did not interfere with political questions; the so-called CDU theologians[17] could interpret Bonhoeffer in the sense of a two-kingdom doctrine that avoided any practical consequences from the conviction that Christians have to obey God more than human persons.[18] Others—like Heino Falcke—used Bonhoeffer's concept of a "church for others" for the statement that the church stands for an "improvable socialism," because "church for others" means to speak for the silent and the silenced.[19]

---

15. Dietrich Bonhoeffer, *Letters and Papers from Prison*, DBWE 8:503.

16. See already in 1955 Albrecht Schönherr, "Bonhoeffers Gedanken über die Kirche und ihre Predigt in der 'mündig' gewordenen Welt," in *Die Mündige Welt I* (München: Chr. Kaiser, 1955), 76–89.

17. Christian Democratic Union. Such "CDU theologians" might be said to include Gerhard Ebeling, Ulrich Duchrow, and Heinrich Bornkamm, among other Protestant and perhaps most Catholic theologians in Germany today. See Hans-Joachim Gänssler, *Evangelium und weltliches Schwert. Hintergrund, Entstehungsgeschichte und Anlass von Luthers Scheidung zweier Reiche oder Regimente*, Veröffentlichungen des Instituts für europäische Geschichte Mainz, Abteilung für abendländische Religionsgeschichte (Wiesbaden: Franz Steiner, 1983), 155ff.

18. Acts 5:29.

19. Heino Falcke, "Christus befreit—darum Kirche für andere." Referat auf der vierten Tagung der Synode des Bundes der Evangelischen Kirchen in der DDR vom 30.6. bis 4.7. 1972 in Dresden, in Peter Fischer, *Kirche und Christen in der DDR* (Berlin: Holzapfel, 1978), 242–55. It was forbidden to publish Falcke's paper in the GDR.

This kind of advocacy was not appreciated by the governing party and its officials. Immediately after Heino Falcke presented his deliberations in a famous speech before the General Synod of the Federation of Evangelical Churches in the GDR in 1972, the leadership of the church was confronted with the expectation that there would be no public reference to this text in the plenary session of the synod or elsewhere.[20]

For the use of Dietrich Bonhoeffer's interpretation of the public role of the church, these years brought a certain kind of culmination. It was Albrecht Schönherr, who in 1971 interpreted the public role of the church in the GDR with the sentence, that it is "church in the socialist society, not against it, not apart from it." Very quickly this well-balanced formula was simplified into the slogan of a "church in socialism." In consequence, Bonhoeffer's formula of the "church for others" became functional for a submission of the church under the communist regime.

Looking back on the relevance of Dietrich Bonhoeffer for Christian existence in the GDR, Albrecht Schönherr with good reason could summarize: "It is not an expression of arrogance but it belongs to the specific situation of the church in the GDR, when we notice as a fact, that in this church Dietrich Bonhoeffer, from the beginning and continuously until the end, was more heard and taken seriously than in the Federal Republic."[21] His statement is echoed by Klaus Gysi, Secretary of State for ecclesial affairs in the GDR from 1979 until 1988, who said in a retrospective on the course of the GDR and its end: "Without the idea of Bonhoeffer, that the church is present for all . . . it would be impossible to understand what happened after 1979. And most of all the role of the protestant churches in the GDR . . . from 1985 to 1990 cannot be grasped without this idea." The consequence drawn by Gysi as a former public servant of the GDR is even more remarkable. He said in 1993: "The capacity to accompany critically the use of power is the most important learning-experience of the churches in the GDR and therefore the most important duty for the public activity of the churches in Germany."[22]

Such a learning process happened also in the West-German churches, but it did so under much easier conditions. But also those churches went through

---

20. Cf. the reports of Albrecht Schönherr and Heino Falcke on these events in Ernst Feil, ed., *Glauben lernen in einer Kirche für andere. Der Beitrag Dietrich Bonhoeffers zum Christsein in der Deutschen Demokratischen Republik* (Gütersloh: Chr. Kaiser Gütersloher, 1993), 115f.

21. Albrecht Schönherr, "Die Bedeutung Dietrich Bonhoeffers für das Christsein in der DDR," in Ernst Feil, ibid., 40–55.

22. Klaus Gysi, "Meine Begegnung mit einem Schüler Dietrich Bonhoeffers, Albrecht Schönherr," ibid., 76–85.

the ambiguities just explained regarding the example of the churches in the GDR. Also Christians and churches in the West were encouraged by the example of Bonhoeffer to evaluate the use of power critically and to take sides for peace and justice, for reconciliation and solidarity. But to be in the world meant for them often enough practically to be apart from the world.

To look forward to future consequences that have to be drawn from Bonhoeffer's legacy for public ethics means therefore again and again, to read the signs of the times in a way in which the submission to God's will is not mixed up with the simple adaptation to given power structures or the existing misuse of power. The arrogance of power executed by today's financial markets, the blindness of political powers with regard to their responsibility for future generations, the transition to global justice and empowerment of the poor or a sustainable way of production and use of energy are some of the fields, for which we not only have to understand Bonhoeffer's image of a "church for others" in the broader sense of a "church with others," but even more to transform it into the vision of an ecumenical "church for the world."

2

Bonhoeffer and Public Ethics: South Africa Notes

John W. de Gruchy

BONHOEFFER AND THE CHURCH STRUGGLE IN SOUTH AFRICA: 1960–1989

When I first engaged Bonhoeffer's theology in the 1960s and 1970s, the church struggle against apartheid had only begun to gather momentum following the Cottesloe Conference. This event, sponsored by the World Council of Churches in Johannesburg in December 1960, was in response to the Sharpeville Massacre[1] earlier that year. Soon after, Beyers Naudé,[2] disillusioned by the negative reaction to Cottesloe by his own Dutch Reformed Church, launched the Christian Institute, an ecumenical foundation motivated by the vision of a Confessing Church in South Africa. In doing so he was influenced by the *Kirchenkampf* and especially Bonhoeffer's role and witness. Several of us younger theologians came under Naudé's influence, and those familiar with Bonhoeffer's legacy began to see Naudé as the South African equivalent, something affirmed by Eberhard Bethge when he visited South Africa in 1973. The Christian Institute led the church struggle until both it and Naudé were banned by the apartheid government in 1977 following the state murder of the Black Consciousness leader, Steve Biko,[3] and Naudé's public identification with Biko and the Soweto Uprising that Biko inspired.

---

1. Sharpeville Massacre: Outcome of a protest march against the notorious Pass Laws that governed the movement of black South Africans, by members of the Pan African Congress on March 21, 1960. Sixty-seven people were shot dead by the police.

2. Beyers Naudé: Dutch Reformed minister who was defrocked by his church for his opposition to apartheid. He founded the Christian Institute in 1962 and was one of the most prominent Christian anti-apartheid leaders during the next decades.

3. Steve Biko: Founder of the Black Consciousness Movement who was murdered by the Security Police in 1977.

To speak about the church struggle in South Africa that emerged in the 1960s and the influence of Bonhoeffer in the process is somewhat misleading and can be misunderstood. Three qualifications need to be kept in mind. The first is that Bonhoeffer's initial influence was limited to a rather small circle of theologians. The second is that many Christian activists were inspired more by Bonhoeffer's political resistance than by familiarity with his theology. The third is that with few exceptions, Manas Buthelezi[4] and Allan Boesak[5] chief among them (both also influenced by Naudé), Bonhoeffer was not widely known among black Christian theologians or activists.

Black Christians had been engaged in the struggle against colonialism and apartheid long before Cottesloe and the formation of the Christian Institute, and thus well before Bonhoeffer's influence on the South African church struggle. During those early struggles, which reached their climax at Sharpeville in 1960, African Christian witness in the public arena was significant, not least through exercising leadership within the African National Congress[6] and later the Pan African Congress.[7] They already knew what white Christians had yet to learn about Christian resistance to oppression and injustice. Only after Sharpeville and the banning of the liberation movements did white Christians begin to take a leadership role by proxy through the Christian Institute and the South African Council of Churches. But this began to change at the end of the 1960s with the emergence of the Black Consciousness Movement[8] led by Biko and the rise and influence of Black Theology.[9] If Beyers Naudé helped some fellow white Christians to discover the relevance of Bonhoeffer, Biko embodied Bonhoeffer's spirit of resistance and political responsibility in reinvigorating black protest and exerting control of the struggle against apartheid. Bonhoeffer spoke most

4. Manas Buthelezi: Lutheran theologian who worked for the Christian Institute and later became a bishop.

5. Allan Boesak: Minister in the Dutch Reformed Mission Church, was an early exponent of black theology and a charismatic leader in the church struggle against apartheid.

6. African National Congress. Was founded in 1912 to coordinate largely black resistance to segregationist policies in South Africa at the time of the formation of the Union of South Africa. It spearheaded the liberation struggle against apartheid and is currently the governing party in South Africa.

7. Pan African Congress. Splinter movement from within the African National Congress led by Robert Sobukwe in 1960. The PAC sponsored the anti–pass law protests that led to the Sharpeville Massacre in 1961.

8. Black Consciousness Movement: Founded by Steve Biko in the late 1960s, partly inspired by the Black Consciousness Movement in the United States.

9. Black Theology: Attempt to develop a contextual theology of liberation in South Africa that distanced itself from both the theology that supported apartheid and the liberal theology that challenged it. It had widespread influence in many churches.

challengingly not to those who were suffering from injustice, but to those who, like himself, were racially privileged. He challenged us to "see things from below, from the perspective of those who suffer," and to do theology from that starting point.

Keeping these qualifications in mind, we can nonetheless say that by the 1980s, Bonhoeffer had become one of the most important non–South African conversation partners in the attempt to respond theologically to apartheid, and to many of the issues relating to public life over which apartheid cast its pall. But just as Bonhoeffer had engaged many issues in his *Ethics*, such as resistance, euthanasia, and human rights, within the framework of his context, so he also helped us in engaging many of the ethical issues over which apartheid cast its dark shadow.

References to Bonhoeffer's writings, selective as they were, demonstrated his relevance as the struggle against apartheid intensified during the two periods of State Emergency rule[10] in the mid- and late 1980s. The recognition that we were in a *status confessionis*, that apartheid was not just evil but also a heresy, and that the illegitimacy of the state demanded that Christians resist and help bring an end to the regime, were all notions we imbibed from Bonhoeffer's witness. His influence was most strikingly evident in the *Kairos Document*,[11] which so categorically rejected the apartheid regime as tyrannical, opposed any cheap reconciliation without justice, and unequivocally called on Christians to take sides with the oppressed in their struggle for liberation. Christian activists, inspired by Bonhoeffer's example, spoke about the need to "put a spoke in the wheel" of an illegitimate government, and sought ways to do so.

It is difficult to quantify the extent to which Christian witness contributed to the ending of apartheid, but it certainly played a significant role, and some if not all of it at least can be credited to Bonhoeffer's influence. By 1989 the victory against apartheid was within grasp with the unbanning of the liberation movements, and in 1990, Nelson Mandela was released from jail. Within four years he had been installed as the first President of the new democratic Republic of South Africa, and a new era was born. Critical in the process was the adoption of a remarkably progressive Constitution and a new supreme Constitutional Court to uphold its values. But also important as a short-term project was the establishment of the Truth and Reconciliation Commission[12] to

---

10. State Emergency rule: Two states of emergency were declared during the mid-1980s as an attempt by the apartheid regime to crush growing dissent and protest.

11. The *Kairos Document* was published in 1986. It challenged both "State Theology" and "Church Theology" while proposing a "Prophetic Theology" that challenged the legitimacy of the apartheid state and called on Christians to actively engage in acts of resistance to the state.

help South Africa deal with its past human rights abuses and foster a culture in which justice could be restored and reconciliation achieved. Those familiar with the earlier process that led to the TRC will know that Bonhoeffer's influence was not unimportant in preparing the ground for this historic, promising, and yet controversial development. But was Bonhoeffer going to be of much use in the new democratic South Africa?

Is Bonhoeffer Still of Any Use? The Cape Town Congress

Those who were present at the Sixth International Congress held at Union Theological Seminary in New York in 1992 may recall the discussion that was held about the possibility of holding the next Congress in Cape Town. At that stage the old apartheid government was still in power, so understandably there were those who felt that the time was not yet right and appropriate. But there was a majority, led by Eberhard Bethge, who felt that Cape Town should be the venue because of the significance of Bonhoeffer's influence during the church struggle against apartheid. Even so, when the Congress planning committee met in Cape Town to consider the theme, they decided to adapt Bonhoeffer's phrase from "After Ten Years": "Are we still of any use?"[13] The question had two interrelated layers of meaning. The first was whether Bonhoeffer's legacy was still of value in a democratic South Africa. The second was whether those theologians and churches that had been engaged in the struggle against apartheid were still of any use in the democratic transformation of South Africa.

At a concluding panel discussion at the Congress, the first question was put to several South African theologians: "Is Bonhoeffer Still of Any Use in South Africa?" The answer was a resounding "yes." But the panelists also made it clear that there were both old and new challenges facing South Africans, and that these would require a fresh engagement with Bonhoeffer. It was not possible to speak too soon about post-apartheid South Africa, as its legacy permeated so much of South African social and political reality despite the ending of statutory apartheid. The challenge to deal with issues of reconciliation and justice would remain on the agenda for many years to come. Questions were raised about the implications for Bonhoeffer's anthropology, ethics, and spirituality in dealing with social agency, as well as both gender and political power relations, as we

---

12. Hereinafter TRC: Established by President Nelson Mandela to facilitate the process of national reconciliation through dealing with the past in a way that brought the truth to light.

13. *Letters and Papers from Prison*, DBWE 8:52.

considered poverty and the scourge of HIV/AIDS as the new *status confessionis* or kairos.

If the answer to the first question about Bonhoeffer's ongoing relevance was an affirmation, the answer to the second, whether we were still of any use, was more ambiguous. It was a widely held view at the time that since the changes that had taken place in South Africa, the ecumenical church and more progressive theologians, some of whom were now in state structures, had withdrawn from public critical engagement with the new government. The situation was by no means hopeless, but there was a growing awareness that speaking truth to power, even in a post-apartheid South Africa, would not be easy and straightforward. There was a growing sense that the notion of critical solidarity that had shaped earlier theological responses to the new government was inadequate to new realities, not least the corruption that always seems to accompany the rise of new power elites. But above all, there was the realization that the transition to a nonracial democracy did not mean that democratic transformation would inevitably follow. Our swords, as Bonhoeffer might have said, were in danger of becoming rusty. So the question discussed at the Cape Town Congress was of considerable importance. Could Bonhoeffer help us recover our prophetic vision and so critically engage the new power realities and the many issues that were now confronting us?

Bonhoeffer and Democratic Transformation in South Africa Today

Looking back over the first decade of the new South Africa in 2005, one of the leading black theologians in South Africa, Tinyiko Maluleke,[14] asked some searching questions about the new political realities facing us, whether, in fact, the quest for national reconciliation had in any significant way fulfilled its promise, and whether we theologians who had been engaged in the struggle against apartheid had, in fact, remained useful. His essay reflected a growing new theological realism about public life that had begun to develop as the new millennium gathered momentum. Gone was the earlier optimism about the achievement of national reconciliation through the work of the TRC, or the ability of theologians and the ecumenical church to have much influence on government policy working from within the structures of the establishment.

---

14. Tinyiko Maluleke: Presbyterian minister who was a professor of theology at the University of South Africa, and now holds a senior administrative position at that University. He is a widely respected political analyst.

The TRC could not possibly have met all the expectations that many people had of its work, but it did achieve much in terms of the mandate given to it by the state. But clearly restoring justice and achieving national reconciliation is an ongoing project that will engage more than this generation. Not only does it require the overcoming of three and a half centuries of colonialism and apartheid rule that negatively affected every sphere of social and personal life, but the task is made more difficult by new challenges and global realities in the new millennium. Chief among these is the economic recession caused by the banking crisis in the United States and Europe, which is having a severe effect on developing countries and emerging markets, and has led to massive unemployment and increased poverty in South Africa. As a result, the shape and character of the democratic future of South Africa are being hotly contested by liberals, socialists, trade unionists, communists, and African nationalists in a way not unlike that which Bonhoeffer would have experienced during the final years of the Weimar Republic. Which raises the question: Has Bonhoeffer become of use again in this historical context?

It is now fifteen years since the Cape Town Congress. Partly in response to the challenges presented there to South African theologians to reengage Bonhoeffer in terms of the new political realities, there has been a growing interest in his legacy, and the circle of Bonhoeffer scholars has widened. Several trajectories in Bonhoeffer's legacy have contributed to the theological debate on the issues facing us, and hopefully influenced Christian engagement. But what I want to suggest is that just as Bonhoeffer provided much-needed resources for our opposition to apartheid as an ideological praxis, so he now provides us with critical insights with regard to democracy and what is meant by democratic transformation. Put bluntly, is the pursuit of and achievement of liberal democracy as championed by the traditionally Anglo-Saxon West capable of bringing about and sustaining a truly democratic society given the realities we now face? This question not only urgently confronts us in South Africa but elsewhere across the African Continent, in North Africa and the Middle East, and I suggest equally so in Europe and the United States, for we are now all profoundly globally interconnected. This was, of course, the question Bonhoeffer himself pondered as he reflected with farsighted vision on the new political order that was anticipated in a postwar Germany when he responded to William Paton's *The Church and the New Order*.[15]

Bonhoeffer knew well enough that western liberal democracy at its best was not about possessive individualism but about the rule of law, the protection

---

15. William Paton, *The Church and the New Order* (New York: Macmillan, 1941; Gateshead-on-Tyne: SCM, 1942), cited in DBWE 16:529–33.

of human rights and dignity, and public accountability. These democratic values he strongly endorsed. But Bonhoeffer was not a liberal democrat. Ruth Zerner once labeled him "a theological de Tocqueville—perceptive, prophetic, aristocratic in temperament, suspicious of the masses, and sensitive to the realities of his time and place."[16] For Bonhoeffer, political authority did not derive "from below" but "from above." Hitler's rise to power epitomized what Bonhoeffer called "populist" or "vulgar democracy" in which individualism and collectivism combined to produce political nihilism. Bonhoeffer's decision to join the resistance, like that of his fellow conspirators, was not motivated by a desire to restore the liberal democracy of Weimar, but arose out of a troubled conscience combined with a deep sense of loyalty to the Fatherland; it was elitist, patriotic, and national in ethos rather than liberal and democratic.

Bonhoeffer did not deny the need to safeguard civil liberties, but insisted that they be grounded at a deeper level and be given greater spiritual substance than that provided for by liberal democratic theory. Fundamental to all else was the rule of law rather than individual liberties. This did not mean that Bonhoeffer was unconcerned about true democratic values, chiefly those that had to do with human rights and dignity, but that he was skeptical about the ability of liberal democracy to deliver these and thereby overcoming the dangers of individual self-interest. Even the Anglo-Saxon liberal democratic tradition was itself in crisis. Having jettisoned its Christian foundations, it had lost confidence in truth and justice and was trying to manage society on the basis of propaganda and pragmatism. What became increasingly important in Bonhoeffer's political ethics was correspondence to reality rather than the absolutes. In fact, the value of Bonhoeffer's contribution to the discussion, as Robin Lovin has recently pointed out, is that he contributes key insights for this task by raising critical questions and helping to keep democratic aspirations realistic.[17]

Bonhoeffer's response to Paton's proposals for a new post–Second World War order may be dated in some respects, but it remains apposite to the current debate. Firstly, his reservations about democracy function as a theological hermeneutic of suspicion, helping us to participate more critically in the contemporary debate. Secondly, Bonhoeffer's theology of sociality and his ethics of free responsibility provide a more adequate theological foundation for democracy and thereby contribute to its contemporary retrieval. Thirdly,

16. Ruth Zerner, "Dietrich Bonhoeffer's Views on the State and History," in A. J. Klassen, *A Bonhoeffer Legacy: Essays in Understanding* (Grand Rapids: Eerdmans, 1981), 149f.

17. Robin Lovin, *Christian Realism and the New Realities* (Cambridge: Cambridge University Press, 2008).

Bonhoeffer's critique raises fundamental questions about the role of the church, not in opposing democracy, but in helping to develop a democratic social order that is just. Fourthly, Bonhoeffer's life and thought have an important contribution to make to our understanding of the role of difference in democratic transformation. Liberal democratic capitalism has become an ideology that rides roughshod over cultural and gender differences. In proclaiming that all are equal, it fails to recognize the extent to which some are more equal than others because of their social location. This raises, in a new way, the question of the relationship between individual or personal identity and the common good, as well as that between global democratization and cultural differentiation.

There are several theological and multidisciplinary projects in which I am involved that seek to engage these issues, and in which Bonhoeffer's legacy certainly informs the thinking of some participants. One is the New Humanist Project, which has focused especially on human solidarity, dignity, rights, and economic justice, and has been responsible for starting a national debate on a special "wealth tax."[18] The second is the Kairos South Africa/Palestine project,[19] which is addressing the issues in partnership with Palestinians in their struggle for justice. A third is the Dinokeng dialogue, which has produced a set of scenarios for the future of South Africa.[20]

A worst-case scenario is that just as the Weimar Republic in Germany collapsed under similar pressures, so the same will happen in South Africa. But there are other more positive possible scenarios that most analysts believe are more likely. There are several mitigating factors that stand in contrast to Germany in the late 1920s. The first is the strength of civil society in South Africa; the second is the widespread support for the Constitution in virtually all sectors of society and the strength of the Constitutional Court; and the third is that despite its many failures and abuses of power, the government remains committed to a just democratic transformation guided by the Constitution. All this might change, but for the present, I believe this is a fair assessment of political reality in South Africa; and sketchy as it is, it provides the context within which we can do

---

18. The New Humanist Project: Multidisciplinary project that I initiated and led, based at the Stellenbosch Institute for Advanced Study. See *The Humanist Imperative*, ed. John W. de Gruchy (Stellenbosch: SUN Media, 2011).

19. The Kairos South Africa/Palestine Project: Joint South African-Palestinian project that provides solidarity for Palestinian Christians. See the special issue of the *Journal of Theology for Southern Africa* 143 (July 2012).

20. The Dinokeng Dialogue: Series of seminars initiated by Dr. Mamphela Ramphele that produced a report on future scenarios for South Africa. See http://www.dinokengscenarios.co.za.

some theological reflection in dialogue with Bonhoeffer and consider the role of the church in helping to bring about democratic transformation both in South Africa and elsewhere in our global community.

3

Public Ethics and the Reception of Bonhoeffer in Britain

Keith Clements

During the autumn of 2011, Britain was convulsed by one of the most bizarre, tragicomic episodes in our public life: the "Occupy the City" campaign which, taking its cue from the "Occupy Wall Street" demonstration in New York, resulted in an encampment of protestors against corporate greed pitching their tents in front of St. Paul's Cathedral in London. There ensued legal measures to evict them, confusion among the Cathedral clergy resulting in several resignations, eventual compromises, and wide public disbelief that the Church had been so wrong-footed and made to appear more concerned with its health and safety rather than the health and safety of the planet at this time of global financial crisis.

This whole episode, however, has simply brought to the surface a deep-seated and long-term malaise in contemporary British society and the churches within it: the lack of any serious, concerted ecumenical attempt, for at least the past decade, at a public theology engaging with the critical issues of the age.[1]

Now it would be pleasing to be able to describe in a quite straightforward way how the reception of Dietrich Bonhoeffer impacted and influenced public ethics in England. That is not possible, however, because it did not happen quite so simply. It would be truer to say that it was a prior and significant

---

1. I must instantly qualify this by noting, first, that there are various think-tanks, advocacy groups, and foundations looking at public ethics, such as *Ecclesia* and *Theos*, although these tend to be marginal to mainstream church life, and to some extent self-marginalizing. Second, within the United Kingdom as a whole Scotland is better served than England, as witnessed by the Centre for Theology and Public Issues in Edinburgh, pioneered by Professor Duncan Forrester and others; and by the greater readiness of the Church of Scotland, as compared with the English churches in recent years, to examine sharply issues like poverty, equality, and international peace and justice. The situation in Britain has been made drastically worse in the last decade by the large-scale dismantling of the ecumenical bodies which, beginning with the British Council of Churches in 1942, had provided an effective forum and platform for the churches' engagement with public and international issues.

concern with public issues that in fact led to the ready reception of Bonhoeffer in Britain. From the start, the posthumous reception of Dietrich Bonhoeffer in Britain was among ecumenical figures who were already wrestling with critical social and international challenges. Two in particular were outstanding. The first was the ecumenical pioneer and social thinker J. H. Oldham, who had known Bonhoeffer personally from the early 1930s, and was study organizer for the 1937 Oxford Conference on "Church, Community and State." He had at the outset of the Second World War started the *Christian News-Letter*, a weekly bulletin of information and comment on a whole range of social and international issues. This continued after the war, and it was in the issue of 14 November 1945 (Number 247) that the first published tribute to Bonhoeffer appeared, over the name of Reinhold Niebuhr.[2] During the war, in 1942, Oldham had also founded the Christian Frontier Council, a forum designed to bring together laypeople, whether committed members of the church or not, who had common responsibilities in secular life and who shared a concern for social order. His stated advocacy of such a group resonates strikingly with Bonhoeffer's perception in his prison writings a year later, of the divorce between the church and the world in which people actually have to live, and the need for a new language of faith appropriate to the contemporary world—even a new meaning for "God."[3] It was Oldham who coined the phrase "the responsible society" as the motif for two whole decades of ecumenical social thinking under the aegis of the World Council of Churches from 1947 till about 1968. Not surprisingly, Oldham was drawn to Bonhoeffer's prison writings when they were published, in fact before they were translated into English, and he drew upon them in his 1953 book, on the meaning of Christianity today, *Life Is Commitment*.

Second, there was George Bell, bishop of Chichester, the great friend of Bonhoeffer during his lifetime and, almost immediately following the news of his death, an advocate of his significance as a martyr. It was Bell who preached the sermon at the memorial service for Dietrich and Klaus Bonhoeffer held in London on July 27, 1945, and broadcast to the world by the BBC. And

---

2. Compare Reinhold Niebuhr, "The Death of a Martyr," *Christianity and Crisis* 5, no. 1 (June 25, 1945): 6–7.

3. "The word God, for example, which is the foundation of everything, has for many people ceased to have an intelligible meaning and lost the power to evoke any emotional response. The only way in which the words used in the pulpit can regain their depth and richness of meaning is that they should be re-enforced by actions in the practical sphere informed by the truths which Christianity asserts. . . ." K. Clements, *Faith on the Frontier: A Life of J. H. Oldham* (Edinburgh: T. & T. Clark/Geneva: WCC, 1999), 413.

it was he who wrote the Foreword to the first English edition of *The Cost of Discipleship*; who constantly spoke in public about what Bonhoeffer meant for the postwar world and church,[4] especially in witnessing to the existence of "another Germany." But Bell was a public theologian in his own right, and indeed concerned with many more issues than those that prompted him to protest during the war, such as the area bombing of German cities. His wartime book *Christianity and World Order* (1940) makes that clear, surveying as it does the whole sweep of issues revealed by the present crisis: modern secularism, peace and war, the universal church and the separated churches; and, even at that early stage, the need for reconstruction and a new order after the war. The postwar years saw Bell's ecumenical activity and stature rise still more with his service as Chairman of the Central Committee of the new World Council of Churches, inaugurated in 1948.[5]

Another, younger, figure who was decisive for the early reception of Bonhoeffer in postwar Britain was the Scottish theologian Ronald Gregor Smith (1913–1968).[6] A devotee of Buber and Kierkegaard, while a minister and army chaplain during the war he had undergone a spiritual and intellectual crisis. The personal reflections he wrote during the summer of 1944—like Oldham's statements two years earlier—at points manifest an uncanny parallel to what Bonhoeffer was writing in prison at exactly the same time: the need for a recovery of God as found in the human Jesus; God as suffering love; and the call for a new kind of church based on honesty, humility, and human solidarity. From 1947 Gregor Smith worked for the Student Christian Movement Press (SCM), of which he became Editor in 1950; and he used his position to ensure the transmission to the English-speaking world of the most significant recent and contemporary continental thinkers, and none more so than Bonhoeffer.[7] Gregor Smith was himself a gifted translator, but, as well as publisher, his chief

4. A senior Anglican churchman told me how as a boy he first heard of Bonhoeffer when Bell came to his boarding school to conduct a confirmation service, and after dinner spoke to the entire school about Bonhoeffer.

5. His book *The Kingship of Christ* (London: Penguin, 1954) was a panoramic sketch of the whole ecumenical scene since the launch of the WCC, including Interchurch Aid and Refugee Service, action for justice and peace, and the role of laypeople. Its concluding chapter, "Christ the Hope of the World," sounds a note familiar to many of us: "The Christian hope is a hope of our earthly calling. The difference between the Christian hope of resurrection and a mythological hope is that the Christian hope sends a man back to his life on earth in a wholly new way which is even more sharply defined than it is in the Old Testament. The Christian, unlike the devotees of the salvation myths . . . etc. But like Christ himself . . . he must drink the earthly cup to the lees . . . etc." (154). Bonhoeffer readers can guess the rest of this piece of holy plagiarism (at least Bell does reference it in a footnote).

6. See K. Clements, *The Theology of Ronald Gregor Smith* (Leiden: E. J. Brill, 1986).

role in the transmission of Bonhoeffer was as an interpreter of his thought—a role encouraged by the close friendship that grew between Gregor Smith (with his German wife Käthe) and Eberhard and Renate Bethge from their arrival in London in 1953. His book *The New Man* (1956) can be reckoned the first really serious theological essay in Britain to use constructively, as distinct from simply cite, Bonhoeffer, with its stress on faith as arising out of history and leading further into historical responsibility.[8]

What did these earlier British recipients and mediators[9] of Bonhoeffer have in common? They were all exercised by public ethics and the need for faith to relate to the social sphere. It is not incidental that they were all known to each other, largely because they were part of the network created by J. H. Oldham. In fact, Jenkins and Vidler belonged to the "Moot," the select discussion group on faith and society led by Oldham for nearly ten years from 1938 and which included sociologists of the stature of Karl Mannheim and literary figures like T. S. Eliot.[10] But further: all these figures had a deep sense of the crisis facing western civilization; a sense of historical moment; of the end of the old Christendom and the impending end of the colonial world; that a new world has to be in the making; and the need for new tools, new plans, new maps. What appealed to them was Bonhoeffer's perception that faith, far from fleeing from this crisis, should rediscover itself in it; that the crucial issue was not the fate of the church but the future of humanity; and that faith should assist, instead of denying, the coming of age of humankind and take responsibility for the next stage of its history.

Moreover, Bonhoeffer was making an impact beyond the normal church boundaries. For example, in 1961 a lawyer of Jewish background, Peter Benenson, was incensed at reports of ill-treatment of political detainees under Portuguese colonial rule. As a result he founded Amnesty International. Benenson made no secret of the inspirational debt he owed to Bonhoeffer.[11]

---

7. *The Cost of Discipleship* (1947), *Life Together* (1954), *Ethics* (1955), *Temptation* (1955), and the chief prize, *Letters and Papers from Prison* (1953), were all published in the UK by SCM. Gregor Smith could not persuade SCM Press to take on *Sanctorum Communio* and *Act and Being* but, having translated *Sanctorum Communio* himself, saw to it that both these works were published by Collins after he became Professor of Divinity at Glasgow University in 1956.

8. Other names that should be mentioned for taking Bonhoeffer seriously include the Congregational theologian Daniel Jenkins, who wrote a positive but not uncritical study of "religionless Christianity," in *Beyond Religion* (1962); and Alec Vidler, the Cambridge historian and editor of *Theology* whose essay "Religion and the National Church" in the volume of essays *Soundings* (also 1962) warned against any idea of the church being concerned only with the "religious" department of life.

9. See notes 7 and 8 above.

10. See K. Clements, *The Moot Papers: Faith, Freedom and Society* (Edinburgh: T. & T. Clark, 2010).

In Britain, public awareness of Bonhoeffer went through a major shift of gears in 1963 with the appearance of *Honest to God* by John Robinson, at that time bishop of Woolwich. *Honest to God* was the religious publishing sensation of the 1960s, and Bonhoeffer continued to be invoked in much of the "secular" theology that ensued in the 1960s and early 1970s. But while Bonhoeffer's prison theology continued to excite, or puzzle, it was a somewhat decontextualized Bonhoeffer who was in the spotlight. For this reason, at this point tribute must be paid to the one, well known to many of us, who from the mid-1960s undertook a lot of the translation of parts of the *Gesammelte Schriften*, the letters, lectures, and papers from Bonhoeffer's earlier period: namely the late Edwin Robertson. Until the appearance of the first English edition of Bethge's biography in 1970—a translation carried out under Robertson's supervision—these selections[12] were the main sources in English for a more thoroughly grounded view of Bonhoeffer, in terms both of his own development and in the history of his time.

One of the results of the highlighting of the prison writings in *Honest to God* and much of the secular theology was, paradoxically, to create a curiosity about what lay behind them. A number of us whose first encounters with Bonhoeffer had been through the prison letters and *Cost of Discipleship* now found ourselves particularly drawn to the *Ethics*, and I think it fair to say that the bulk of the serious work done in Britain on Bonhoeffer in the past forty years has either been on the *Ethics* or the ethical implications of the Bonhoeffer corpus as a whole. I do not think this is simply because, as Karl Barth and others have alleged, we Britons are congenitally Pelagian. But we are pragmatic rather than speculative and it is the concretion of revelation that Bonhoeffer so emphasized, and its bearing on ethical formation, which has appealed so strongly. Certainly a good number of the Ph.D. theses written in Britain have been on Bonhoeffer's ethics, and so too the more significant published studies, in particular Stephen Plant's *Bonhoeffer* (2004). If I may be permitted to mention my own earlier work, *A Patriotism for Today* (1984 and 1986), this was an attempt, in the light of Bonhoeffer's career and theology, to rescue the notion of national loyalty from that of unquestioning nationalism and racial ideology, in order to transform it into a mature, clear-headed and critical form of communal responsibility. Because of its publication date, a lot of people have assumed it was written primarily as a reaction to Prime Minister Margaret Thatcher's nationalistic

11. Interestingly, Benenson (1921–2005) as a boy was privately tutored by W. H. Auden, who would later dedicate his poem "Friday's Child" to the memory of Bonhoeffer.

12. *No Rusty Swords* (London: Collins, 1965); *The Way to Freedom* (London: Collins, 1966).

exploitation of the Falklands/Malvinas war of 1982. I have to say, however, that I was well into the writing before that episode. Margaret Thatcher just came along to illustrate my point. Bonhoeffer by then was already important as a theological resource for many of those supporting the South African struggle against apartheid and engaged in the peace movement in the context of the Cold War.[13]

Bonhoeffer as a courageous figure is certainly highly regarded in Britain today. His statue, along with those of nine other twentieth-century martyrs, stands above the great west door of Westminster Abbey. But at the moment we are not sure what to do with him and his theology, beyond obtaining a supply of striking aphorisms. That is because we are not at all sure what to do with ourselves as a nation and a society and as churches, an uncertainty symbolized by the fracas at St. Paul's Cathedral.

We do not have a sense of historical moment as the first recipients of Bonhoeffer had. Moreover, the assumed postwar consensus about Christianity as supplying the bedrock morality of our society and civilization has largely gone in face of a much more pluralist and secular ethos. And a key question facing Britain today is how faith may, if at all, now have a role in the formation of public ethics. The philosopher Mary Warnock, a member of the House of Lords, and one who has been in the forefront of public debates on bioethical issues such as embryo research and euthanasia, in 2010 published a book with a title interestingly twisted from John Robinson's in 1963: *Dishonest to God*.[14] Warnock, while not unsympathetic to religion as a source of moral values to the individual, and as supplying a rich vein of cultural enrichment through liturgy and religious art, is highly critical of any corporate role for the church or other religious bodies in the formulation of public policy and its legislative encoding. The danger of any religion, she argues, lies in its claim to absolute immutable moral knowledge which, if justified, would give its adherents a special place or right to instruct others on how to behave. "The only meaning . . . is that people who *are* religious, who *do* hold the requisite metaphysical or supernatural beliefs, should be given special authority over the rest."[15] Yet this, she asserts,

---

13. Mention should also be made of the ecumenical program on Justice, Peace, and the Integrity of Creation (JPIC), which in Britain and in other countries made a permanent impact even at the local parish and congregational level. The instigation of the JPIC process, especially in the "two Germanys" in the 1980s, owed much to the memory of Bonhoeffer's 1934 call for an ecumenical council of all the churches to declare against war. Bonhoeffer's instrumentality was therefore significant in originating the process but less well known at the more popular level.

14. Continuum 2010.

15. Ibid., 165.

is what the Roman Catholic Church does when it instructs parliaments which side to support on moral issues, "and it is what the other churches demand too, in offering 'guidance' on which way to vote in a general election." Democracy must be alert to every sign of encroaching theocracy. For our purposes we can leave aside the question of whether Warnock is operating with a too narrowly defined understanding of what the democratic process involves, but she is certainly representative of a large body of secular opinion that sees any faith-reference as a threat to the autonomy that is the hallmark of operating in the public forum in a liberal, western society where reason and its examination of actual experience are the unconditional requirements. On the other hand we have institutional churches, and certain theological movements such as the self-styled "Radical Orthodoxy" school in Anglicanism, which are overly anxious to demonstrate that there is a secure body of revealed truth, utterly different from anything the world might offer, which alone can supply the basis for a sound and fulfilling human society: the church teaches the way, and itself exemplifies what the world should be like. Caught between these antagonisms, the public realm seems destined to become a battleground between secularists wishing to assert human autonomy, and religious institutions desirous of asserting authority. In between, however, on the street of actual life, there are a lot of people for whom the issue is neither autonomy nor authority, but authenticity: the authentically human, what makes for human fulfillment in community. They are found in local politics, in environmental groups, in ordinary neighborhood communities, in caring for the homeless, in campaigning for international development—and they are found among those camping on the steps of St. Paul's. That camp is not anti-church. Indeed there is about it something almost akin to the call of the Macedonian, "Come over and help us!" (Acts 16:9).

Someone whom I regard as speaking for all such people "on the street" is Rebecca Hickman who in a recent essay, "In pursuit of egalitarianism: and why social mobility cannot get us there,"[16] writes:

> To help the most marginalised, and help them gladly, we need an ethic born of love, kindness, sympathy and generosity. *These words currently reside at the outermost fringes of political discourse.* Qualities that we praise and seek in our personal relationships and conduct, we dismiss as sentimental or sources of inefficiency in the design of public services and the organisation of the economy.[17]

16. Published by Compass – Directions for the Democratic Left (www.compassionline.org.uk).

There are many in that "no-man's land," or on the street, who welcome the contribution of faith groups in the struggle to ensure that the language "born of love, kindness, sympathy and generosity" is *not* marginalized to the fringes of political discourse. They know that such values will *not* automatically flourish in the supposedly liberal society, prey to so many powerful economic and political interests. They have to be stood for, spoken for, struggled for, and lived, by whoever believes in them for whatever reason.

Perhaps, therefore, only now are we at a point where Bonhoeffer's challenge might be felt in full strength: not so much on this or that particular ethical issue but right across the board in a recognition of the significance of what he calls the "penultimate." At its most creative, I suggest, a future reception of Bonhoeffer in Britain will, like the earliest one, be among those who see that the struggle for authentic humanity and the witness of faith are engaged with the same reality, if not always working from the same point or consciousness. The churches are rightly concerned to retain their identity and calling as witnesses to the gospel of Christ in its specificity and finality. But, unsure of their status in a secular and pluralist society, they are susceptible to two temptations: either, to retreat from the world as it is into a self-enclosed space in which the absolute verities can be contemplated and enjoyed in unchallenged fashion; or, to seek to impose directly what they regard as these absolute truths on the world around them. Bonhoeffer's full-blown recognition of the ultimate, yet of the rights of the penultimate realm as the place where the coming of the ultimate requires patient preparation, remains crucial for preserving that space in the public realm where faith can be in dialogue with all who seek justice, peace, and human fulfilment and dignity.

Bonhoeffer writes in his *Ethics*:

> To give the hungry bread is not yet to proclaim to them the grace of God and justification and to have received bread does not yet mean to stand in faith. . . . The entry of grace is the ultimate. But we must speak of preparing the way, of the penultimate—for the sake of those who have failed with their radicalism that denied penultimate things, and are now in danger themselves of being pushed back behind penultimate things, as well as for the sake of those who remained stuck in penultimate things, who have made themselves comfortable with them, and who must now be claimed for the ultimate. In the

17. Ibid., 19, italics mine.

end, however, perhaps we speak of penultimate things primarily for the sake of those who have never achieved these penultimate things, whom no one has helped to gain them, for whom no one has prepared the way, and who now must be helped so that the word of God, the ultimate, grace, can come to them.[18]

That, I suggest, constitutes a basic theological charter for seeking a public ethic for a new generation.

18. DBWE 6:163–64.

4

Bonhoeffer and Public Ethics in the USA

Larry Rasmussen

To address Bonhoeffer and Public Ethics in the USA, I will illustrate with Bonhoeffer's reception among Union Seminary students in the years of my tenure, 1986–2004.[1] My evidence is thus anecdotal, but I think it holds up in view of similar testimony by others.

In those years a highly diverse and sometimes fractious student body only assembled in the same room if the course were a required one—for example, a first course in biblical studies or in systematic theology. Sometimes, although not often enough, a cross-section of the seminary also gathered for worship in James Chapel. The politics of identity ruled, whether racial-ethnic identity, gender identity, or the tensions between economic and political liberals and radicals.

The exception to the lack of a diverse cross-section in electives was the Bonhoeffer course. For reasons of history, I taught it in the Bonhoeffer Room.[2] But for some years, that space was too small. Bonhoeffer always drew a crowd.

In addition to their attraction to Bonhoeffer, the crowd shared a passion for issues in social, or public, ethics. That, of course, continues the long-held focus of Union students and faculty.

But why and how did the Union cross-section in this course mirror, in microcosm, the reception of Bonhoeffer on matters of public ethics in the USA?

Here is an educated guess. The writing assignment in most iterations of the Bonhoeffer course was six reflection papers per student during the semester. Each reflection addressed a different Bonhoeffer text and each revealed the

---

1. For reference to the actual series of formal public lectures—The Bonhoeffer Lectures in Public Ethics, which are held annually in Germany and North America, the latter of which were launched and held at Union Theological Seminary for a number of years—see the Foreword to this volume, page xii.

2. Formerly called the Prophets' Chamber when Bonhoeffer occupied it in 1939.

writer's explicitly stated point of view as she or he grappled with that text. In broad brushstrokes, the results were these.

I thought the feminists would be aghast at the wedding sermon in *Letters and Papers from Prison*[3] and Bonhoeffer's conservative Prussian patriarchalism in portions of *Ethics*. They were. Yet at another level, they resonated deeply with Bonhoeffer's theological ethics of relationality or sociality. His treatment of community and the other in Christ placed every sister and brother in the same moral framework on the same terms. Feminists found this theology of sociality and solidarity more basic for them than Bonhoeffer's cultural patriarchalism.

The evangelicals in the class were drawn to *Discipleship* and *Life Together*, both Christocentric, both demanding texts, and both attending to close Christian community over against the wider world as a disciplined faith-based alternative to it.

The social justice cohort—they cut across the class constituencies—were drawn to *Letters and Papers* and to *Ethics* and the resistance, both in the church struggle and the military-political conspiracy.

African Americans found in Bonhoeffer the only dead white male European theologian who thought he had something important to learn from blacks and their cultures. They were also moved by a witness who, though in very different cultural contexts and histories, paralleled Martin Luther King's in striking ways, not least in their common attraction to Gandhi.

Koreans and South Africans at Union were largely from the ranks of student opposition groups in their home countries that opposed to their own governments, so the Bonhoeffer of both faith-based and patriotic resistance drew them.

Roman Catholics, Episcopalians, and Lutherans were often, despite their love/hate relationship with their respective denominations, were still "mother church" people. They were surprised that the rather dense text of *Sanctorum Communio* was also such a rich one. Bonhoeffer's ecclesiology resonated with them and instructed them.

Perhaps nobody in this conference audience finds any of this surprising. But recall that, for most of the students, this was their first course in Bonhoeffer studies. And recall that these are highly disparate texts—*Act and Being* bears no obvious resemblance to *Life Together*; *Discipleship* is not, on the surface, from the same hand that penned *Sanctorum Communio*; *Letters and Papers from Prison*, and *Ethics*, are not *Life Together* and *Discipleship*.

---

3. "Wedding Sermon from the Prison Cell," *Letters and Papers from Prison*, DBWE 8:82–87.

In the end, however, the disparate readings as grappled with by a diverse readership were all framed by a common attraction. Each week the readings included a considerable chunk of Eberhard Bethge's biography. And the common attraction was the integrity of a life and the power of its witness in a terrible time.

In sum, the reception of Bonhoeffer in and for matters of public ethics in the USA—those fluid identity groups and their respective struggles and passions—is mirrored in the experience of Union students' articulated personal encounters with Bonhoeffer.

In what passes for retirement, I taught a semester at the Lutheran Theological Seminary at Philadelphia. I was requested to include a Bonhoeffer course. Rather weary of writing extensive comments on six papers per student, I looked forward to a small class—maybe fifteen or twenty—and I expected them to be a rather homogeneous lot—Lutheran, white, male and female. I walked in the first day to the largest elective class, maybe fifty or sixty, that, for all its diversity, including denominational diversity, made me wonder whether I had time-traveled back to Union.

The integrity of a life and the power of its witness, together with the ways in which disparate texts intersect the location and passions of disparate peoples—this both reflects Bonhoeffer's reception in and for public ethics in the USA and is the reason for it.

5

Bonhoeffer and Public Ethics from the Perspective of Brazil

Carlos Ribeiro Caldas, Filho

What is the contribution of Bonhoeffer's theology for a public theology in Brazil? What are the lessons the great Brazilian Christian church, Catholics and Protestants alike, must urgently learn from Dietrich Bonhoeffer's theology? I approach this question from my personal history. Thirty years ago, when I was a freshman in the Presbyterian Theological Seminary, Bonhoeffer's book *Discipulado* (*Discipleship*) came into my hands and had a profound impact on me. After that I read eagerly all the Bonhoeffer books that had been translated into Portuguese at that time: *Vida em comunhão* (*Life Together*) *Tentação* (*Temptation*), *Orando com os Salmos* (*The Prayerbook of the Bible*) and *Resistência e submissão* (*Letters and Papers from Prison.* Dietrich Bonhoeffer's theology became very important in my personal theological formation, and I quoted it in a number of sermons and lectures over the years. Then, about twenty years ago, perhaps due to a kind of patriotic spirit, I also began to study Latin American theology, especially the Theology of Integral Mission. My dissertation was about the theology of contextual evangelization of Orlando Costas, the well-known Puerto Rican theologian and missiologist. So, for some years my main intellectual-academic and theological-spiritual concern was the theology of integral mission as produced in the existential, historical, political, economic, cultural, religious *Sitz im Leben* of Latin America. Recently I began reading Bonhoeffer again, and started thinking about how to establish a relationship between Latin American theology and the theology of Dietrich Bonhoeffer, and published some essays about that.

To speak about Bonhoeffer and public ethics in the particular context of Brazil, I will first comment on the relevance of his theology to the Brazilian Christian church as a whole.

THE IMPORTANCE OF CONFESSION

All of us know that Bonhoeffer was from a Lutheran background. He received a solid formation in the Lutheran tradition. In his writings he never tried to hide his Lutheranism. From this point I conclude that in Brazil, Christians must learn from Bonhoeffer about the importance of knowing their own theological and confessional traditions. It is important always to have in mind that Christianity is much more than a rational credo that is known only theoretically. Bonhoeffer would be the very first to criticize such an understanding of Christianity. He gives us this imperishable lesson with the dramatic story of his life and death. Christianity is discipleship, the following of Jesus Christ. Christianity has to do not only with ideas, but with life, with flesh and blood. Nevertheless, as there are many different confessional traditions within the great Christian family, it is important that we know our own particular tradition. Bonhoeffer knew his tradition and, if he was not proud of it, neither was he ashamed of it. Thinking about the relationship Bonhoeffer had with his own confessional tradition leads me to conclude that those who study his theological legacy must learn to be better Reformed, Baptists, Pentecostals, Catholics, and so on. The knowledge of a given confessional Christian tradition must never be an end in itself. Rather, it is intended to be a way to make us aware of our particular denominational ethos, never forgetting that what really matters is to be a disciple of Jesus Christ.

This lesson has particular importance for the Brazilian context, where there are so many Christians who, consciously or not, have become more worshipers of their theological traditions than followers of Jesus Christ himself. Bonhoeffer was a Lutheran, but he was wise enough to understand that the theologian must understand the historical context, and not only repeat what was said centuries earlier. In Bonhoeffer's case, this was patently obvious, but in the Brazilian context many theologians simply do not see like this, and they limit themselves to repeating what the "divines" of old had said.

THE ECUMENICITY OF THE CHURCH

The other side of the coin is that Bonhoeffer the confessional Lutheran Christian was at the same time wise enough to see the importance of the *oecumene*. He knew how to work with Christians of other traditions such as Anglicans and Reformed, to name only a few. Note that I described Bonhoeffer with the word "Christian," not "Evangelical" or "Protestant." This is intentional. I am absolutely convinced that Bonhoeffer has too much to offer to all traditions under the great umbrella of Christianity to limit him to only one. His relevance and appeal is as much to progressive ecumenical Protestants as to conservative evangelicals, as much to Pentecostals in general as to Catholics. In his youth, the young Dietrich spent some time in Rome and became amazed at traditional Catholic liturgy, and then, many years later, he led the underground seminary in Finkenwalde following a monastic model offering the seminarians of the *Bekennende Kirche* a blend of Lutheran, Benedictine, and Pietist formation. From this it is clear that in Bonhoeffer's theology the church is absolutely important. It cannot be forgotten that the ecclesiastical question was pivotal in his whole theology. That he was always concerned about the church is demonstrated by the fact that his doctoral thesis, *Sanctorum Communio*, was about the church. Later, his *Life Together* again shows how important the church and Christian community life was for him. Reading Bonhoeffer, one is convinced that he really believed in the importance of the *One, Holy, Catholic and Apostolic Church*. In Bonhoeffer we find the sound example of a confessional Christian and an ecumenist who worked actively in the formative days of the ecumenical movement.

In Brazil it is very common that many believers become so proud of their denominational tradition that they have their eyes closed to the beauty and to the good in other Christian traditions. In other countries there are many Catholic theologians who are Bonhoeffer experts. For the time being we do not have them in Brazil. But from Bonhoeffer we should learn the lesson of the importance of the church universal. This is especially important in Brazil where the ecumenical movement is not so large. For the majority of evangelical conservative—even fundamentalist—Christians, the ecumenical movement is something dangerous because it is seen as theologically liberal. But what they have in mind is more a caricature of the ecumenical movement than a true picture of it. From Bonhoeffer's theology one learns that the kingdom of God is greater and more important than the particular denominational tradition to which one belongs, and that there are important issues we must face together—in other words, "united we stand, divided we fall." But this should not force us to prioritize or homogenize under any particular theological or denominational tradition.

The Practical Dimension of Spiritual Life

We can observe a pattern in the lives of all important leaders in Christian history, Christian men and women who have succeeded in leading important movements of reform and revitalization in Christianity. All of them were people who took very seriously in their lives the importance of living a sound spirituality. There are so many examples that could be remembered here: St.

Bernard of Clairvaux (1090–1153), a very gifted man who was a strategist and lived as a deep Christian mystic at the same time; St. Francis of Assisi (1181–1226), just one of the reformers before the Protestant Reformation, who lived a strong Christocentric spirituality; in more recent times, the Rev. Martin Luther King Jr. (1929–1968) and John M. Perkins (1930), two of the most well-known American civil rights activists, who were always involved in difficult political questions, but never forgot to cultivate their spiritual relationship with the Lord. This very same lesson is learned from Bonhoeffer's theological production and from his life as well. It is not an exaggeration to affirm that Bonhoeffer was one of the greatest Christian spiritual masters of the mid-twentieth century. The aforementioned experience of the theological seminary in Finkenwalde, and his small but quite good introduction to the Psalms, *Prayerbook of the Bible*, remind us of an essential lesson: the feeding of spiritual life is the fuel that motivates one to get involved in practical and public questions as committed Christians who are convinced that Christian faith has a word to say about public issues such as economics and politics. Before we as Christians get ourselves involved in such questions we must spend time in silence in the presence of God, meditating upon the Scriptures—this is the lesson we learn from the Finkenwalde experience. In the Brazilian context this lesson is absolutely important. Bonhoeffer taught us that the practice of spirituality is important for living the Christian mission—a spirituality that is not an escape from this world, but which is the fuel for Christians engaged in showing the love of God in this world.

The Relationship of the Private and Public Aspects of Christian Faith

Since 1974 when the American theologian Martin Marty first published the expression "public theology," many theologians around the world have been concerned about the relationship of Christian faith and Christian theology to public questions. This discussion is of absolute importance for the world today. This is not an easy task for theologians. It is very easy simply to speak about questions like world poverty and the environment, and it is not necessary to be a Christian to be concerned about these issues. The difficulty for theologians is to speak about such issues without losing the *proprium* of Christian faith. And it is equally necessary to speak in debate about public issues with a humble spirit and a sincere and honest willingness to learn from people from other fields of knowledge—even from people of other faiths. It is not the aim of this essay, however, to discuss the method of public theology. Rather I want to show that

Dietrich Bonhoeffer was concerned about public theology many years before Martin Marty coined the expression. Bonhoeffer was a public theologian *avant la lettre*. In Brazil the tendency is still to think of Christian faith only in a private, individualistic, and otherworldly way.[1] The "salvation of the soul" is the only and major concern for the majority of Catholics, Evangelicals, Pentecostals, and Neo-Pentecostals alike. This understanding of Christian faith is more Greek than Hebrew, because it has to do more with Plato than with the Bible itself. In a dramatic contrast, Bonhoeffer teaches us that Christian faith has something to do with the public, not only with the individual. According to Bonhoeffer, the Christian church must have a political presence, not only a "spiritual" one, as the majority of evangelicals in Brazil think. In his theology Bonhoeffer was wise enough to perceive that the Christian gospel has a word to say to this world, not only about the world to come. As far as I understand it, this was due to the strong Christocentric aspect of Bonhofferian theology, that is to say, Bonhoeffer took seriously the implication of the doctrine of Incarnation. And since ecclesiology is based on Christology, the church in mission in the world must learn how to "incarnate" itself in the struggles and complexities of human existence. Therefore, in Bonhoeffer's theology both the private and the public aspects of Christian faith are held together, and walk hand in hand on the road of life.

CARE FOR THE DOWNTRODDEN AND OPPRESSED OF SOCIETY

Even though Bonhoeffer was born to a wealthy family—he had a *natu nobilis*—he learned very early in his life that Christians have a responsibility to the oppressed and downtrodden of society. His pastoral experiences as a youth pastor in Germany and in Spain, and also the year he spent in New York, helped to open his eyes to the imperative of Christian care for those who are living in difficult situations.[2] This particular aspect of Bonhoeffer's theology and life practice is of great importance for Latin American theology, both Liberation Theology and the Theology of Integral Mission. Perhaps what I stated previously about Bonhoeffer can be repeated now: Bonhoeffer was somehow at the same time a kind of liberation theologian and an Integral

---

1. Is there in English such a word as "verticalistic" to describe this sort of spirituality?

2. This aspect of Bonhoeffer's biography is quite interesting: there were plenty of Protestant churches for white Caucasian people in the New York of the 1930s. In spite of this, the young Dietrich, a white German Lutheran male, decided to attend a Black Baptist congregation, Abyssinian Baptist Church in Harlem! Of course this experience had an impact on his social sensibility, as was fully demonstrated in the years to come, especially during the war, in his actions toward the Jews.

Mission theologian *avant la lettre*. In order to understand that, one must remember that Bonhoeffer, faithful to his Lutheran theological formation, was greatly influenced by Martin Luther in his comprehension of the immanence of God—the Christian God who reveals himself in Jesus of Nazareth is the God who suffers. So, the Christian God revealed in the Scriptures and in the person of Jesus is never, by any means, the impassible Aristotelian God. The majority of Brazilian evangelicals—there are literally many millions of them!—are concerned only about the soteriological question, by which they mean the "salvation of the soul." They need urgently to learn this lesson from Bonhoeffer. As far as this particular dimension of Bonhoeffer's theology and its relevance for Brazilian Christianity is concerned, it is helpful to remember some very well-known expressions of Luther's theology: Luther spoke about the *theologia crucis* in contrast to the *theologia gloriae*. In Brazil nowadays, due to the pervasive influence of the Pentecostal movement, including in the Catholic Church (through the Charismatic Renewal Movement), the Christian message broadcast on radio and television[3] virtually twenty-four hours a day from January first to the last day of December is one of "victory," "success," and "stop suffering."[4] This is the Brazilian version of a *theologia gloriae*. In such a context it is necessary to rediscover the Christian concern for the downtrodden and oppressed of our society. This teaching is not a monopoly of Liberation Theology. Dietrich Bonhoeffer taught the importance of this concern many years before Rubem Alves and Gustavo Gutiérrez started to talk about it.

PUBLIC ETHICS AND NOT ONLY PERSONAL ETHICS

Brazilian evangelicals are by and large concerned only about questions of individual, personal ethics, which are usually framed in the negative: "you shall not drink beer," "you shall not dance," "you shall not smoke," and so on. The questions of a public ethic are not considered to be important. Bonhoeffer teaches the importance of a public ethic. For Bonhoeffer, ethics is not a moralistic question. He taught ethics from a theological basis, and did not simply repeat the mores of a so-called Victorian tradition. In his *Ethics* he taught that such moralistic comprehension serves only an egocentric convenience, not the cause of the gospel. This is unfortunately very common in Brazil. By and large the Brazilian evangelicals have lost their prophetic voice, sacrificing it on the altar of personal convenience or the convenience of their churches.

3. In Brazil there are several Pentecostal and Catholic TV channels and radio programs.

4. "Stop suffering" is the motto of the Universal Church of the Kingdom of God, a mammoth Brazilian Neo-Pentecostal church, organized in the 1970s, which is nowadays present virtually all over the world.

Bonhoeffer took that point to the ultimate consequence, when he moved from confession to conspiracy, paying for that boldness the price of his own life. Only a few Christians are ready to pay such a price, the price of martyrdom. Nevertheless, what Brazilian Christians cannot forget is that from Bonhoeffer we learn about the importance of public ethics and the necessity for the Christian church to raise her voice on behalf of the voiceless. I mention a practical example, for the sake of the non-Brazilian readers of this essay. There are many Congressmen in the Brazilian Congress nowadays, including some Senators in the Brazilian Senate, who are active members of evangelical congregations. They are not only churchgoers. But almost all of them (if not all) are always in favor of the government in every vote. It does not matter what the issue is, they are in favor of the government. The only exception is when it is a question related to sexual issues, e.g., homosexual rights and the right of women to abortion.[5] To say that is not to say that these questions are of little importance. But the point is, first, that churches and Christian legislators should have a distinctive voice. Then they should demonstrate that Christians have views on important public questions, and not act as though these are the exclusive prerogative of a given government administration. Christians must learn to raise their voices and to give prophetic testimony. If personal ethics is important, public ethics is equally so.

The Promise of Bonhoeffer's Theology in Brazil

It is a very well-known fact that the theology produced by Dietrich Bonhoeffer dealt with a wide range of subjects in the theological spectrum. In these *loci* one can find robust and profound discussions varying from Christology to ecclesiology, from study of the nature and of the being of God to social ethics. All these topics are helpful to the current *Sitz im Leben* of the large evangelical Brazilian church. But for the purposes of this essay the last aspect—Bonhoeffer's theological, social, and political ethics—is more important.

All the aforementioned aspects of Bonhoeffer's theology are highly important, with a potential to have a decisive effect on ethical discussions in Brazil. That is because Bonhoeffer's theology is not merely an abstract and theoretical stratospheric discussion that takes place only in the realm of ideas. Rather, it is a theological discussion about the concreteness of life, from a distinct Christocentric perspective.

5. In Brazil in the last ten years the presidency of the country has been in the hands of the Labor Party (PT, *Partido dos Trabalhadores* in Portuguese), a left-wing party. The tendency of a left-wing party is to be more liberal in questions like the right to abortion and the rights of minorities, such as homosexuals.

The discussion about public theology is still in its infancy in Brazil.[6] There is still a lack of a concrete theoretical and conceptual basis for the construction of a Christian public theology in Brazil that takes seriously the question of social ethics. The purpose of this essay has been to show that such a basis can be found in the theology developed by Dietrich Bonhoeffer. It is my conviction that this is the strongest, but not the only, contribution from Bonhoefferian theology to Christians in Brazil. This is the special promise of Bonhoeffer's theology to the country. Christians in Brazil, whether they are Catholic or Protestant, Evangelical, Pentecostal, or even Neo-Pentecostal, can present a healthy contribution to public affairs in the country if they engage themselves in a mission informed by Bonhoeffer's theological social ethics. My prayer is to see the day when this will come true.

6. At present there are only a few published texts in Portuguese about the history, method, and the *proprium* of public theology. The work of Professor Rudolf von Sinner, a German-Swiss theologian at the Lutheran School of Theology in São Leopoldo (in the Brazilian "Deep South"), has succeeded in pioneering the discussion about public theology in the country.

6

Bonhoeffer's Social Ethics and Its Influences in Japan

Kazuaki Yamasaki

This chapter addresses the influences of Bonhoeffer's ethical thought in Japan and on the Japanese people from 1945 to 2010. In Japan there were only 350,000 Protestant and Catholic Christians in 1937, less than 0.5 percent of the whole population. Now there are around 960,000 Christians (0.8 percent) in the country, and not growing. So Japan was not a Christian country before 1945 or after World War II.[1]

The ecumenical and universal Bonhoeffer who belongs to the whole Christian church is the Bonhoeffer most of the world knows today. That said, it would seem on the face of it difficult for Bonhoeffer's ethical thought to have an impact on a non-Christian society like Japan. Recognition of the importance of such thought would seem to depend on its relevance to Japanese society and on whether it has a solid academic foundation within that society. Both of these conditions obtain in Japan today.

Bonhoeffer's ethical thought is ultimately centered on Christ. The more we are grounded firmly in Christ, the more we will become liberated from human restrictions, as well as, paradoxically, from religious laws. The liberating process through this Christocentrism is expressed when he wrote of being "without God before God and with God," or of "non-religious Christianity in a world come of age." I would argue that Bonhoeffer offers significant Christian ethical thought here and now, an ethic that is valid not only for people of other faiths but also for the secular society in which most Japanese live. That is why Bonhoeffer's name has gained resonance throughout the world after World War II, ranging from the West to Asia, Africa, and Latin America. Moreover,

---

1. After the defeat in the war, the number of Christians in 1947 was around 310,000, less than 0.4 percent of the population. So, Japan was a non-Christian country before and after the war, unlike Korea, our nearest neighbor. In Korea there were about 13,760,000 Christians in 2005, some 30 percent of the whole population.

47

Bonhoeffer's influence extends ecumenically beyond Protestantism, and crosses over ideological boundaries to the former East-European socialist countries. The significance of Bonhoeffer has long been globally recognized.[2]

But how has a Bonhoeffer reception been possible in Japan, and what are the outlines of that reception?[3] During the Asia-Pacific War of 1931–45,[4] there was no person comparable to Dietrich Bonhoeffer in Japan. There was no church struggle as in the German Confessing Church, much less a plan for a *coup d'état*, i.e., political resistance with power and violence such as the attempt to kill Hitler on July 20, 1944 in Germany. To understand the attitude of the Japanese churches toward a figure like Bonhoeffer after the war, the peculiar position of Japanese Christians during the war must first be understood.[5]

Generally speaking, Japanese Christians before and during the Asia-Pacific War had a minority complex. They therefore wished not to become isolated from the Japanese majority. Besides that, during the prior war, the Russo-Japanese War of 1904–1905, Christianity was considered to be the religion of the enemy, for it was imported from America and Europe. Now, during the new war with the western powers, Japanese churches and Christians wanted to prove themselves as patriotic and perfect subjects of the Emperor. Willingly or unwillingly, the leading persons of the United Church of Japan at that time cooperated with the national authorities and promoted a militaristic national policy based on the Emperor system, *Tennō*, in order to protect their churches and members.

I classify the behavior of Christians during the wartime into five types: positivists, seclusionists, cooperationists, suffering martyrs, and passive resistors.

---

2. Although Bonhoeffer's ethical thought is ecumenical and universal, it cannot be guaranteed that Bonhoeffer will ever be fully accepted by Japanese society. Even if Bonhoeffer should not be fully accepted in Japan, Bonhoeffer's ethical thought in the non-Christian majority at least gives off a fragrance of Christ, and works as the salt of the earth and light of the world in a secular Japanese society.

3. On Bonhoeffer's reception in Japan, cf. K. Yamasaki, "Um Gottes willen—für die Welt. Dietrich Bonhoeffer in Japan, Wahrnehmungen und Wirkungen," in *IBG Bonhoeffer-Rundbrief* 82 (March 2007): 33–55.

4. The Asia-Pacific War, the so-called "15 Years War," began not with World War II in 1941, but with the Sino-Japanese War in 1931, continuing until the Japanese capitulation in 1945.

5. Here I deal with this theme mainly in the Protestant church in Japan, which was not able to protest more at that time, and not in the Catholic Church in Japan, except insofar as what would generally apply to Japanese Christianity would also apply to the Catholic Church. For very important literature about this theme, cf. Miyata Mitsuo, *Authority and Obedience. Romans 13:1-7 in Modern Japan*, trans. Gregory Vanderbilt, American University Studies, Series VII Theology and Religion, vol. 294 (New York: Peter Lang, 2009). It treats the kind of interpretation and preaching on Romans 13 that had been done by the leading Christians not only during the last war, but also from the beginning of Christian missionary work in the 1850s.

Christians during the war should have been the minority who did not kneel down before Baal; they should have resisted the militarism of the *Tennō* system. However, aside from a few exceptions, they were not worthy of the name "Christian."

The theology of Karl Barth had already been introduced before World War II by clergymen such as Masatoshi Fukuda (1903–1998), Tasuku Matsuo (1903–1938), Kagami Hashimoto (1903–1943), and Masahisa Suzuki (1912–1969). In general, the German Confessing Church movement against the *Reichskirche)* was already known to some Japanese Christian circles.[6] They obtained a considerable amount of information about the German church struggle, and even a brief biography of Martin Niemöller was written in Japanese then. The Japanese Barthians before the war did not act politically like Karl Barth, who openly challenged both church and state until he was deported to his native country, neutral Switzerland. During the war, the Japanese Barthians remained silent, quietist, or "seclusionist." They were involved in neither the confessional nor the political struggle against the militarism of *Tennō*. Instead, they merely conformed in a "cooperationist" way to the national policy of that time in order to prevent the church from being oppressed by the state.

The "Positivists" were those Japanese so-called Christians who wanted to accomplish the militaristic national policy vigorously, and staunchly supported *Tennō*, combined with the Samurai warrior code, *Bushidō*, the twin guides of modern Japanese fascism. They were, so to speak, a Japanese type of "*Deutsche Christen.*" They mixed Christianity and the Japanese Emperor system and were convinced, heretically, that the Japanese national myth was identical to and compatible with Christian faith. For example, they insisted that the Emperor, as a divine human, is the same as the incarnate Jesus Christ. This type of Christian adapted to the times and, as a result, promoted militaristic national policy in collaboration with national authorities. After the War they said that they had been unable to stage an act of resistance, even had they wanted to, because of their overriding concern for the security of their churches and members. There we find their motive for self-justification. In any case, they repeated their pattern of adaptation and assimilation and followed a path of flattery and affirmation of the country's political and military Shintō leadership. These positivists might have protected their churches and their members; however, in

---

6. Professors of political science at Tokyo University, e.g., Prof. Shigeru Nanbara (1889–1974) and Prof. Toyohiko Hori (1899–1986).

the process, they sacrificed the church and her members. The true nature of the church was lost and irrecoverable.

The "seclusionists" divided the matter of this world neatly into two spheres, the sphere of "Caesar" (the state and nation, politics, war, and so on) and the sphere of God, citing Matt. 22:21: "Then pay to Caesar what is due to Caesar, and pay to God what is due to God." The seclusionists wanted to stay in the world of God and faith. They retreated, hiding from the secular world and the times. They kept silent politically, wishing only to lead a quiet Christian life, managing in the sphere of this world not to see, and neither to hear nor to speak. Their nonpolitical Christian life had nevertheless a political meaning, namely it was nothing but tacit approval of the policy and actions of the state. The seclusionists resembled pseudo-Lutheran quietism in their stance, appealing to the "two kingdoms doctrine" of Luther, but only willing to take responsibility in the kingdom of God, and not in the kingdom of this world.

Among Japanese Christians during the Asia-Pacific War, there truly were a very few suffering martyrs. These came primarily from the Holiness church groups, Christians who were persecuted and oppressed because of their fundamental Christian faith. Their fight took the form of a reactive and passive disobedience against political interference with religion, and blatant acts of oppression from the authorities, rather than any sort of proactive resistance for human dignity and fundamental human rights, peace, or democracy. Under intense oppression and severe persecution, these suffering Japanese Christians did not abandon their faith. Instead, they held on to it as a witness of Christ unto death.

There were very few and very exceptional Christians among those who committed acts of passive resistance. Some of these passive resistors were members of Non-Church-Christianity (*Mu-kyou-kai*), who have no church organization. They criticized the national policy of imperialism and the *Zeitgeist* of fascism. They advocated absolute pacifism against war and expressed anti-militarism and anti-imperialism during that difficult time for "two J's," one might say, namely, for Jesus and for Japan. For example, Sensaku Asami (1868–1952) was arrested and fought his trial until the end of the war, and Osamu Ishiga (1910–1994) refused military service as a conscientious objector.[7] Remarkably, the resistance of Tadao Yanaibara (1893–1961)[8] was based not only on his Christian faith in the ultimate, but also on his academic recognition

---

7. Beside Non-Church-Christians, there were about five Japanese Watch Tower people at that time, such as Junzo Akashi (1889–1965) with a few Jehovah's Witnesses, who were heretical in Christianity but determinedly refused to have a gun after enlisting in the army.

of social sciences in the penultimate. However, those acts of resistance did not take the path of political violence but rather that of pacifism.

The aforementioned factors all need to be borne in mind when considering the Japanese encounter with Bonhoeffer after the war. Under the new constitutional system,[9] some conscientious Christians, mainly Barthian scholars, began to undertake a contemporary comparative study of the German Confessing Church struggle and the Japanese United Church (of Christ) during the Nazi and *Tennō* periods respectively. While studying the details of the German church struggle, they realized anew the importance of Karl Barth, particularly his political statements and activities, and at the same time encountered Dietrich Bonhoeffer's life and thought for the first time.

Japanese Christians did not know of the existence of Dietrich Bonhoeffer until 1950. As they got to know him they were amazed at his dramatic life and martyrdom, and marveled at his brilliant theological ideas. So far as I can tell, Bonhoeffer was introduced to Japan for the first time in October 1950 by an American Missionary, D. A. Glugston, who taught at Kwansei Gakuin University, one of the leading Christian universities in Japan. He published an article about Bonhoeffer's life and death according to Eberhard Bethge's account in a small-circulation magazine. However, it was in the pages of the monthly magazine of a leading Protestant publishing company named Shinkyo, *Gospel and World*, through which Bonhoeffer became really widely known to

---

8. T. Yanaibara, Professor of Economics and Colonial Political Science in Tokyo University during the war. Because of his critical teaching against Japanese militaristic imperialism he was dismissed. But after the war he was reinstated and elected in 1951 as President of Tokyo University.

9. On August 15, 1945, Japan accepted the Potsdam Declaration and unconditional surrender. After the end of the war, Japan received the current Constitution as a part of the occupation policy of the American army. The new, post-WWII Constitution was thus substituted for the Great Japanese Imperial Constitution, which was drafted during the Meiji period in 1889, and therefore called the "Meiji Constitution." The present Japanese Constitution has three fundamental principles. The first principle is that the sovereignty of the nation resides in its people. Japan was no longer under the monarchical sovereignty of the Emperor, but a new form of the symbolical imperial system was established by assuming that the sovereign people, by their general will, accept the Emperor as the symbol of Japan. The second principle is pacifism. In the preamble of the Japanese Constitution, the right to live in peace is expressed. And Article 9 states that Japan renounces war and will never maintain military power and war potential. But on the occasion of the Korean War (1950–53), the National Police Reserve was founded in 1950, and was reorganized in 1952 as the National Security Force, both of them predecessors of the current Self-Defense Forces set up in 1954. The third principle of the Constitution is respect for fundamental human rights. So the freedom of religion was asserted constitutionally for the first time as a fundamental human right. And to secure religious freedom, the principle of separation of religion and state was also consolidated. Cf. T. Miyazawa, *Verfassungsrecht (Kempō) Japanisches Recht 21*, trans. R. Heuser and K. Yamasaki (Cologne: Carl Heymanns, 1986).

the Japanese church, in January 1955. Through this publishing house almost all Bonhoeffer works have been published in Japanese. This direct textual encounter with Bonhoeffer by Japanese Christians as well as Bonhoeffer's real introduction into Japanese society was facilitated by Japanese Barthian scholars after the war.[10]

These same Barthians held the United Church of Christ responsible for her conformity to the militarism of the Emperor political system during the war, as opposed to being faithful to the Christian message and worldview. They also subjected themselves to a thoroughgoing self-criticism and expressed radical repentance. They took on themselves the responsibility of the United Church of Japan for supporting the war. Untiring efforts in this regard found expression on Easter Sunday, March 26, 1967, as "The Confession of Responsibility of the United Church of Japan during World War II."[11]

These Barthians studied Bonhoeffer and introduced his life and works in Japanese. They became the first generation of Bonhoeffer researchers and founding members of the Japanese Bonhoeffer Society in 1978. They became involved in political and social problems of democracy, peace, and human rights. In what follows, I would like to briefly present the history of the reception of Bonhoeffer in Japan.

The works of Dietrich Bonhoeffer have established a classical place for themselves in Japan, both as part of Japanese literature and now through the English translation, DBWE. In the 1960s, the major works by Bonhoeffer (*Sanctorum Communio, Act and Being, Creation and Fall, Discipleship, Life Together, Ethics, Letters and Papers from Prison,* together with selected Bible studies and ecumenical works) were translated into Japanese in nine volumes as *The Selected Works of Dietrich Bonhoeffer.* The Bonhoeffer boom occurred in the 1960s and continued through the 1980s in Japan.

There are in fact multiple Japanese readerships of Dietrich Bonhoeffer. The Japanese Christian churches are roughly divided into evangelicals and progressives. Both groups seem to be drawn to the pious Bonhoeffer of the

---

10. Cf. K. Yamasaki (responsible for Japanese literature), *Internationale Bibliographie zu Dietrich Bonhoeffer* [*International Bibliography on Dietrich Bonhoeffer*], ed. Ernst Feil with assistance of Barbara E. Fink (Gütersloh: Chr. Kaiser, 1998). There is a more detailed Japanese Bonhoeffer bibliography, but only available in Japanese, viz., K. Yamasaki, Japanese Bibliography of D. Bonhoeffer, in Osaka City University, *Journal for Jurisprudence and Political Science* 26. no.1 (1979) and Japanese Bibliography of D. Bonhoeffer 1979–88, in Shikoku Gakuin University *Treatise* 70 (1988).

11. Regrettably, there is no official church denunciation of the Japanese Emperor system. Also, this confessional document is issued under the name of Masahisa Suzuki (1912–1969), the moderator of the United Church of Christ in Japan, not the United Church of Christ in Japan itself.

second period of his life, *Discipleship* and *Life Together*. As for the third period of his life, progressive Christians read *Ethics* and *Letters and Papers from Prison*, whereas evangelicals are cautious about *Ethics*. Evangelicals do however read *Letters and Papers from Prison*, precisely because political remarks of Bonhoeffer are rarely found there. The Bonhoeffer boom declined in the 1990s. The Dietrich Bonhoeffer Society in Japan has a membership of almost one hundred, and its annual journal, *Bonhoeffer Studies*, published its twenty-eighth issue in 2011. I believe that Bonhoeffer's works have become a twentieth-century Christian classic in Japan.

The completion of the *Dietrich Bonhoeffer Works English Edition* calls to mind the last days of Professor Heinz-Eduard Tödt in 1989/90. He devoted a great deal of his scarce time but remarkable energy during that period to the editing and publishing, for the coming generations, of the German *Dietrich Bonhoeffer Werke*; it is perhaps the defining theological classic of the twentieth century. As the chair of the German editorial board until his death, when he was succeeded by Professor Wolfgang Huber, Professor Tödt led a team of editors who provided detailed footnotes and other scholarly apparatus that laid a new foundation for Bonhoeffer scholarship, even as far away as East Asia.

The English Language Section of the International Bonhoeffer Society is to be congratulated upon the completion, with the same passion and determination, of the English version of the *Dietrich Bonhoeffer Works*. As for Japan, the complete translation of DBW into Japanese would face considerable financial obstacles.[12]

Thanks to DBWE, Bonhoeffer can now be read in English, thus giving a new impetus to Bonhoeffer studies, not only in the English-speaking countries but right across Asia as well, for it has indeed made his writings and thought available to the whole world. A number of his works, but not all, have already been translated into Korean and Chinese languages.[13] Although advanced Asian students of Bonhoeffer are still required to read his texts in German, the availability of his works in English will be a helpful resource to Asian scholars who are more familiar with English than German, as well as opening access for a broader Asian general readership.

The particular way in which Bonhoeffer has informed the ethical debate in Japan must be understood in terms of the matrix in which the following

12. Even the original German DBW would have been impossible without the financial support of the foundation of Professor Loges, the father of Dr. Ilse Tödt.

13. Cf. also K. Yamasaki, "Wirkungen und Rezeption in Asien," in *Bonhoeffer Handbuch*, ed. Christiane Tietz (Tübingen: Mohr Siebeck, forthcoming).

converge: the Japanese Emperor system (*Tennō*) in both its openly militarist and postwar form, Dietrich Bonhoeffer's thought and action under the German equivalent of *Tennō*, and the issue of war and peace for Japan and the Japanese people.[14]

The core point of the German church struggle, against which Karl Barth and Dietrich Bonhoeffer fought, is definitely shown in the Barmen Theological Declaration. It was to flush out the heresy of the various branches of the German Christian movement and to expose the pseudo-religiosity of Nazism;[15] it was a peaceful but firm and articulate resistance for the sake of the church. The church struggle was a struggle for the first and the second commandments of the Decalogue: "I am the Lord your God, . . . you shall have no other gods before me. You shall not make for yourself an idol. . . . You shall not bow down to them or worship them, for I the Lord your God am a jealous God. . . ." (Exod. 20:2-5). This cause is found summarized in the New Testament in the phrase from Peter's discourse, that the church and Christians are to "obey God rather than men" (Acts 5:29).

On the postwar Barthian analysis, the war responsibility of the United Church of Japan lay at the point where that church did not cling exclusively to the living God of the Bible as the one and only God; rather, alongside the living God they worshiped the Emperor, who is not God, and they obeyed the national authority as true God, instead of subjecting their individual and collective consciences to the Holy Spirit. In other words, the fatal error of the United Church of Japan then was that they accepted the deification of the Emperor and Emperor-worship, which are closely associated with Shintōism, the religion of the imperial family and "national Shintō," the principal shrine of which is Yasukuni, the ancestral shrine of all the war dead of Japan.[16]

14. Cf. M. Miyata, "Bonhoeffer und Japan," in *Freiheit kommt von den Tosabergen* (Frankfurt: Otto Lembeck, 2005). It is the most important article on Bonhoeffer and the Japanese Emperor system, to be found in German. See also Shozo Suzuki, *Ökumenische Studien* and *Evangelium-Wirklichkeit-Verantworutung. Dietrich Bonhoeffers Theologie in Auseinandersetzungen mit japanischer Theologie und Tennōismus bei Kitamori und Takizawa* (Berlin: LIT Verlag, 2011).

15. Bonhoeffer had warned in a radio broadcast manuscript, "Wandlungen des Führerbegriffes" (DBWE 12: 266–82, esp. 279–80) on February 1, 1933 that the Leader (*Führer*) could become a "misleader" (literally, a seducer *Verführer*), and therefore an idol (*Abgott*). Its original manuscript is said to have already been completed on January 27, 1933.

16. During the Asia-Pacific War, Japanese men called up for military duty would often observe a kind of funeral service in acceptance of their possible death in the presence of their next of kin. At such moments, and often in letters home, a common parting greeting was, "We shall meet again at the Yasukuni Shrine." Yasukuni is the central war memorial and chief shrine in Shintō. As such, it is the most visible expression of the *Tennō* tradition, uniting the official state religious cult with veneration of both

The Emperor (*Mikado*, literally "honorable gate," i.e., from earth to heaven) was believed to be *Arahitogami*, a living Man-god (hypostatic apotheosis), a descendant god and son of *Amaterasu*, the "great goddess" (Sun-goddess). The Emperor is the highest priest in *Shintō* (from Chinese *shen-taó*, literally "way to heaven") and is thus both the object and subject of Shintō worship. In the 1930s, the imperial political system was reunited with national Shintō as the official state-religion under the military dictatorship of army General Hidekei Tojo in what became the Japanese equivalent of fascism, *Tennō*. Religious freedom was trampled underfoot, and separation of the state and religion was not followed; rather a Shintōistic theocracy was imposed on all the institutions of society in a manner similar to the Nazi "coordination" (*Gleichschaltung*).

Through studies of Bonhoeffer and the German church struggle, Japanese Christian scholars and the church have learned a still sharper critique of *Tennō* and its remnants today. We have also acquired an unshakable political ethic with which to address the symbolic imperial system and the current "Yasukuni problem," now long after World War II.

What are the main elements of Bonhoeffer's social-public ethic as it relates to our struggle against this shadow *Tennō*, our struggle for peace and against the Emperor's political system, which has a pseudo-religious character? Bonhoeffer's ethical thought provides us with a criterion that is valid here and now. I call his ethical thought "a responsible ethic in accordance with God's reality." This ethic is completely different from the so-called "new situation ethics," which was introduced in Japan in the 1960s, and became the predominant ethic of that generation. According to Joseph Fletcher, "all is

the Emperor and the military might and honor of the state. The Yasukuni Shrine has become the focus of a resurgent interest in *Tennō* on the part of Japanese youth in a nation that is constitutionally pacifist. Some observers attribute this resurgent cult of the war dead to lacunae in history texts and instructions in the Japanese schools where mention of Japan's military aggression and crimes against occupied peoples have often been passed over in silence. The documentary confirmation in the 1970s that several convicted and executed Japanese war criminals are interred and named at Yasukuni has made the shrine the focal point of diplomatic difficulties with countries formerly occupied by Japan, such as the two Koreas, China, and Taiwan. See Saki Noguchi, "'Is It Trendy to Be Right Wing?' Asks Article, Netizens React," *Japan Crush* (31 October 2012), http://www.japancrush.com/2012/stories/is-it-trendy-to-be-right-wing-asks-article-netizens-react.html; "Japan's Yasukuni Shrine," *BBC News*, Asia (18 October 2012), http://www.bbc .co.uk/news/world-asia-19987251; Yoko Wakatsuki, "Shrine visit could inflame tensions between Japan, China," *CNN* (17 October 2012), http://www.cnn.com/2012/10/17/world/asia/japan-china-shrine-visit; Martin Fackler, "Japanese Politician's Visit to Shrine Raises Worries," *New York Times*, Asia-Pacific (17 October 2012), http://www.nytimes.com/2012/10/18/world/asia/japan-opposition-leader-shinzo-abe-visits-war-shrine-a-possible-message-to-neighbors.html?_r=0.

permitted as long as there is love."[17] Situation ethics, which was imported into Japan without any reference to Christian tradition and background, posited an ethical universe in which good and evil do not exist *a priori* but depend on the situation: something becomes either good or evil *a posteriori* under the particular circumstances. All that is needed for situation ethics is a consideration of timing, fittingness, and a calculation of the probable cost-benefit of a given course of action.

Eberhard Bethge recognizes that Bonhoeffer's ethic builds a bridge between "norm ethics" and "situation ethics."[18] Bonhoeffer's responsible ethic in accordance with the reality of God is not a "servile attitude toward the facts."[19] Bonhoeffer's responsible ethic in accordance with God's reality is not slavery to a situation without and apart from Christ. It is an ethic that impels Christians and the church to wrestle with the realty of God through Christ.

If we observe the whole of Bonhoeffer's life and thought, there exist norms of good and evil in his ethic *a priori*. One would fight against Nazism and the Nazi regime, but not simply hypothetically, struggling with historical phantoms of evil. Depending on a situation, he might take the violent way according to his responsible ethic in response to God's reality through evangelical freedom, following Jesus Christ. But violence is violence, evil is evil to the last. Murders, use of violence, acts of fraud including lies are evil to the last, even if the actions are prompted by self-defense, however legitimate and justifiable these actions are. That is why we have to carry our liability and responsibility for the better evil chosen among only evil choices. Whether we are ready to take ownership for our actions or not, that is the point that divides Bonhoeffer's responsible ethic in accordance with God's reality from the simple situation ethics of Fletcher. That is why Bonhoeffer's ethic is called an ethic of responsibility.

Bonhoeffer's ethical thought is not designed only for "borderline situations" or *in extremis* cases encountered in time of war or revolution. Bonhoeffer's ethical thought is still valid in a democratic society and relevant in a normal peacetime life. In what follows I will explain how his ethical thought operates as an ethic of resistance, or restoration or reconstruction, in Bonhoeffer's own special case and as an ethic of peace today.

17. Joseph F. Fletcher (1905–1991), Episcopal priest and theologian, author of *Situation Ethics: The New Morality* (Nashville: John Knox, 1966).

18. Cf. Eberhard Bethge, *Dietrich Bonhoeffer: A Biography*, rev. ed. Victoria J. Barnett (Minneapolis: Fortress Press, 2000), 717.

19. *Ethics*, DBWE 6:222.

At a time when there were disputes and conflicts about peace, justice, and human rights in the society, that is, after the 1960s, the society needed drastic, even revolutionary change. Thus Bonhoeffer's radical "ethic of resistance" functioned within this framework. When the instability and insecurity settled down, the trendy Bonhoeffer researchers, who have a partial interest in one side and one period of Bonhoeffer when he determined to take part in violent resistance against the Hitler regime, felt that Bonhoeffer and his radical political theology seemed to have become a thing of the past.

Bonhoeffer's ethic of resistance was always quoted when justice was trodden upon, human rights were suppressed, and peace was threatened. In Japan, Bonhoeffer was misunderstood, or only half understood, at the time of the campus riots; at that time, Bonhoeffer's ethic of resistance was abused by justifying violence. Also in Korea, Bonhoeffer is much discussed and has always been mentioned in the "Korean struggle for democracy" and "theology of the oppressed" (*Minyung* theology).

However, Bonhoeffer's ethical thought is valid not only for such cases as an ethic of resistance. Bonhoeffer's ethical thought still holds good where fundamental human rights are somehow respected, even if not perfectly, where democratic systems keep functioning, and peace is maintained. In other words, in "the world come of age" Bonhoeffer's ethical thought is still available and relevant as an ethic of reconstruction, of rebuilding, of restoration.

We find quite conservative descriptions appearing here and there in the *Ethics* manuscripts when Bonhoeffer was deeply engaged in the political resistance. For example, we easily recognize his conservative attitude in the *Ethics* manuscript chapter about "the four mandates" theory, particularly concerning the relations between "state and church."[20] Some historians (H. Mommsen and others) criticize the conservative tendencies, which clearly existed within both the resistance group in the counterespionage department (*Abwehr*) of the *Wehrmacht* (Armed Forces) and the Bonhoeffer-Dohnanyi circle, one of the civilian resistance groups.[21]

The conservative elements supposed to be in Bonhoeffer's manuscript are not items of reactionary conservatism, but of sound conservatism in order to reconstruct and maintain German society and the ethical norms that were

---

20. DBWE 6:288; DBWE 16:523ff.

21. Cf. Hans Mommsen, "Der Widerstand gegen Hitler und die Deutsche Gesellschaft," in *Der Widerstand gegen den National-Sozialismus. Die Deutsche Gesellschaft und der Widerstand gegen Hitler*, vol. 685, ed. Jürgen Schmädeke and Peter Steinbach (Munich and Zurich: Piper, 1986). Thus the same plans for constitutional and administrative reform of the resistance groups of the 20th of July 1944, ibid. See also Klaus-Jürgen Müller, "Nationalkonservative Eliten zwischen Kooperation und Widerstand," ibid.

deliberately and ruthlessly destroyed by the Nazis before and during the war. Those conservative bits and pieces found in Bonhoeffer's political thought as the ethic of reconstruction must be evaluated in comparison with his ethic of resistance. I interpret these two sides—the ethic of resistance and ethic of reconstruction—to constitute the whole ethical thought of Bonhoeffer's unfinished *Ethics*. Thus Bonhoeffer's ethical thought would be valid as the ethic of resistance for the turbulent period and the borderline situation, where dictatorship and terrorism dominate, and where liberty, justice, and human dignity are infringed. On the other hand, Bonhoeffer's ethical thought is also valid as the ethic of reconstruction for normal everyday life where a real degree of democracy, peace, human rights, and prosperity may be enjoyed. In such conditions we may live an ordinary life without checking our own conscience all the time with glaring eyes. In a reconstructed peaceful life and society, we follow Christ simply, obeying the law and commandments according to the ethic of reconstruction.

Bonhoeffer's own special case must also be considered in terms of the particular decisions he faced and the alternatives that were open to him. He came across Christian pacifism for the first time while he studied abroad at Union Theological Seminary (1930/31), and after that he became a defender of Christian pacifism at home and abroad. He advocated nonviolent resistance not only in the German church struggle at home, but also in ecumenical gatherings abroad; recall his famous peace address in Černohorské Kúpele in Slovakia (then part of the former Czechoslovakia) on July 26, 1932, and his peace message at the Fanø conference in Denmark on August 28, 1934. He longed to go to the East to meet Gandhi and to learn his practice of *Ahimsa* (nonviolence) and *Satyagraha* (grasp of truth).

But once the Second World War broke out, Bonhoeffer began formulating his new ethic of responsibility in his *Ethics*. He undertook this project because the normative ethic of his *Discipleship* book had become unsuitable for the new reality of the world and God's call for him. Indeed for Bonhoeffer to participate in the military conspiracy against Hitler and the Nazi regime as a follower of Christ was made possible only when his new ethic of responsibility had been constructed in accordance with the new reality of God he had come to see—the God of the suffering, visible only "from below." His ethics of responsibility, in accordance with God's reality, is surely the necessary condition for his political resistance. Yet the new ethic does not become the sufficient cause and condition for him to take part in plans for the assassination of Hitler and the *coup d'état*.

Bonhoeffer's participation in the conspiracy would have been practically impossible without his exemption from military combat service, which he secured, ironically, by being inducted into German military counterintelligence under Admiral Canaris. Bonhoeffer's incredible talents and his special family circumstances also played a great role and placed him in a position in which the decision not to participate would have taken a sheer act of the will. For example, Bonhoeffer's family included a high-ranking official with the Lufthansa state airline, a judge, a lawyer, and a scholar of the first order who could get the inside information on the Nazi regime and even approach the center of the power. Such a condition was not usual, a position in which not many Christians could be found. With the many gifts and talents given to Dietrich Bonhoeffer from God, much responsibility and hardship would be required of him.

Bonhoeffer believed that he followed Jesus Christ by faith through allowing Christ to form within his own spirit ("conformation"), and that, though he trespassed the law of God in evangelical freedom for the sake of others, the law would be fulfilled in the deeper dimension of its original intent. It is this ethic of responsibility in accordance with God's reality that admits various ways of resistance against the Nazi regime or its equivalent in one's own historical reality. Therefore, Bonhoeffer neither justified his role in the conspiracy nor judged those who did not participate in it.

Dietrich Bonhoeffer's ethic of peace is the fruit of his ethic of resistance and restoration, and it is this dimension of his ethic that is of the greatest import for Japan and the Japanese church today. Bonhoeffer's ethical thought on peace did not fall into a kind of dogmatic principled pacifism throughout his life. There remains, on the one hand, his ethical thought on peace and pacifism, and, on the other hand, acceptance of nonviolent resistance as an indispensable type of pacifism. He never renounced the principle of either of these positions. It was in God's grace and evangelical freedom that Bonhoeffer took his political responsibility and its necessary risk of resistance by force and violence in accordance with God's reality. On the other hand, however, he sets a limit to an absolutist claim to nonviolent pacifism.

Bonhoeffer's ethical thought on peace offers important insights. Once a war has begun, there might be a situation where the very resistance against the war needs to take a form of force and violence to stop it, as in Bonhoeffer's case. Therefore, it is crucial to realize that we have to work hard for peace before injustice and violence erupt into war. In other words, it is in time of peace that we are called to the pacifism of nonviolent resistance as Bonhoeffer was called to it before the outbreak of war. What we say and do for peace in time of peace to maintain peace and to prevent war is far more important than what we say and do for peace after the outbreak of war. The legacy of Bonhoeffer still speaks to the Japanese people today. The legacy of his pacifism in the time of peace and of his resistance for peace in the time of war is a very important resource for Japanese Christians.

In conclusion, I find that Bonhoeffer's ethical thought is of crucial importance in my country, both for theologians and for political scientists in the following two respects. First, though the quasi-religious political system of the Japanese Emperor and resurgent *Tennō* is admittedly a specifically Japanese problem, it is also a universal problem in that it contradicts the first and second commandments of the Decalogue, a tendency found in some form in all societies today.

Concerning the endeavor to achieve peace, we have the peaceful postwar Constitution of non-armed pacifism (Paragraph 9). This also is a uniquely Japanese situation, but perhaps gives Japan and Japanese Christians an opportunity to lead the world in living out an ethic of peace, even if it might mean nonviolent resistance to an aggressor state. We must therefore wrestle with the peace problem nonviolently. It is simply our task. We are called to achieve nonviolent pacifism and peacemaking in a secular world as ecumenically and as globally as possible, reaching across religious-ideological boundaries that separate us.

Finally, Bonhoeffer lived the latter part of his life in a Germany ruled by the Nazis. He responded to the reality of God responsibly and died a martyr's death. For us Christians in Far East Asia, Bonhoeffer is still present, though he lived sixty-eight years ago and very far from Asia, as long as we also live "here and now" in Christ, responding to God's reality, just as Bonhoeffer did. The distance of space and difference of time between Bonhoeffer and ourselves is overcome only through the presence of Jesus Christ in him and in us. And this is also true for the coming generations in Asia and the world.

7

B. Translation as Bonhoeffer Interpretation

Cultural Elements in Theology and Language: Translation as Interpretation

Hans Pfeifer

The Dietrich Bonhoeffer Works edition is not only a very carefully edited set of books but is also a remarkable translation from the German. It is in fact a faithful facsimile of the German edition. A few additions were made, because during the time of its editing new Bonhoeffer material was discovered and was published in the Dietrich Bonhoeffer Yearbook in German and consequently translated for the English series. There are other additions, both commentaries necessary for the English reader and also the results of recent research. But basically the English edition is a replica of the German.

To achieve this, a very definite procedure was necessary. For both the German and English languages have their own special traditions and cultures. Each language has something like an individual personality, coined by its own history, formed by the development of spiritual and epistemological characters of a special kind. All participants of this conference have ample experience in this field, and are familiar with the necessity to bridge more or less deep trenches of separation and distance. Translation, however, is based on the conviction that it is possible to transfer contents of mind from one language into the other. Those who are used to this may not realize it anymore, because we all have come to develop our own personal English, if we are German, and vice versa. But when it comes to written texts, we are again confronted with a new wall to climb. It means to comprehend and appropriate a set of words and ideas that have no exact parallel in the other language, be it the target or the original language. For this very reason a lot depended on skillful and diligent translation, which was provided for by employing translators as partners of the editors, and also by the reviewing of drafts by German readers, mostly the editors of the volumes in question.

When we look at the kind of literature we are confronted with in the *corpus Bonhoefferianum*, we soon realize that his academic language and set of ideas are rather complicated and owe a great deal of their phrasing to the long history of European intellectual development. But, in addition, in his letters he writes a rather refined German, which again is differentiated and sometimes full of allusions from the German culture of his time and its manner of expression. And in this context I am not yet speaking of disguised hints, which were necessary to remain undetected by German censors, but to texts and trains of thought that are very elaborate. Often the facts behind a given text were not easy to discover and communicate to the translators. And, in any case, translating German style into English can be hard. Let me just give an example.

How do you translate "Sehr geehrter Herr Professor," or "Sehr verehrte gnädige Frau" into English? Strictly speaking you cannot, even though this is an everyday figure of speech. And these were relatively simple problems. But these simple examples bring basic problems to light, which are not easy to solve even though German and English are closely related languages.

But this is only the external problem, so to speak. For it is not surprising that theology and church life had its own linguistic development, which was distinct from theological or confessional differences. I will spell out a few. For example, the word *Gemeinde* has no exactly corresponding word in English. Neither "parish," nor "congregation," fully match what is meant by the word of the sister language.

Or consider this: Bonhoeffer in America is very often considered to be a Lutheran, except by those who want him to be Reformed. He was neither totally. Rather, he was a Protestant theologian belonging to a church that was a union of both. He was indeed deeply inspired by Luther. But, at least in the beginning, it was Luther as he had been rediscovered by Karl Holl, who saw in Luther the discoverer of the religious individual who lived following his conscience. I wonder whether this is what first occurs to the mind of a Lutheran in America when asked what Lutheranism means for him. In later years Bonhoeffer discovered the Lutheran confessional writings, which, I understand, are highly valued in American Lutheranism. But for Bonhoeffer, this was connected to Luther's doctrine of the state, or rather, the relationship between state and church, making both of them pillars of God's order in this world. This function of the church for Bonhoeffer was relevant for the

Confessing Church as well. Even when he spoke about the church becoming independent of the state, he still saw in both, mandates which, together with other institutions, were God-given orders for the life of the community. Nowhere did he ever advocate for the right of a people to find its own method of political organization.

At this point we are dealing with one of the most nauseating problems in translating texts like those Bonhoeffer left us. The greatest problems for translation are not to be found in the theological terminology Bonhoeffer employed. Theological words and texts are less complicated to translate, because they tend to go back to common Latin roots. Nontheological language, however, confronts us with the problem of finding the highest possible equivalent for any given word or meaning. The possible result of this process is that we may never fully arrive at true equivalency.

If some of us who were not directly involved in the editing and translating of this Bonhoeffer series have sometimes asked, why it took so long before another volume was published, and if some became a little anxious because they were waiting for texts to use in their research and to quote in publications (and of course, sometimes draft translations led to debates between a translator or editor and other Bonhoeffer scholars), I hope that by now it has become apparent what an extraordinary amount of work was necessary to carry this through.

Let me also mention some more problems that come up in letters or personal notes. In every exchange of letters, facts are implied that need not be mentioned because both partners have the necessary knowledge. Sometimes, and this is more important, there was reference to matters that should not be understood by the political censors, to which all letters were subjected. And then of course there were more or less important affairs in general life at any given time, not significant enough to be mentioned in historical writings, but the knowledge of which would help to understand the content of a letter. As the liaison person between the German and English editions, which I have been for thirteen years, I have followed and participated in a great deal of this work. I came to understand some of the troubling situations that arise when decisions have to be made on the basis of assumptions that may not be judged with certainty to be totally relevant. I would like to personally thank those who took on the trouble and time-consuming work to accomplish this translation, both Germans and Anglo-Saxons.

Finally, I would like to say something about different approaches to the process of translating. In theory, one makes a major distinction between two ways of translating. One approach is the kind of translating that aims to remain faithful to the individual *words*, in the sense that words used in a comparable way should be chosen for the translation. To use the example I have already mentioned, "parish" or "congregation" can be used for the German *Gemeinde*. The second approach aims for a most careful presentation of the *meaning* in the words, perhaps eventually using completely different words or expressions that are believed to help the reader understand the meaning even in its finest shades and implications.[1] Such translation may help to get the meaning of a whole sentence or passage. But the problem with this approach is twofold. First, different words can be used to translate the same German word, and that makes it hard to compare passages with each other. The index loses its significance. Second, such translations make quotations more complicated or sometimes impossible. In general the translators used the first kind of translation, thus making it easier to use the English text for further study. But in this case, as described above, the task of finding the best translation according to verbal affinity gets much more complicated than in the second approach. Finding verbal affinity is often much more difficult than trying to describe the meaning of a text in one's own words. And for that reason, cooperation with German readers was important; in fact it demanded of them a great deal of time and thought. But all of them were prepared to do this, so long as their language capacity was sufficient.

BONHOEFFER AND THE CULTURAL BREACH

Since we are talking about the translation of Dietrich Bonhoeffer's writings, I would like to suggest going back to Bonhoeffer himself regarding the question about the effect of a culture on theology, and the challenge of understanding between different cultures. Bonhoeffer is helpful, as he experienced remarkable changes in dealing with the cultural elements in theological differences and exchange. In 1929 H. Richard Niebuhr published a book with the title "The Social Sources of Denominationalism," in which he argued that divisions between Christian groups or churches parallel social divisions. In his conclusion he stated that unity of the church would depend on the gospel of the fatherhood of God and the brotherhood of men.[2] One year later Dietrich Bonhoeffer arrived in New York and began to study American theology. Although

---

1. The first approach is "the most possible rendering, most faithful to the text, which follows the original as closely as possible," while the second is a "free construction directed at the sense of a text employing the linguistic and stylistic peculiarities of the target language in the sense of a transmission (*Übertragung*) . . ." See *Der Literaturbrockhaus* in 8 vols., ed. Werner Habicht and Wolf-Dieter Lange (Mannheim: Bibliographisches Institut, 1995), 8:157f.

2. H. Richard Niebuhr, *The Social Sources of Denominationalism* (New York: Holt, 1929), 278.

Bonhoeffer of course knew of H. Richard Niebuhr, we don't know whether he had read this book. But we do know that he arrived with high hopes and expectations. He wanted to see the "cloud of witnesses"[3] realized, or actualized, in a country with many different Christian groups and churches. He envisioned churches that devoted their life to God without restrictions, and in which Christian faith was lived convincingly. It is not surprising that these high expectations were disappointed, but the deep dismay that Bonhoeffer felt astonishes. Perhaps one reason for his dismay is that Bonhoeffer couldn't imagine people speaking about God without going back to Holy Scripture. In the German churches, too, Bonhoeffer felt that while there was much talk about Scripture, the deepest meaning had gone, and God in his holy truth was not present in many German church services. This assessment may sound harsh, but I believe it to be the perspective of the young Bonhoeffer.

Bonhoeffer's criticism fell also on Union Theological Seminary, where he found not enough deep theological seriousness. It is said that he asked Reinhold Niebuhr whether only sociology was taught at this Seminary. In short, young Bonhoeffer, in his first encounters with theology and church life in the States, judged these new cultures and churches from his own intellectually solid but culturally limited experience and historical knowledge. What we see here on the side of young Bonhoeffer is a remarkable lack of distinction between theological questions as such, and the problem of differentiated shaping of society and culture under different social, cultural, and even political conditions, and how this differentiation bears on theological issues. His contact with Anglo-Saxon churches and theology could have become a complete failure right there.

But then the unexpected happened. Bonhoeffer made friends at Union, one of whom was Frank Fisher, an African American. Frank invited Bonhoeffer to go with him to his church, the Abyssinian Baptist Church, in Harlem. (I would like to know what Frank thought or had in mind when he made this move.) And all of a sudden, the scene changed completely; Dietrich was overwhelmed. Here he found Christian faith, Christian life, sincerity and probably humility, such as he had never seen before. This was the cloud of witnesses he had been hoping for. So after all, Dietrich, though full of European humanist and particularly German presuppositions, was capable of recognizing something genuinely Christian in a completely different cultural context, something that was to become of the greatest significance for his future life.

---

3. See Hebrews 12.

Is there not some significance in this, when it comes to reading and translating German theological texts into English? Somehow the same inspiration is required for English-speaking translators when confronted with so German a theologian as Dietrich was. It is openness to the genuine, to the authentic, even in a completely different culture, that is an important condition for translating and editing in general, and for translating Bonhoeffer in particular. And in my understanding and experience of the procedures that were followed in this project, it is precisely this openness that makes of the DBWE edition in its outlines and goals such a remarkable work of scholarship. And when I say this I have in mind the fact that German culture, and its way of thought and sentiment, does not always come naturally to the English-speaking reader. All the more we Germans appreciate the understanding that is seen in the editorial effort of DBWE.

Back to Bonhoeffer. He was not a person to give up easily. Now he began to study and contact his new academic environment. Students who met him remembered that though he was already qualified to be a visiting lecturer, he accepted them as equals, and he soon made friends with Paul Lehman and Frank Fisher and also with other European students like Jean Lasserre and Erwin Sutz. But not only this. Clifford Green has recently investigated Bonhoeffer's studies during his second semester in 1930 and was able to demonstrate how diligently and persistently Bonhoeffer began to learn about the theological and cultural settings of church and theological thought in this country. Paul Lehmann became a close friend of Bonhoeffer and supported his critical approach to American mainstream theology, hoping that this young and intelligent German theologian might help him introduce Karl Barth's theology of crisis into the studies of Union Seminary and in other parts of the country. Bonhoeffer himself summed up his time in the States as the beginning of an entirely new way of thought and Christian life that led to an entirely new outlook on life and his own theology.[4] And his late remark, that he had changed his life by the experiences abroad, refers to this too.[5]

Some years after that, Bonhoeffer came to the States a second time. As is well known, his free work and teaching were barred by the Nazi police in 1939, World War II was under way, and Bonhoeffer, being a conscientious objector, was liable to get into serious trouble. He was forced to find new space for this living and teaching. So he accepted the invitation to come to the States for a period of teaching and working. But instead of staying, he decided to return to Germany. He chose not to be separated from his students, his church, and

---

4. Letter to Max Diestel, November 5, 1942, DBWE 16:367–68.
5. See letter to Eberhard Bethge, July 21, 1944, DBWE 8:485–87.

his family during a possibly long period of warfare. But, having returned, and realizing how much trouble Lehman and Niebuhr had had in finding financial support to guarantee his visit, but probably also for other reasons, he set about using his recent experiences to write a paper about church life in the States, and to make a comparison between the two different cultures.

This paper was published as "Protestantism without Reformation."[6] In it we find him further advanced in dealing with the question of the unity of the one church and the differences between denominations. He studied the historical background of churches in America and came to the conclusion that the greatest difference between Protestantism in the States and Protestantism in Germany was that German churches were still very much stamped by the Reformation period while American Protestant churches had an altogether "post-Reformation" character. And he was sure that the different relationship between Christians in the States and in Germany should be related to this point. Interesting is his remark, that German churches had a closer relationship to government, but that the influence of churches on politics and government in the USA was much bigger and more successful. Bonhoeffer then developed a criterion for mutual acceptance and cooperation between different churches and denominations: As long as, on the basis of Jesus Christ, unity is seen as both the origin and goal of different Christian groups, there the life and work of Christians can grow.[7] Bonhoeffer did not belittle the differences between denominations and confessions, seeing them instead as part of the interim, the "penultimate,"[8] which is the character of all things in history. I speak about this now, because I see this as a relevant characteristic of the Christian multitude, and an important guiding principle in the business of translating Bonhoeffer.

After returning to Germany, Bonhoeffer began to sum up the result of this second contact with the American universe, and wrote the article already mentioned. At that time he was already occupied with the question of a new reconstruction of the churches after the overthrow of Hitler's dictatorship, which he felt sure was about to happen. This time he looked at Christian life in the States as a possible model for a future setup of the German churches. He concluded that the churches in Germany would have to follow their own tradition that had been valid before the Nationalist Socialist corruption of thought and life in Christian thinking. But he also found it extremely helpful

---

6. DBWE 15:438–62. See esp. 438 n. 1, concerning Bonhoeffer's notes for this paper, edited by Victoria Barnett, "Notes at the Conclusion of the Diary," first published in *Dietrich Bonhoeffer Jahrbuch* 4 and then in DBWE 15:238–45.

7. DBWE 15:444.

8. See "Ultimate and Penultimate Things," *Ethics*, DBWE 6:146–70.

and thought-provoking to study the history and social setting of church life in the States. He dealt with the public role of churches in Europe and the States, discussed the difference of calling Christian communities *denominations* of churches, and assumed that the main difference between churches in Europe and the States lies in the fact that European churches had experienced a reformation while churches in America mainly had come into existence after the Reformation had already happened. Bonhoeffer's investigations, like those of H. Richard Niebuhr, are based on historical, sociological, and theological methods and criteria, and this made them extremely helpful in the case of comparative study and work such as translations are built upon. For example, at one point, Bonhoeffer discusses the difference of the relationship between church and state in Germany and the U.S. He concludes that, though the relationship between state and church is much closer in Germany than in the States, the influence of churches on public life is much stronger in the States than in Germany. At one point Bonhoeffer discusses democracy with the result that, according to his impression, individual rights are at least as well protected in the German system (of course in the time before Hitler) as in the United States. He tends to draw the conclusion, that though church life and public life are very different in the two political systems he is investigating, both have values and failures that can be rated as more or less equal. But the most important point is that, despite all differences, God has set a common goal for both forms of Christendom: "Where unity [of the churches] is contemplated as both origin and goal, there the life and work of Christendom can grow, seeking and finding the unity of the split up churches on the basis of the life and work of Jesus Christ, in whom the unity of the church is fulfilled."[9] In his studies, Bonhoeffer came to the conclusion that a comparative study needs to avoid putting one's own theological tradition in the center of the study, and that diligence and objectivity is essential, but that, in the end, a theological point of view has to be found that makes it possible to constitute a unity of Christian language and beliefs in two completely different cultures.

Thus Dietrich Bonhoeffer can then be seen as an excellent example for the task of translating theological thoughts and issues from one language into another, in other words, translating German texts into English. His willingness to become fully involved in the life and thought of English theology, his being prepared to encounter totally different ways of being Christian, his trying to understand the problem from within its own history and life, rather than just from his own presuppositions, made him a Christian witness not only for

---

9. DBWE 15:445, translation Pfeifer.

Germans but for the whole *oecumene*. And in this disposition he also became an example for translating and editing his work into English. So if one wants to evaluate the work and capacity of the editorial board and the team of translators of DBWE, Bonhoeffer himself can be an adequate guideline. I would like to emphasize that the editorial team has met this example, following Bonhoeffer by existentially entering into the cultural, historical, and theological otherness of his time, culture, and person, believing that there is a deep unity, which rests not with humans themselves but within the life and resurrection of Jesus Christ.

8

Discovering Bonhoeffer in Translation: New Insights from the Bonhoeffer Works, English Edition

Reinhard Krauss

I would like to begin with a biographical note. Many years ago, I was a theology student at the University of Tübingen in Germany, enrolled in my first seminar. For the duration of the entire semester, each of the weekly two-hour sessions was devoted to the study, analysis, and discussion of a single monograph: Dietrich Bonhoeffer's doctoral dissertation *Sanctorum Communio*. This intense intellectual exercise concluded with an oral exam at the end of the semester. The professor was quite satisfied with my responses, and I sensed the exam was about to draw to a close. However, before proceedings concluded, and at the risk of doing some damage to my expected grade, I could not help but confide to the professor some uneasiness I had about the course. "We have studied *Sanctorum Communio* for over four months now," I said with some hesitation, "and yet I am left with a vague feeling that I have not yet fully grasped all the nuances of Bonhoeffer's ecclesiology." To which my examiner kindly responded: "Do not be overly concerned. This sensation is quite normal after reading *Sanctorum Communio*." My relief was immense—on multiple levels. I was even more relieved when I learned, sometime afterwards, that none other than Karl Barth had openly confessed that he had been worried whether, in his own theological exposition of the community of saints, he would be able "even [to] maintain the high level reached by Bonhoeffer."[1] A few years later still, in 1990, I then learned from John Godsey that the International Bonhoeffer Society was looking for an additional translator for one of the volumes of a new English edition of Bonhoeffer's works. Regarding the specifics, he advised me to contact Clifford Green, the editor of the volume. In making the initial contact,

---

1. Karl Barth, *Church Dogmatics* IV/2, Sections 67–68: *The Doctrine of Reconciliation*, Study Edition 26, 22nd ed. (Edinburgh: T. & T. Clark/Continuum International, 2010), 30.

I recall harboring the secret hope that the volume in question would not be *Sanctorum Communio*. It turned out to be *Sanctorum Communio*!

These personal memories of how I came to participate in this extraordinarily rich intellectual venture of a new English translation of Dietrich Bonhoeffer's collected writings may serve as a hermeneutical entry point to reflect on both the general and the particular ways in which this translation project was shaped by the primary goal of all translation, namely to achieve a consonance of meaning between the author and the reader of a given text. This consonance of intended and received meaning between author and reader is, of course, the inherent purpose of any text. Its successful attainment is contingent on a multiplicity of variables, such as the respective linguistic milieus, the historical settings, and the socioeconomic contexts of both author and reader. Translation adds multiple layers of complexity and potential impediments to the achievement of this necessary consonance of meaning between author and reader. To be critically aware of, to pinpoint, and to creatively reduce, minimize, or ideally even eliminate such communicative impediments—this is the world the translator inhabits in her or his work.

The translator's first and primary task is to elicit the accurate and nuanced meaning of the source text within its own linguistic milieu. This includes the diligent effort to develop an intimate familiarity with the author's specialized vocabulary, specific word usage, grammatical nuances, idiomatic conventions, and linguistic idiosyncrasies. This aspect of a translator's work entails a hermeneutic circle in which the linguistic nuances and subtleties of a given source text continue to emerge more fully throughout the translation process itself. Thus one could paradoxically say that one cannot begin to translate a text until one has finished translating it. The posture of the translator, seeking to plumb the linguistic depths of meaning of a given source text, was eloquently expressed by the British novelist and translator Iris Murdoch in her 1967 Leslie Stephen Lecture:

> If I am learning [a foreign language], I am confronted by an authoritative structure which commands my respect. The task is difficult and the goal is distant and perhaps never entirely attainable. My work is a progressive revelation of something which exists independently of me. Attention is rewarded by a knowledge of reality. Love of [the foreign language] leads me away from myself towards something alien to me, something which my consciousness cannot take over, swallow up, deny, or make unreal. The honesty and humility required of the student—not to pretend to know what

one does not know—is the preparation for the honesty and humility of the scholar who does not even feel tempted to suppress the fact which damns his theory.[2]

The process Murdoch describes is that of learning a foreign language, but the underlying posture that is of concern here also accurately describes the translator's approach to a given text, even in cases where the translator is a native speaker in the source language.

Applied to the specific case of this project, Dietrich Bonhoeffer's German is shaped by the academic terminology and conceptuality of the early decades of the twentieth century, the linguistic conventions acquired from a family belonging to the upper-middle-class, highly educated elite of German society, as well as the distinctive personal traits of his own writing style and thought patterns. Each of these three categories marking Bonhoeffer's distinct "sociolinguistic" location presents the translator with a conceptual gulf to be bridged within the German source text itself, even before the task of casting Bonhoeffer's thoughts into the structural and conceptual mold of another language, in this case English. The terminology and conceptuality of German theological discourse has evolved and markedly changed since the days of Reinhold Seeberg, Adolf von Harnack, and Ernst Troeltsch. German sociologists and social philosophers likewise no longer employ the categories and linguistic conventions of Max Weber, Ferdinand Tönnies, and Alfred Vierkandt. The task of translating Bonhoeffer's texts into contemporary English adds an additional layer to this challenge of bridging the linguistic and conceptual gap across three-quarters of a century. At the time of his writings, Bonhoeffer and his academic contemporaries in the English-speaking world were, of course, already separated by the linguistic barrier and significant differences in conceptuality. This initial gap has been widening ever since due to the same evolutionary processes within the respective academic disciplines in both the German and the English-speaking worlds.

Similar challenges present themselves in translating Bonhoeffer's nonacademic vocabulary and style into contemporary English. Throughout the translation process, translators were cognizant of the fact that the intended readers of the new English translation would come from a broad spectrum of social, cultural, and linguistic traditions. We also had to assume that the majority of readers would not be thoroughly familiar with the details of political,

---

2. Iris Murdoch, "The Sovereignty of Good over Other Concepts," in *The Sovereignty of Good*, 2nd ed. (London and New York: Routledge, 2001), 77ff., 89. Originally published as *The Sovereignty of Good over Other Concepts: The Leslie Stephen Lecture, 1967* (Cambridge: Cambridge University Press, 1967).

economic, and cultural matters in Germany in the first half of the twentieth century, nor with the social milieu, the customs, and the literary, musical, and artistic tastes of a highly educated family in the upper echelons of German society during that era. In this regard, the critical apparatus in the new edition is indispensable. The historical and cultural background information it supplies provides a crucial frame of reference for understanding the nuances and subtleties of the translated texts.

Having outlined some of the particular complexities of this translation project, I would now like to highlight some of the specific ways in which the translation took shape within this matrix. Particularly helpful in the early stages of the project were extensive face-to-face consultations in which nearly all translators and editors were able to participate. In a series of multi-day gatherings, crucial issues were addressed in vigorous discussions intended to develop both a methodological consensus and a set of practical tools for the project. Among the topics addressed was the need for linguistic consistency across all volumes of the series. Another issue was the question of the appropriate balance between historical fidelity and the need to render Bonhoeffer's concepts and thoughts in natural contemporary English, or the balance between "formal correspondence" and "dynamic equivalence" of the translation, to use the helpful terminology coined by the translation theorist Eugene Nida.[3] Further discussions focused on the proper translation of several key terms in Bonhoeffer's vocabulary that presented particular challenges due to the lack of a direct English equivalent. Many foundational methodological decisions and practical tools, such as glossaries and style guidelines, emerged from this intensive early consultation phase. Common to all the discussions was an underlying consensus that the language of the new translation ought not to draw attention to itself, but function in the strictly subservient role of making Bonhoeffer's thoughts as transparent and accessible as possible to contemporary English-speaking readers. The common goal of the translators in this, as in any translation project, was the "revelation of something which exists independently"[4] of the translator, to use Iris Murdoch's perceptive expression again; in this case to "reveal" Bonhoeffer's theological arguments, concepts, and insights to an English-speaking audience as unfiltered as possible.

---

3. Eugene A. Nida and Charles R. Taber, *The Theory and Practice of Translation* (Leiden: E. J. Brill, 1969), 200, 201; see also Eugene Nida, "Principles of Correspondence," in *Toward a Science of Translating: With Special Reference to Principles and Procedures Involved in Bible Translating* (Leiden: E. J. Brill, 1964), 156–92.

4. Ibid., note 2.

The question of the proper translation of gendered language may serve as one important example to illustrate the practical challenges and the operative translation strategies that were used in pursuing this goal. Throughout his writings, Dietrich Bonhoeffer liberally and consistently uses male nouns and pronouns to refer to human beings collectively or typologically. In some instances, the context makes it clear that Bonhoeffer's male-gendered language in reference to human beings is intentional, such as when he refers to his seminarians in Finkenwalde who were, in fact, all men.[5] However, in the large majority of cases in which Bonhoeffer is not referring to a specific group comprised of men only, he also uses male nouns and pronouns to refer to human beings generically. Likewise, in speaking about God, Bonhoeffer exclusively employs male-gendered language. In so doing, he follows the theological and linguistic conventions of his era. Like his contemporaries in the first half of the twentieth century, Bonhoeffer was not yet conscious of the critical theological issues that have since been raised by feminist theology both in Germany and in the English-speaking world. In light of these developments and the resultant changes in theological terminology toward more gender-inclusive language over the past several decades, what is the most appropriate way to translate Bonhoeffer's gendered language for a contemporary English-speaking audience? "Most appropriate" is to be understood, in light of the preceding considerations, as a translation that allows a contemporary English-speaking reader to hear Bonhoeffer's authentic voice and intended meaning.

Given the historical facts, it would be inappropriate to translate Bonhoeffer's gendered language in every instance with gender-inclusive expressions in English. This would create the false, misleading, and historically inaccurate impression of Bonhoeffer as a proto-feminist, especially in cases where such English expressions sound forced and stylistically awkward. On the other hand, the blind rule of translating Bonhoeffer's gendered expressions in each case with a gendered expression in English might let Bonhoeffer appear, again historically inaccurately, as an active proponent of a chauvinistic agenda, thereby misleading the English-speaking reader about an issue that in Bonhoeffer's time had not yet come to the fore of theological reflection. Translators and editors had strong and at times divergent views on how to steer this delicate course between the Scylla of Bonhoeffer, the proto-feminist, and the Charybdis of Bonhoeffer, the hopeless chauvinist. The judgment calls of how to translate specific instances of gendered expressions in Bonhoeffer's texts accordingly varied somewhat with each translator and editor. However, our work was guided by the common attempt to minimize the use of gendered

5. DBWE 5:30, note 6; 52.

language in English in line with contemporary usage except in cases where Bonhoeffer either referred to or implied men or women only, or where the resulting English expression would be stylistically awkward, thus drawing the reader's undue attention to the language instead of the meaning.

The question of gendered language in Bonhoeffer's texts and its functional equivalent in contemporary English is but one of the numerous challenges encountered by all the translators and editors of this project. Other factors impacting the translation were specific to individual volumes or particular personal factors that translators and editors brought to our common task. In concluding my remarks, I would like to reflect briefly on two such aspects that were specific to my own biographical background and social location.

Unlike the majority of translators participating in the project, I am a German native speaker. It is rare, and at times frowned upon among translators and translation theorists, to translate from one's native language into a secondary language. The reasons are obvious: the range of vocabulary, stylistic sensibilities, and the overall mastery of a secondary language will always, at least to a certain degree, remain inferior to one's native language. However, this disadvantage is counterbalanced by the ability of a translator working with a source text in her or his native language to comprehend nuances of meaning, style, and idiomatic usage more accurately than is ever possible for a non-native speaker. The ideal configuration would be a collaborative arrangement between two bilingual individuals, one a native speaker in the source language and the other a native speaker in the target language. Throughout the project, I considered it a distinct advantage, not just personally but more importantly in terms of the quality of the resulting translation, to be able to work within precisely this configuration. For each of the four volumes in which I participated as a translator, it was most beneficial to work with editors who were English native speakers. Intensive collaborative consultations between native speakers in both the source and the target language made it possible to thoroughly examine the stylistic, conceptual, and historically conditioned nuances of Bonhoeffer's German, as well as craft the most stylistically and conceptually appropriate equivalents in contemporary English. Future translation projects might consider adopting such an arrangement intentionally by actively recruiting teams of translators and editors comprising native speakers in both the source and the target language.

Lastly, I would like to comment on the fact that for the duration of my work on the Bonhoeffer Works translation project, I also was engaged in parish ministry. This contextual setting of pastoral ministry had a significant impact on the hermeneutical task of deciphering Bonhoeffer's linguistic and conceptual world. The close reading and intensive reflection on Bonhoeffer's texts over more than a decade likewise exerted a positive formative influence on my understanding and practice of pastoral ministry. Especially important in this regard is Bonhoeffer's emphatic insistence on the sociality of the church as a constitutive ontological category rather than an accidental attribute. Being called to the practice of pastoral ministry in a culture in which "church shopping" is considered entirely unobjectionable, and Christian denominations vie with each other for "market share," Bonhoeffer's foundational concept of "Christ existing as church-community" (*Christus als Gemeinde existierend*) provided an important ecclesiological and Christological horizon for preaching, teaching, and congregational mission. Being engaged in pastoral ministry also served as a daily reminder of both the brokenness and the essential worldliness of the community of saints, one of Bonhoeffer's crucial theological insights. Even at the height of his most abstract thinking, Bonhoeffer never makes a separation between academic theology and the practice of the church. In the midst of his doctoral dissertation on the sociological structure of the church, for example, he raises the critical question of the silence of the church vis-à-vis the proletariat—a question that incidentally earns him his doctoral supervisor's only serious rebuke.[6] Bonhoeffer's theological program is at once intellectually demanding, spiritually challenging, and eminently practical. At its very core, Bonhoeffer's theology presses toward the practice of the church as the embodied and worldly presence of Christ. In our age of worldwide economic instability, an alarming increase of inequities between the rich and the poor, and the growing threat of a global ecological catastrophe, Bonhoeffer's clarion call to the church is as important and urgent as ever. It has been a privilege and a labor of love to help make that voice be heard more fully and clearly in the English-speaking world.

However, all translation, including this one, is like the attempt to paint a bird in flight. It can be nothing more than an imperfect and temporary aid for those who, for reasons of station or circumstance, are as yet unable to watch the real bird soar. The degree to which readers of the new English translation will be inspired to read the German original will ultimately be the true measure of whether we as translators and editors have succeeded in our task.

---

6. Bonhoeffer, *Sanctorum Communio*, DBWE 1:8; 10 n. 34; 271f. n. 430.

9

Bringing Voice to Life: Bonhoeffer's Spirituality in Translation

Lisa E. Dahill

INTRODUCTION

For English-speaking readers curious about the spirituality of Bonhoeffer, the translation of the Dietrich Bonhoeffer Works English Edition (DBWE) is a signal event. The "B" series in particular—volumes 8 through 16[1]—gathers for the first time in English the full range of just the sort of writings spirituality scholars covet for the fine-grained access to Bonhoeffer's life and heart they open: here we see the texture of his thinking and relationships, how his voice moves into and through and behind the more familiar formal language of his published writings. Above all, the study of spirituality listens—through such layers and complexities of texts and artifacts—for the visible and vanishing traces of the God-experience disclosed or evoked here: What does Bonhoeffer's experience of God contribute to broader streams of Christian spirituality, and how do these fragmented texts "work" to mediate glimpses of the triune One to new generations of disciples?[2]

As a scholar of spirituality, I am privileged to have been invited into these texts with the intimacy and nuance required by the practice of translation. As sole translator of *Conspiracy and Imprisonment: 1940–1945* (DBWE 16)[3] and

---

1. I am informally including DBWE 8, *Letters and Papers from Prison*, here as part of the "B" series since its letters and other documents stand—logically and chronologically—as the culmination of the arc traced in volumes 9–16.

2. This essay assumes but cannot more fully outline the hermeneutical complexity of such listening to (or for) the spirituality mediated in a particular text or other artifact of Christian study. For an introduction to the study of Christian spirituality as a scholarly discipline, see the essays collected in *Minding the Spirit: The Study of Christian Spirituality*, ed. Elizabeth A. Dreyer and Mark S. Burrows (Baltimore: Johns Hopkins University Press, 2005), as well as David B. Perrin, *Studying Christian Spirituality* (New York and London: Routledge, 2007).

one of a team of translators of *Letters and Papers from Prison* (DBWE 8),[4] I—like all those involved in editing and translating the DBWE volumes—have wrestled with words, sentences, documents, and the stretching, shifting limits of language for years in the process of listening to these texts in English. This process has nourished my capacity to listen as well to Bonhoeffer's spirituality in the last five years of his life as it comes alive in these texts. In this essay I will begin with broader comments on the significance of DBWE and translation for the study of spirituality and then move into particular features of Bonhoeffer's spirituality I glimpse in these texts from the end of his life.

TRANSLATING SPIRITUALITY: ON VIOLINS AND VOICE

The fact that translation is not somehow static or mechanical but a primary form of interpretation is well known. In my work on these volumes I have been curious about the metaphor of "voice" in the process of translating. I have attended to questions of voice both in the process of translation itself (as my collaborators, editors, and I in a given volume or across the DBWE volumes tried to convey a consistent sense of Bonhoeffer's tone and cadence into English) and on a more metaphoric level: how a human voice—here, Bonhoeffer's—gives expression to a person's spirituality.

First, in terms of language: How shall a translator or group of translators establish and convey, across a given volume or the breadth of Bonhoeffer's life and genres of writing, the sense of a consistent, maturing voice? How, further, shall we convey in English the ranges of tone, shadow, emotion, and authority in that voice, as well as the even greater diversity of voices also present in these volumes—letters from loved ones and professional colleagues, official documents, even the cold voices of Nazi interrogation reports? Attention to such questions is of course among the important tasks of volume editors also, and of the general editors and editorial board overseeing the entire project. I note it here both because attunement to voice is perhaps the most important—and ephemeral—aspect of the translator's distinctive vocation and because it is a primary means of access to a given spirituality.

The liturgical musician and scholar Kathleen Harmon writes,

> The sound a body projects is the consequence of interior properties and relationships. Sound reveals this hidden interiority. The

---

3. DBWE 16.
4. DBWE 8.

> appearance of a violin, for example, tells us nothing about its true value; only its sound can reveal the quality of the wood from which it is made and the condition and tension of its strings. Sound reveals interiority in a way that our other senses cannot. . . . Sound binds together interiorities that would otherwise remain unknown to, hidden from, and disconnected from one another.[5]

As with violins so with human beings: a person's voice reveals his or her interiority—the soul, the unique acoustics of a body. And sustained attention to that voice (in both literal and metaphoric senses) makes possible increasing intimacy with the subject whose voice is heard, even when such hearing takes place via written texts. Just as attention to the voice (i.e., the "word") of God for Christians requires listening deeply to the divine heart and being as disclosed through Scripture, so attunement to a human other—say, a person whose writing one is translating—also requires attending to the nuance and timbre of this person's voice. By listening carefully over time to the subtleties of Bonhoeffer's voice as conveyed in his writings, translators begin to sense the interiority (in Harmon's sense) that these texts reveal; and through their capacity to notice and convey what is characteristic of that voice they attempt to create texts that evoke such resonance in turn in new generations of readers in English.

This capacity to notice and pay formal attention to what is most resonant in the voice/s of a person or community one is studying is itself also, scholar Mary Frohlich asserts, a form of "interiority." In fact, Frohlich proposes such attunement on the part of the scholar as the defining methodological criterion of the study of spirituality.[6] To attend adequately to the interiority of one's

5. Kathleen Harmon, *The Mystery We Celebrate, the Song We Sing: A Theology of Liturgical Music* (Collegeville, MN: Liturgical Press/Pueblo Books, 2008), 24f. Don Saliers reflects on the significance especially of the human voice in "Sacred Sound," *God's Grandeur: The Arts and Imagination in Theology*, ed. David C. Robinson, S.J., The Annual Publication of the College Theology Society, vol. 52 (Maryknoll, NY: Orbis, 2006), 53–58.

6. In "Spiritual Discipline, Discipline of Spirituality: Revising Questions of Definition and Method" (*Minding the Spirit*, 65–78), Frohlich develops the category of "interiority" as a way of naming the "uniquely defining methodological principle of the academic discipline of spirituality" (75). She means by *interiority* that self-awareness and self-differentiation which alone makes intimacy possible, the capacity for being fully present to another person or text or reality *on its own terms*. Only by means of such deeply self-aware grounding in one's own lived relationship with the fullness of reality—including, for Christians, the triune God, the church, and the world one loves—can a scholar of spirituality establish the necessary "means of access" to the textures of the interiority of the research subject under study. To use her definition of the material object of such study, namely, "the human spirit fully in act": "We cannot know 'the human spirit fully in act' except *as* the human spirit in act. We cannot recognize the constructed expressions that radically engage the human spirit except on the basis of our own radical

subject on his or her or their own terms requires precisely the sort of internal space and receptivity that will allow (as in the vacuum of the inner ear, the cave of the human heart) the echoes of some other's interiority (the body of a violin, the nuance of a letter's tone) to resound clearly. Precisely this quality of interiority—the capacity to resonate with another's mediated voice—thus marks not only the study of spirituality but the practice of translation too as a contemplative process of listening.

"Improving" Bonhoeffer vs. Letting Him Stand: The Case of Gender-Language

How one is most effectively to convey that voice into another language—in another time and place—is not however a simple question. In addition to the usual puzzles of tone, idiom, register, etc., a translation alert to questions of spirituality also runs up against the problem of discerning when Bonhoeffer's parochialism hinders readers' capacity to hear through his words their intended, gospel-conveying meaning, thus requiring subtle or drastic emendation (as in the earlier DBWE volumes' consistent use in English of gender-neutral or -inclusive language even where Bonhoeffer uses or even seems to intend a masculine-only reference)—as opposed to where such "improvements" keep readers from encountering the real Bonhoeffer whose writing did not attend to such questions. Discerning a way through the particular question of gendered language has occupied the DBWE editorial board from the beginning of the project, but its shape depends on the prior determination of whether a given text (or an entire volume, or the series as a whole) is/are being translated primarily as "spiritual" texts or classics, meant to function for readers in ways conducive to their hearing the presence of God through them, or as "historical" documents primarily intended to open a window into the human Bonhoeffer with his limits (as we might perceive them) intact. The series as a whole has tipped roughly toward gender-inclusive language in the "A" volumes (published and often intended for the church more clearly as spiritual texts) and toward retaining Bonhoeffer's masculine-language bias in the "B" volumes (seeing these more as resources for historical study). While volumes 1–5 and 7 can thus work as devotional resources in the contemporary church among those who find masculine-normed language alienating of the complex mystery

engagement" (73). Similarly, a translator cannot adequately give new expression to Bonhoeffer's voice except on the basis of a capacity for sustained receptivity to—indeed, interior resonance with—that voice on its own terms.

of G*D,[7] nevertheless in these volumes in English it can be difficult to determine precisely how *Bonhoeffer himself* framed such questions; conducting an accurate analysis of, e.g., Bonhoeffer's spirituality of gender would be nearly impossible for a reader limited to these DBWE texts.

DBWE as Resource for Teaching Bonhoeffer's Spirituality

As a feminist scholar reading Bonhoeffer, I am grateful for access to the German texts and for aspects of the later DBWE volumes' retention of his masculine usage. As a teacher of Christian spirituality, however, it is those earlier DBWE volumes—with gender-neutral language for both humans and God in English—that I find most helpful in the seminary classroom and, even more so, in congregational teaching. Consider, for example, the difference between these two excerpts from *Life Together*, the first from the original translation by John W. Doberstein[8] and the second from the DBWE translation:

> The Christian, however, must bear the burden of a brother. He must suffer and endure the brother. It is only when he is a burden that another person is really a brother and not merely an object to be manipulated. The burden of men was so heavy for God Himself that He had to endure the Cross.[9]
>
> However, Christians must bear the burden of one another. They must suffer and endure one another. Only as a burden is the other really a brother or sister and not just an object to be controlled. The burden of human beings was even for God so heavy that God had to go to the cross suffering under it.[10]

These questions of gender-language are just the beginning of the gift of DBWE in teaching, however. These lines from *Life Together* in DBWE 5 appear within a complex set of editorial notes and introductions providing invaluable interpretive help for my U.S. students, layers of scholarship that allow our discussions of Bonhoeffer's spirituality—in any of the volumes—to be informed

---

7. In my view, the use of non-gender-specific language rightly includes avoiding masculine pronouns for God in English. Bonhoeffer's use of such pronouns for God reflects pre-feminist German usage *and* the grammatical gendering of German nouns. In twenty-first-century American English, theological terminology is moving away from gendered God-language, recognizing that, because English has shed nearly all use of grammatical gender, retaining the masculine for God conveys an ideological bias.

8. Harper & Row, 1954.

9. Harper & Row edition, page 100.

10. *Life Together*, DBWE 5:100.

by critical attention to his context, intellectual forebears, and originality of thought. Precisely because they want to understand this spiritual teacher as fully as possible, even my most devotionally inclined students pore over the notes and cherish these critical editions.

SPIRITUALITY IN TRANSLATION

Finally, circling in to the core of the essay, I present aspects of Bonhoeffer's spirituality in the years 1940–1945 that I have discovered through translating these two volumes. They are (a) how his practice of Bible reading was shifting during the conspiracy period (from DBWE 16); (b) the impact on him of Maria's Yes to his proposal of marriage in the winter of 1943; and (c) his experience of the cell and the empty space of human longing (from DBWE 8).

(A) BIBLE READING (DBWE 16)

As is well known, Bonhoeffer's love of Scripture and commitment to a disciplined daily practice of prayer with the Bible permeates his spirituality from the early 1930s through his imprisonment. This love and intimate knowledge of Scripture shows up on nearly every page of his writings, and its power to shape his thinking and action is a cornerstone of his preaching and discernment. What is less well known is that in the conspiracy period Bonhoeffer was experiencing a disconcerting freedom from Bible reading. We read in several letters from the early 1940s how his Bible reading was becoming more occasional, less strict:

> Sometimes there are weeks in which I read very little of the Bible. Something prevents me from doing so. Then one day I pick it up again, and suddenly everything is so much more powerful, and I can't let go of it at all. I do not have a clear conscience about this. . . . But then I wonder whether perhaps even this aspect of being human is and shall be borne by the word of God. Or do you think—actually I think this myself!—that one should force oneself? Or is that in fact not always good? We must talk about this sometime.[11]
>
> I am amazed that I am living, and can live, for days without the Bible—I would then perceive it not as obedience but as autosuggestion if I were to force myself back to it. I understand that such autosuggestion could be and is a great help, but I fear that I

---

11. DBWE 16:133 (January 1941). By return mail (DBWE 16:137), Eberhard notes that he is "startled" at this news.

would thereby falsify an authentic experience and in the end still not be experiencing authentic help. When I then open my Bible again, it is new and delightful to me as never before, and I only wish I could preach again. I know that I only need to open my own books to hear all that can be said against this. I do not wish to justify myself either, but I realize that I have had much richer times in the "spiritual" sense. But I sense how an opposition to all that is "religious" is growing in me. . . . I am not religious by nature. But I must constantly think of God, of Christ; authenticity, life, freedom, and mercy mean a great deal to me. It is only that the religious clothes they wear make me so uncomfortable . . . because I believe that I am on the verge of some kind of breakthrough, I am letting things take their own course and do not resist.[12]

Such writings open a more nuanced view of Bonhoeffer's spiritual practice while revealing the roots in his own prayer of what he would later articulate as "nonreligious" Christianity.

(b) Darkness and Yes

That the conspiracy period represents a time of gathering heaviness is manifest. We can see across the seven DBWE 16 circular letters to the scattered Finkenwalde community a shift of tone from the clarity and warmth in pastoral care of the first two letters[13] to the heartbreaking condolence portraits of each newly fallen Finkenwalde brother stretching from August 1941 to March 1942,[14] and then to the paralysis and numbness of grief named in the final circular letter, dated November 29, 1942.[15] The parallel progression of condolence letters to widows and parents of fallen comrades demonstrates the weight such grief surely brought Bonhoeffer. This is a landscape devoid of hope

---

12. DBWE 16:329 (June 1942). Yet see also, e.g., DBWE 16:78 (October 1940): "I rejoice here [at Ettal] in daily morning prayer. . . . Such well-organized days make work and prayer as well as my interactions with people easy for me and spare me the spiritual, physical, and mental hardships resulting from disorder." See also DBWE 16:72 (August 1940), DBWE 16:153f. (February 1941), and the March 1942 circular letter on the practice of meditation (DBWE 16:254f.). In January 1943 he writes to Maria, "the *Daily Texts* . . . are very dear to me" (DBWE 16:388).

13. DBWE 16, letters I/6 and I/47.

14. See DBWE 16, letters I/119, I/137, and I/144.

15. See DBWE 16, letter I/212. The sixth pastoral letter (I/155) doesn't include farewell portraits of any fallen brothers but treats the question of the Finkenwalde community members' concerns about "legalization" into the Reich church.

beyond the grit of the conspiracy itself; the essay "After Ten Years," written at the turning of the 1943 New Year, reveals a similarly tough-minded struggle for spiritual orientation in the midst of chaos.[16] And the German edition of *Conspiracy and Imprisonment* (DBW 16) closes more or less on this note, trailing off into the records of interrogations and Nazi documents in the prison period.

But the discovery of previously unpublished letters from Bonhoeffer to Maria von Wedemeyer from fall 1942 and especially winter 1943 recasts our entire perception of this period.[17] This earliest correspondence between the two, culminating in their promises of engagement for marriage, reveal an entirely different side of Dietrich—indeed, a whole new voice, one suddenly jubilant *and* hesitant, human, his perception of the world suddenly dawning into joy and hope and falling in love.

In mid-January 1943, after turmoil involving the difference in their ages and Maria's own discernment of a way forward, she writes, "Today I can say Yes to you from my entire, joyful heart."[18] And by immediate return mail Dietrich writes,

> May I simply say what is in my heart? I . . . am overwhelmed by the awareness that a gift without equal has been given me—after all the confusion of the past weeks I had no longer dared to hope—and now the unimaginably great and blissful thing is simply here, and my heart opens up and becomes quite wide and overflowing with thanksgiving and shame and still cannot grasp it at all—this "Yes" that is to be decisive for our entire life.[19]
>
> [And a week later] Now the letter is here [as she reaffirms her commitment to him] . . . I thank you for it and thank you anew each new time I read it, indeed to me it is almost as if I were experiencing now for the first time in my life what it means to be thankful to another person, what a profoundly transforming power gratitude can be—it is this Yes—this word so difficult and so marvelous, appearing so seldom among mortals—from which all this springs—may God from whom every Yes comes grant that we may speak this Yes

---

16. DBWE 8:37–52.

17. These ten letters from late October 1942 to March 1943 are all from Dietrich to Maria; her responses are noted in footnotes but her letters do not appear. These letters are additions in DBWE 16 to the DBW contents (I/206a, 208a, 209ab, 214a, 215abc, and 220ab), scattered between pages 366 and 394 of the volume and progressing at the outset from formal ("Miss von Wedemeyer/Sie") to intimate address ("Dearest Maria/du . . . with much love").

18. DBWE 16:383; this line from her letter of January 13, 1943, is cited in footnote 2.

19. DBWE 16:383 (January 17, 1943).

always thus and always more and more to one another throughout our entire life.[20]

We know of course from the published prison correspondence between Maria and Dietrich how well matched these two were emotionally and intellectually despite the difference in age and education.[21] But what we glimpse only now—by these *first* letters set within the otherwise horrific months of the 1942–43 winter—is the impact this new love made on Dietrich: the gift of a future of real hope and joy. The emotion in these early letters is like nothing else in this volume: full of awe, rapturous. If *spirituality* refers to the experience of being fully alive—or to the way one channels one's life-energy[22]—then these letters are surely one of the clearest glimpses of Bonhoeffer's conspiracy spirituality: the power of God's Yes, experienced in human love right in the heart of pain and grief.

(C) DBWE 8: THE CELL, EMPTY SPACE

Much has been written—powerfully—of Bonhoeffer's prison spirituality, from his nonreligious interpretation of the Bible to his practices of prayer and ministry, and from the new language finding voice in poetry to the gratitude unfolding to the end.[23] I will note two additional motifs visible in the portion of DBWE 8, Part II, that I translated, from summer 1943 to winter 1944.

THE CELL

First, I am struck by how Bonhoeffer engages the experience of the cell itself. We know of his initial shock at imprisonment and can readily imagine why words like "torment" and even "suicide" haunt him in this initial period.[24] This experience of profound claustrophobia—the cell as, of course, prison—is the

20. DBWE 16:387 (January 24, 1943).

21. Cf. Dietrich Bonhoeffer and Maria von Wedemeyer, *Love Letters from Cell 92: The Correspondence between Dietrich Bonhoeffer and Maria von Wedemeyer, 1943–1945*, ed. Ruth-Alice von Bismarck and Ulrich Kabitz, trans. John Brownjohn (Nashville: Abingdon, 1992).

22. See, e.g., Ronald Rolheiser, *The Holy Longing: The Search for a Christian Spirituality* (New York: Doubleday, 1999).

23. Cf. Ralf K. Wüstenberg, *A Theology of Life: Dietrich Bonhoeffer's Religionless Christianity*, trans. Douglas Stott (Grand Rapids: Eerdmans, 1998); Peter Zimmerling, "Die Spiritualität Bonhoeffers in den Gefängnisjahren: Beten, das Gerechte tun und auf Gottes Zeit warten: Ein Werkstattsbericht," in *Dietrich Bonhoeffer, Mensch hinter Mauern: Theologie und Spiritualität in den Gefängnisjahren*, ed. Rainer Mayer and Peter Zimmerling (Giessen/Basel: Brunnen, 1993), 35–68; see also the marvelous essays on Bonhoeffer's prison poetry contained in *Who Am I? Bonhoeffer's Theology through His Poetry*, ed. Bernd Wannenwetsch (London/New York: T. & T. Clark, 2009).

essential underpinning to any attempt at speculating on a "prison spirituality," as it underlies both the nearly unbearable poignancy of his longing for release and the actual physical and spiritual conditions within which he was forced to live the rest of his life.

This is not the only way he is able to conceive of this cell, however. In September 1943 he writes to his parents,

> The stormy world events in recent days [the invasion and capitulation of Italy] . . . race through one's body here like electricity, and one wishes to be able to accomplish something useful someplace; but at the moment that place can only be the prison cell, and what one can do here plays itself out in the realm of the invisible, and there of all places the expression "doing" is quite inappropriate. I sometimes think of Schubert's "Münnich"[25] [monk] and his crusade.[26]

Bonhoeffer is not the first to compare a monastic cell to a prison cell, or vice versa; and the power of the Christian prison tradition from St. Paul through Martin Luther King Jr. and the Berrigan brothers testifies to the continuing spiritual power of Christians imprisoned for the sake of the gospel in the world. The fact that Bonhoeffer makes this connection not conceptually so much as musically, aesthetically, and contemplatively adds texture to the image: Dietrich the monk cloistered[27] away in this cell not by vows though no less by

24. See, e.g., DBWE 8:70–74 (May 1943, private notes): "Separation: from people/ from work/ from the past/ from the future/ from God" (71); "time as help, as torment, as enemy./boredom as expression of despair" (73); "discontent—tension/ impatience/ yearning/boredom/ night—deeply lonely// apathy/ urge to be busy, variety, novelty/ dullness, tiredness, sleeping—against [this] strict order as antidote// fantasizing, distortion of past and future/ suicide, not out of a sense of guilt, but because I am practically dead already, the closing of the book, sum total" (74).

25. *Letters and Papers from Prison*, DBWE 8, reproduces a misspelling (*Münich*) from the German editors' footnote 6 at this point, but Bonhoeffer's text at DBW 8:158 has the correct "Münnich" in quotation marks. The spelling "Münnich" is the Middle High German form of the Standard High German "Mönch." See DBW 8:158, n. 6: "Ein Münich ["Mönch"] steht in seiner Zell. . . ."

26. DBWE 8:155. Note 6 translates the text of Franz Schubert's song, "The Crusade": "A monk is standing in his cell/ its window grill is gray./ So many knights in armor bright/ are riding through the field./ The hymns they sing are pious songs,/ a choir earnest and fine./ Amid them flies, in silk so soft,/ the banner of the cross,/ the banner of the cross./ They mount the ship, so high above/ the shorelines of the sea./ Its path is green, it runs away,/ will soon be but a swan./ The monk looks through his window still/ and contemplates their fate./ 'I am like you a pilgrim yet'/ though I but stay at home./ Life's pilgrimage through waves' deceit/ and stinging desert sand/ is nothing but a crusade into the promised land,/ the promised land."

conviction, standing at his gray window grill and watching those who are able out acting in the world, their movements still free. And his well-known letter to Eberhard two months later on the prison cell as a powerful image of Advent adds liturgical shape to the experience:

> Now comes Advent, a time during which we share so many beautiful memories. You were the first to open for me the world of music making, as we did for years during the Advent weeks. By the way, a prison cell like this is a good analogy for Advent; one waits, hopes, does this or that—ultimately negligible things—the door is locked and can only be opened *from the outside.* That has just occurred to me; don't get the idea one cares much about symbolism here![28]

Here the attempt to reinterpret the prison cell first coming to expression in the September letter to his parents allows him to experience the intimacy of friendship and memory—centered paradigmatically in the celebration of Advent—in, of all places, the cell that is keeping him *from* the fullness of this familiar mutual presence. This longing for tangible connection *even here* to the life of faith now so irretrievably distant shows up again in the same letter, a few lines later: "I have quite spontaneously experienced Luther's instruction to 'bless oneself with the [sign of the] cross' at morning and evening prayer as a help. There is something objective about it for which a person here particularly longs."[29]

EMPTY SPACE

Yet this craving for tangible signs—a prison door as image of Advent, the physical sign of the cross on one's body—does not imply for Bonhoeffer an incapacity for life in the even more profound *emptiness* of longed-for connection that the prison experience (and the war itself) creates. He clings to such signs not because they somehow fill this void but because they help him hold it open. He writes, again to Eberhard, in December:

> In my experience there is no greater torment than longing. Some people have been so shaken from early on in their lives that they can no longer, so to speak, manage any great longing. They have given

27. In his July 1944 poem "Stations on the Way to Freedom," he will use the language of "hands . . . fettered."

28. DBWE 8:188f. (November 21, 1943).

29. DBWE 8:189.

up extending their inner "bowstring" of tension over long periods of time and create for themselves surrogate pleasure that can be more easily satisfied. That is the . . . ruin of all spiritual fruitfulness. It truly may not be said that it is good for people to be beaten up by life early and often. In most cases it simply breaks a person. To be sure, such people are better hardened for times like ours but also infinitely coarser. If *we* are forcibly separated from the people we love, then we *cannot* procure for ourselves a cheap substitute. . . . The substitute repulses us. We simply have to wait and wait; we have to suffer indescribably from the separation; we have to experience longing practically to the point of becoming ill—and only in this way do we sustain communion with the people we love, even if in a very painful way.[30]

Then, addressing this time both Eberhard and Renate at Christmas Eve 1943, he writes

. . . there is nothing that can replace the absence of someone dear to us, and one should not even attempt to do so; one must simply persevere and endure it. At first that sounds very hard, but at the same time it is a great comfort, for one remains connected to the other person through the emptiness to the extent it truly remains unfilled. It is wrong to say that God fills the emptiness; God in no way fills it but rather keeps it empty and thus helps us preserve—even if in pain—our authentic communion.[31]

The space of emptiness—cavernous—that holds open one's communion with an impossibly distant beloved: this is the inner void, the inner "cell" if you will, that alone makes possible for Bonhoeffer a life of sustained love and hope. The external cell imaged as monastic, or as a glimpse of Advent, thus paradoxically itself helps Bonhoeffer structure the spirituality its very confinement imposes on him.

Conclusion

The last five years of Bonhoeffer's life provide shape to what I have asserted elsewhere is his "Christmas spirituality":[32] the capacity to give voice to the

---

30. DBWE 8:227 (December 18, 1943). Italics in original text.

31. DBWE 8:238 (December 24, 1943).

presence and love of a God incarnate precisely in the rubble, the war, the cell. Translating these volumes has allowed me to see how incarnational Bonhoeffer truly is, how closely his theological insights are interwoven with his emotional, historical, and relational contexts—the same thickness of experience every Christian lives in.

Even more than Bonhoeffer's time, our time urges attention to the ecological dimension of such a Christmas spirituality.[33] We who listen to Bonhoeffer's voice and translate it for new contexts, both linguistic and enacted, do so in the face of what ethicists and activists are calling the greatest moral and spiritual crisis our species and culture have ever faced. We need theologians able to help us say Yes to hope even in the face of numbness, as grief and loss and extinctions mount; we need spiritual leaders able to hold open terrifying, bewildering empty space—the loss of the world we have known and the entitlements we cling to—and not keep filling those inner and outer voids with false substitutes. We need teachers of prayer who can teach us too, carbon-addicted Americans, to give thanks for the barest gifts of food, of love, birdsong and sky and touch.

Precisely here, in the empty space opened up in prison and war, this incarnational Bonhoeffer was able to give voice to gratitude in increasingly polyphonic ways: from ending nearly every letter to his parents in both volumes "your grateful Dietrich," to the essay on gratitude written in 1940,[34] to the outpouring of gratitude to Maria in January 1943, to the place he gives consciously to gratitude even in prison and as the awareness of his death moves ever closer.[35] It is never glib. The stench and the shock, the longing and love,

---

32. Dahill, "Particularity, Incarnation, and Discernment: Bonhoeffer's 'Christmas' Spirituality," *Studies in Christian-Jewish Relations* 2, no. 1 (2007): 53–61; and "Bonhoeffer's Late Spirituality: Challenge, Limit, and Treasure," *Journal of Lutheran Ethics* (December 2006): http://www.elca.org/What-We-Believe/ Social-Issues/Journal-of-Lutheran-Ethics/Issues/December-2006/Bonhoeffers-Late-Spirituality- Challenge-Limit-and-Treasure.aspx. DBWE 16 and 8 reveal the richness of his theological engagement with the seasons and themes of Advent and Christmas in both 1940 and 1943; see the pastoral letter of December 1940 (DBWE 16:105–8) and the Christmas 1940 meditation on Isa. 9:6-7 (DBWE 611–17), as well as the 1943 Advent/Christmas letters to Eberhard (DBWE 8:188f., 226–37) and to his parents (DBWE 8:224–26). His emerging nonreligious interpretation through May and June of 1944 culminates in the July 21 articulation of "the profound this-worldliness of Christianity" (DBWE 8:485–87). See also his naming in *Ethics* of "penultimate" reality using Advent metaphors (DBWE 6:160–68); the "ultimate," then, is imaged here as the great Christmas arrival: Christ the *telos* of all life, here and now.

33. For an expansive treatment of the scope of these questions (including attention as well to Bonhoeffer's ecological significance), see Larry Rasmussen, *Earth-Honoring Faith: Religious Ethics in a New Key* (New York: Oxford University Press, 2013).

34. "On Gratitude among Christians" (DBWE 16:489–92).

music and prayer and the lonely world come of age all rise to voice in him, resonating from the emptiness of that prison cell out into hearts and lives he could never have imagined. And we translating, listening, hear through his voice echoes of that great *cantus firmus* of God's Yes to human reality, sung in the incarnation of Jesus Christ right into the heart of the world's brokenness: the firm song, firm ground on which even we can stand. How will the voice of God echo through us in turn? How will our voices enact God's Yes to life on Earth?

---

35. DBWE 8:509–11, 514–16, 551. See also his final poem, "By Gracious Powers" (DBWE 8:548–50).

10

C. Historians Interpreting Bonhoeffer

The Bonhoeffer Legacy as Work-in-Progress: Reflections on a Fragmentary Series

Victoria J. Barnett

The 2011 conference on which this volume is based examined the numerous aspects of Bonhoeffer's life and thought that continue to impact Christian life and witness around the world. Yet to a very great extent, future scholarship will be based primarily on the *Dietrich Bonhoeffer Werke / Dietrich Bonhoeffer Works*: the sixteen-volume collection of his papers, correspondence, and theological writings. These volumes will remain seminal to any understanding of his work, life, and legacy not only theologically, but historically (for our understanding of Bonhoeffer, his church, and his times, including the history of Nazi Germany and the Holocaust) and biographically (for our understanding of his person).

As the very existence of sixteen volumes shows, Bonhoeffer's life is an extraordinarily well-documented one, as is the historical period during which he lived. Yet, despite the vast documentation and the countless books that have been written about Bonhoeffer, his life and work remain fragmentary in many ways, and the series illustrates that as well. In this brief essay I wish to discuss the relationship between these fragments and the whole, particularly when we reflect on how Bonhoeffer will be understood by coming generations.

The Bonhoeffer legacy is best approached as a work-in-progress. I have spent hundreds of hours in the past years reading through these works, both in German and in our translations. There are thousands of pages, hundreds of letters, seventy-one sermons, Bible studies, lecture notes, and papers he prepared to deliver at international conferences, the polished and finished theological works as well as the countless threads of thought and reflection that appear in the odd letter or draft. Part of this process has entailed understanding the life in German, and then trying to imagine how all this can best be conveyed and understood in English. This is not just a matter of translating the language but of conveying the times, the culture, the church, and most importantly, the ways in which this man understood his faith. The world in which Bonhoeffer lived is gone, and, to a great extent, so is the understanding of church and faith that shaped him and his students. This poses a particular challenge not only to translators but to historians and theologians.

There is something both moving and unsettling about the process of reading through someone's life chronologically, day by day, week by week, year through year. When one is in the thick of this work the big picture vanishes from sight. The Bonhoeffer volumes contain both the grand narrative and the pieces of that narrative, which include the documents that one would expect to be preserved as well as drafts and notes that I suspect he would have thrown away if he had known we would be doing this with them. Early in the process of assembling Bonhoeffer's writings, Eberhard Bethge made the decision to include everything, from the rough drafts to the polished pieces—the attempts, the successes, the failures. Inevitably one loses sight of the forest and even the trees and is immersed in the microcosmic level. This is where the role of general editor is somewhat unique, because I have been looking not just at entire documents but at sentences and translation choices and the placement of semicolons. It is analogous to when a sharp-edged stone falls into tumbling water and over the course of time is worn down and reshaped. It is the task of the historian, the biographer, and the theologian to describe the stone and the water and the currents that form it and the end result. But in the midst of the actual documents, one is immersed in the process of the changes in the stone. It is here that we can sometimes see the actual moments of change in his life and thought: those moments where a new concept emerged, where he clarified something, or where a decision was made that determined the course of his life. On the level of grand narrative we look for those great turning points: the decision to study theology, the decision to go to London, return to Germany, enter the resistance, or become engaged to Maria von Wedemeyer. Yet up close in these volumes we see how even these major turning points emerge slowly, as they would obviously emerge over the course of a life, as the steady accumulation of small fragmentary moments that eventually quicken into a moment of crisis or decision. Bonhoeffer himself apparently struggled sometimes with making decisions. In his New York diary in the summer of 1939—having just made what was arguably the most momentous decision of his life, to return to Germany—he wrote: "It is strange that in all my decisions I am never completely clear about my motives. Is that a sign of lack of clarity, inner dishonesty, or is it a sign that we are led beyond that which we can discern, or is it both?"[1]

Several years ago I was invited to deliver the annual Raoul Wallenberg lecture at Muhlenberg College, and I spoke about the complexity of Bonhoeffer's life and thought, titling my lecture "Unfinished Hero." This is how I have come to think of Bonhoeffer: as an unfinished hero. This is a fragmentary series, not just because it's the compilation of many different kinds of writing over a protracted period of time, but because the circumstances of history compelled Dietrich Bonhoeffer to live a very unfinished and fragmented life.

The fragmentary and turbulent nature of his life is evident in even the briefest biographical outline between 1932 and 1945. In 1931 he returned from his year of study at Union Theological Seminary and became active in the ecumenical movement while preparing for the parish ministry as well as for an academic career. Each of those activities was affected radically by the Nazi rise to power in 1933 and the subsequent battle within German Protestantism about a nazified theology and the attempts to nazify the church. At the height of this battle, Bonhoeffer left Germany to serve two German-speaking congregations in London. In the spring of 1935 he returned to Germany to lead Finkenwalde, one of the five illegal Confessing Church seminaries that had been set up after the Dahlem synod. In the fall of 1937 Finkenwalde was closed by the Gestapo, and in the two following years Bonhoeffer continued to educate his seminarians "underground." In 1939, as it became clear that another European war was imminent, Bonhoeffer began to explore the possibility of emigration in short visits to London and to New York. That summer he traveled to New York but stayed only five weeks, returning to join his students. In early 1940 he became part of the German resistance and made several trips abroad on its behalf in the early years of the war. In 1943 he was arrested and imprisoned. His period in prison, from 1943 to 1945, was marked by moments of hope, uncertainty, and despair, and it was during this time that he wrote some of the letters, poems, and theological reflections that have since captured the imagination of Christians around the world.

Even this short synopsis reminds us of what a very unusual career and life track Bonhoeffer had. It was imposed upon him by circumstance—by the chaotic, terrible, oppressive, violent years of National Socialism—but it is also very much the outcome of his own decisions, principles, and beliefs. The fragmentary nature of his life, however, is always revealed in conjunction with another aspect that emerges from these volumes: the portrait of a man of

1. DBWE 15:227.

continuity and consistency. While his life changed dramatically, it did so in part because he remained firmly on one path throughout this period. He showed great political clarity about the evils of Nazism from the very beginning. It is striking that this political clarity is articulated primarily in the language of civil liberties, not in theological language. The centrality of Bonhoeffer's perspective on civil liberties derives, I think, from three sources: from his family, from his ecumenical perspective (the early critique of National Socialism that came from the ecumenical movement was also framed largely in terms of civil liberties issues),[2] and his period of study in the United States. At the same time, he was deeply and consistently opposed to the nazification of his church, and in the process of articulating that opposition, he developed the theological argumentation that draws a firm line between the elements of faith and the ideological distortion of those elements. This process began already in 1932, as the growing prominence of the National Socialist party was generating a more nationalist theology among some German theologians. As volume 11[3] illustrates, Bonhoeffer was already engaged in debates with people like Emanuel Hirsch and Paul Althaus during this period. His critique of *völkisch* theology continued in the years that followed and is particularly evident in volume 14,[4] both in his statements about the challenges facing the Confessing Church and in his lectures to his students. These volumes document not only Bonhoeffer's role in these events, but give a detailed and up-close portrait of the German *Kirchenkampf* and its impact on theological students and clergy, as well as an indispensable portrait of the ecumenical movement during the 1930s and 1940s.

Above all, they reveal intriguing fragments of Bonhoeffer's personality. He truly practiced a deep and committed faith, but he also seems to have been a person of great uncertainty and caution, both in terms of how he made decisions and where he chose his battles. When I was interviewing Confessing Church members for my first book,[5] I usually asked them if they had known Bonhoeffer and, if so, what their memories of him were. The most moving response came from Stefanie von Mackensen, who was active in the Confessing Church office in Pomerania and knew him from his Finkenwalde period. Recalling a person of straightforward goodness and decency, she simply said: "Seine Güte."[6] But I should add that most of the people I asked told me that

---

2. Cf. my commentary on this in "Christian and Jewish Interfaith Efforts during the Holocaust: The Ecumenical Context," in *American Religious Responses to Kristallnacht*, ed. Maria Mazzenga (New York: Palgrave Macmillan, 2009), 13–31.

3. DBWE 11: *Ecumenical, Academic, and Pastoral Work, 1931–1932* (2012).

4. DBWE 14: *Theological Education at Finkenwalde: 1935–1937* (2013).

5. *For the Soul of the People* (Oxford: Oxford University Press, 1992).

they had never heard of him until after 1945. That often surprises people today, but it's an important element of the Bonhoeffer story to remember. From our perspective he is a central figure in the German church struggle and the resistance movements, but in fact in his own times he was a marginal figure. Those who knew him, both in the German churches and in the ecumenical community abroad, were tremendously impressed by him; his students and colleagues in Germany turned to him for leadership and his international friends trusted his reports about the true situation in Germany. Yet, he was very young (only twenty-six years of age in 1933) and just beginning his career; because he was not a bishop or an established theologian, there were a number of people in the church struggle who simply did not know him or did not take him seriously. Moreover, he traveled in and out of Germany throughout the 1930s, and during his most active years in the Confessing Church, from 1935 to 1939, he was working with small groups of illegal seminarians in a very remote region of Germany. He remained on the margins of his church and was a troublesome figure for his church leadership, both during the Nazi era and after 1945, when his record of resistance drew a sharp and uncomfortable contrast with the compromising behavior of so many Protestant leaders under National Socialism.

Even this record of resistance, however, must not be viewed ahistorically. From within the Bonhoeffer opus, he seems to have been the central voice against what was going on—yet there were others in the German Protestant churches who were in fact far more outspoken against the regime, particularly on behalf of the Jews, during the 1930s, including Friedrich Siegmund-Schultze, Elisabeth Schmitz, Otto Möricke, Julius von Jan, and Paul Schneider. This larger context is necessary if we are to understand Bonhoeffer's own writings accurately; when he writes in "After Ten Years," for example, that he and his co-conspirators have been "silent witnesses of evil deeds," he means it.[7]

But the reality of all this—and I think we often lose sight of this when we discuss Bonhoeffer's legacy—is that he did not get the whole job done. He did not finish his work, his theology, and he was not given the opportunity to reflect back on it. His life was cut brutally short at age thirty-nine. As moving and brilliant and remarkable as so many of these writings are, they remain fragments in a very real sense. Bonhoeffer did not complete his *Ethics*; Eberhard Bethge pieced it together and then reorganized it several decades later after more research had been done.

6. "His goodness."
7. Cf. DBWE 8:52.

Poignantly, Bonhoeffer himself seems to have known that it would fall to Bethge to complete things. "Personally," he wrote Bethge from prison in 1943, "I reproach myself for not having finished the *Ethics* (at the moment it is presumably confiscated), and it comforts me somewhat that I told you the most important things. Even if you were not to remember it any longer, it would nevertheless resurface in some way indirectly. Furthermore my thoughts were, of course, still incomplete."[8] This—and so many other passages—reminds us of the central role played by Eberhard Bethge in these collected works and in the life of Bonhoeffer himself.[9] Bonhoeffer himself knew that in Bethge he had the great good fortune to find one of those rare friends that are truly a gift in life: someone who understood him, enjoyed his company, and put up with what Bonhoeffer felt were his faults ("how grateful I was that with so much patience and forbearance you bore my tyrannical and self-serving manner, which often made you suffer, and everything with which I sometimes made your life difficult."[10]) It is striking that in life—and certainly after death—Eberhard Bethge was the friend who helped Bonhoeffer think things through. In the same letter Bonhoeffer shared some of his theological reflections and then wrote: "If only I could talk to you about it every day. Truly I miss this more than you can imagine. The origin of our ideas often lay with me, but their clarification entirely with you. Only in conversation with you did I find out whether an idea was of any use."[11]

It was a two-way street. As Bethge told me himself in a 1995 interview:

> I think that Dietrich made me independent to a large degree. He did that because he gave you self-confidence and always expected more of you than you thought you could do—and then you found that you could do it. . . . I never thought of myself as a great theologian. . . . I only wanted to be a pastor. And that he said to me: you know how to preach, you do know how to preach. . . . And he also taught me to write letters . . . and he thought that I was a very good observer.

Bonhoeffer chose his friend well. Eberhard Bethge was indeed a very good observer, as well as a conscientious and thorough biographer, and he was

---

8. DBWE 8:181.

9. Cf. my essay, "Die Biographie: Eberhard Bethges Gestaltung von Dietrich Bonhoeffers Vermächtnis," in *Eberhard Bethge: Weggenosse, Gesprächspartner und Interpret Dietrich Bonhoeffers*, ed. Martin Hüneke and Heinrich Bedford-Strohm (Gütersloh: Gütersloher, 2011), 83–101; as well as John de Gruchy, *Daring, Trusting Spirit: Bonhoeffer's Friend Eberhard Bethge* (Minneapolis: Fortress Press, 2005).

10. DBWE 8:181.

11. Ibid., 182.

Bonhoeffer's equal in integrity. We would have had a very different Bonhoeffer if we were only now beginning to compile and edit this series—that is, without the guiding hand of Eberhard Bethge. Bethge's hand and his understanding of Bonhoeffer's theology are so woven into the *Bonhoeffer Werke* that it is sometimes difficult to distinguish where Bonhoeffer stops and Bethge begins. This was a process that already began in the compilation of the Bonhoeffer papers: many of the documents in the *Nachlass* are not in Bonhoeffer's hand or even from his typewriter, but were transcribed and typed up by Bethge after 1945.

And there were places where Bethge filled in the blanks. Looking at this series from the perspective of the historians, we must acknowledge Bethge's decisive hand in shaping the Bonhoeffer we know. On balance I think we've been remarkably fortunate to have had Eberhard Bethge—and Albrecht Schönherr, Otto Dudzus, and the others who knew Bonhoeffer during the 1930s—contribute their impressions, share their notes, and help shape the picture we have today. But what this means is that the sculpting of the legacy began with Eberhard Bethge—who after 1945 continued to interpret Bonhoeffer's theology and develop it further in the process of handing it over to us. What we received from Bethge doesn't seem fragmentary—and yet it is.

Bonhoeffer knew that life by its very nature is somewhat fragmentary, but that the times in which he lived had rendered it even more so, upending the lives of his generation:

> . . . from our own experience we have learned that we cannot even plan for the next day, that what we have built up is destroyed overnight. Our lives, unlike our parents' lives, have become formless or even fragmentary. Nevertheless, I can only say that I have not wanted to live in another time than ours, even though it tramples on our outward happiness. More clearly than in other ages, we realize that the world is in God's wrathful and merciful hands.[12]

Bonhoeffer's words here show a graceful acceptance of being led, a reliance on God's mercy and forgiveness. These features permeate his writings throughout these volumes, and it is this aspect of Bonhoeffer that caught me when I first encountered him, as so many do, when I read *The Cost of Discipleship* as a college student.

It is this kind of faith, not just the pathos of an interrupted life, that makes so many of us want to fill in the blanks of the Bonhoeffer story. The irony of

---

12. DBWE 8:387.

the completion of the *Bonhoeffer Works* is that these volumes both help us fill in the blanks and remind us of the questions that cannot be answered. Dietrich Bonhoeffer remains an unfinished hero, a man whose theology has energized Christians around the world for over sixty years now. He was someone who—as Bethge wrote in the preface to the biography—did what was demanded of him, who met the challenges of his times and acted in response to the needs of his family, friends, students, and, not least of all, his God. He made compromises, but he acted with as much faith and integrity as he could muster. He tried to be a model to his students. He fled to safety only to return to Nazi Germany and to the resistance. He ended up in prison, where he acknowledged (and this is what I think we miss when we cling to a heroic picture of him that makes no allowance for complexity) the profound failure of European Christianity, of his church, nation, and culture. Yet he did not lose his faith, and he found a language to express that faith that continues to make sense to us today in our broken world. It is not a triumphalist faith, because in the wake of the Holocaust such a faith is not possible. And for that very reason I think that Bonhoeffer offers the most authentic theological voice we have from that era. That is the voice that emerges from these volumes—in its fragments and as a whole.

11

The American Protestant Theology Bonhoeffer Encountered

Gary Dorrien

I have been asked to speak about American theology in the 1920s. Who was the most distinguished American theologian of the 1920s? It was not Walter Rauschenbusch,[1] who died in 1918. It was not Henry Nelson Wieman[2] or Reinhold Niebuhr,[3] who were just getting started in 1930. Harry Emerson Fosdick[4] was famous by then, but nobody regarded him as an important

---

1. Walter Rauschenbusch, 1861–1918, minister, Second Baptist Church, New York, prof. NT interpretation, Rochester Theological Seminary, 1897–1902, prof. church history there, 1902–18; principal works: *Christianity and the Social Crisis* (New York: Macmillan, 1907), *For God and the People: Prayers of the Social Awakening* (Boston: Pilgrim, 1910), *Christianizing the Social Order* (New York: Macmillan, 1912), *Dare We Be Christians?* (Boston: Pilgrim, 1914), *The Social Principles of Jesus* (New York: Macmillan, 1916), *A Theology for the Social Gospel* (New York: Macmillan, 1917)—*Dictionary of American Religious Biography*, ed. Henry Warner Bowden, adv. ed. (Westport, CT: Greenwood, 1977), hereafter DARB, 375f.

2. Henry Nelson Wieman, 1884–1975, prof. of philosophy, Occidental College, 1917–27, prof. philosophy and religion, University of Chicago Divinity School, 1927–47; active retirement, 1947–75; principal works: *Religious Experience and Scientific Method* (New York: Macmillan, 1926), *The Wrestle of Religion with Truth* (New York: Macmillan, 1935), *The Source of Human Good* (Chicago: University of Chicago Press, 1946), *Man's Ultimate Commitment* (Carbondale, IL: Southern Illinois University Press, 1958), and *Intellectual Foundation of Faith* (New York: Philosophical Library, 1961)—DARB, 509f.

3. Reinhold Niebuhr, 1892–1971, Evangelical and Reformed minister, Detroit, 1915–28; assoc. prof. philosophy of religion, Union Theological Seminary, New York, 1928–30 and prof. of applied Christianity there 1930–60; editor, *Christianity and Crisis*, 1941–66; principal works: *Leaves from the Notebook of a Tamed Cynic* (Chicago: Willet, Clark & Colby, 1927), *Moral Man and Immoral Society* (New York: Scribner, 1932), *An Interpretation of Christian Ethics* (New York: Harper & Brothers, 1935), *The Nature and Destiny of Man*, 2 vols. (New York: Charles Scribner's Sons, 1941–43), *The Children of Light and the Children of Darkness* (New York: Charles Scribner's Sons, 1944), *The Structure of Nations and Empires* (New York: Charles Scribner, 1959)—DARB, 332ff.

4. Harry Emerson Fosdick, 1878–1969, minister, First Baptist Church, Montclair, NJ, 1908–15; part-time instructor, Union Theological Seminary, New York, 1908–15, prof. of practical theology there,

theologian. The correct answer is Douglas Clyde Macintosh,[5] who taught for many years at Yale, who blended Chicago School empiricism and evangelical liberalism, and who convinced Niebuhr, inadvertently, that getting a doctorate in theology would not be worth the trouble.

The 1920s were not an interesting period for American theology, but that does not mean that Bonhoeffer was right about theology in this country.[6] In Germany, theology was dramatic, controversial, and abounding in the language of crisis. The first name for the Barthian revolt was "crisis theology." It was a reaction against the slaughter and destruction of World War I, the pro-war boosterism of liberal German theologians, and the conceits of bourgeois culture. Karl Barth, writing in 1920, declared that before the kingdom of God could become real to modern Christians, "there must come a crisis that denies all human thought." German theologians from Schleiermacher to Harnack conveyed the impression of being comfortable with God and proud of their sophistication. Crisis theology was about shattered illusions and the experience of emptiness before a hidden God.

Nothing like that occurred in the United States, until the 1930s. American theologians did not have to interrogate the trauma, humiliation, disgrace, and colossal destruction of a world war fought on their native ground. The U.S. tried to stay out of the war; liberal Protestant leaders campaigned against intervening; and after America entered the war, most Social Gospel leaders

1915–34; assoc. minister, First Presbyterian Church, New York, 1919–25, Park Avenue Baptist Church (Riverside Church after 1931), 1926–46; active retirement, 1946–69; principal works: *The Manhood of the Master* (New York: Association, 1913), *The Meaning of Prayer* (Boston: Pilgrim, 1915), *The Modern Use of the Bible* (New York: Association, 1924), *The Secret of Victorious Living* (New York: Harper & Brothers, 1934), *On Being a Real Person* (New York: Harper & Brothers, 1943), *Living These Days: An Autobiography* (New York: Harper & Brothers, 1956), *A Preaching Ministry: Twenty-one Sermons Preached by Harry Emerson Fosdick at the First Presbyterian Church in the City of New York, 1918–1925*, ed. David Pultz, foreword and afterword by J. Barrie Shepherd (New York: First Presbyterian Church, 2000)—DARB, 163f.

5. Douglas Clyde Macintosh, 1877–1948, instr. philosophy McMaster University, 1903–04, prof. biblical and systematic theology, Brandon College (Manitoba), 1907–09, prof. at various ranks theology and philosophy of religion, Yale University Divinity School, 1909–42; active retirement 1942–48; principal works: *The Problem of Knowledge* (London: G. Allen & Unwin, 1916), *God in a World at War* (London: G. Allen & Unwin, 1918), *Theology as an Empirical Science* (New York: Macmillan, 1919), *The Reasonableness of Christianity* (New York: C. Scribner's, 1925), *The Pilgrimage of Faith in the World of Modern Thought* (Calcutta: University of Calcutta Press, 1931), *Social Religion* (New York: C. Scribner's Sons, 1939), *The Problem of Religious Knowledge* (New York: Harper & Brothers, 1940), *Personal Religion* (New York: C. Scribner's Sons, 1942)—DARB, 282f.

6. DBWE 10:307–10.

preached Wilsonian sermons about making the world safe for democracy. For a while they celebrated that the war turned the U.S. into a great power.

Such is not the makings of a crisis theology. We did, however, get a different kind of Social Gospel movement after the war turned out differently than progressive Americans had expected. In the early 1920s, leading Social Gospel theologians and ministers such as Fosdick, Ward,[7] Charles Macfarland,[8] Kirby Page, and Vida Scudder contended that the victorious powers betrayed the cause of a decent world order by wreaking their vengeance on Germany. Many who had given pro-war sermons in 1917 vowed never to do it again. Contrary to many renderings of this story, the Social Gospel did not fade away in 1918. It had its strongest influence in the churches in the 1920s and 1930s, when it preached anti-war idealism and League of Nations internationalism. By the mid-1930s nearly every mainline American Protestant denomination had issued a declaration never to support another war. That is a measure of the influence of Social Gospel idealism; Reinhold Niebuhr became famous by turning against it.

Liberal theology and the Social Gospel were not the same thing. In the late nineteenth and early twentieth centuries, there were prominent liberal theologians who were not Social Gospelers and prominent Social Gospelers who were not theologically liberal. Liberal theology overthrew the principle of an external authority establishing or compelling belief on any particular thing, while the Social Gospel taught that Christianity has a mission to transform the structures of society in the direction of social justice. By 1920, however, these two movements had so thoroughly merged that hardly anyone claimed to be one but not the other. Albert Knudson,[9] a liberal theologian, had little feeling

7. Harry F. Ward (1873–1966), with Charles Macfarland co-authored the "The Social Creed of the Churches" in 1907 for the Methodist Federation for Social Action later the Methodist Federation for Social Service, predecessor organization of the Federal Council of Churches. Known as the most outspoken "fellow traveler" among American clergy and member of the "United Front" of political and labor organizations that included the American Communist Party. Taught theology at Boston University until joining the faculty of Union Theological Seminary, New York, where he served until retirement in 1941.

8. Charles S. Macfarland, from 1914 General Secretary of the Federal Council of Churches.

9. Albert Cornelius Knudson (1873–1953), prof. church history University of Denver, 1898–1900, prof. philosophy and English Bible, Baker University, 1900–02, prof. English Bible and philosophy, Allegheny College, 1902–06, prof. Hebrew and OT exegesis, Boston University, 1906–21, prof. systematic theology there, 1921–43; active retirement 1943–53; principal works: *The Religious Teaching of the Old Testament* (New York: Abingdon-Cokesbury, 1918), *Present Tendencies in Religious Thought* (New York: Abingdon-Cokesbury, 1924), *The Philosophy of Personalism* (New York: Abingdon-Cokesbury, 1933), *The Doctrine of God* (New York: Abingdon-Cokesbury, 1930), *The Doctrine of*

for the Social Gospel, but by the 1920s he felt compelled to pretend otherwise. More importantly, by the time that America intervened in World War I, the conflict between modernist church leaders and an increasingly organized fundamentalist movement made it impossible for theological conservatives to be *in* the Social Gospel movement. Then the Presbyterian and Northern Baptist churches exploded over modernism versus fundamentalism.

American fundamentalism was overtaken by dispensationalist and other forms of premillennial eschatology; and older forms of confessional orthodoxy were alien to Social Gospel liberalism. The liberals who led the struggle against fundamentalism in the 1920s deeply regretted that they had to spend so much time doing so. Fosdick and Mathews[10] were emphatic on this subject. To them it was frustrating, and embarrassing for the church, that anybody still believed in biblical inerrancy. They hated that they had to spend so much time battling over this topic, which helps to explain how Niebuhr and his generation completely lost sight of tens of millions of conservative evangelicals who were still out there, somewhere, after they left the mainline churches.

For most of the twentieth century there were three dominant schools of liberal theology in this country, and all were thriving when Bonhoeffer arrived at Union. Evangelical liberalism was the mainstay of American theology, and its chief intellectual center was Union Seminary. Personalist idealism was the second type, which had a strong influence in the Methodist churches and was centered at Boston University. The third type was Chicago School empiricism, centered at the University of Chicago Divinity School.

The evangelical liberal tradition sustained the original merger that gave rise to liberal theology. Logically and historically, American liberal theology was a fusion of Protestant evangelicalism and Enlightenment rationalism and humanism. From its Enlightenment heritage, it emphasized the authority of modern knowledge, championed the values of humanistic individualism and democracy, and was usually too Kantian or empiricist to make metaphysical

---

Redemption (New York: Abingdon-Cokesbury, 1933), *The Validity of Religious Experience* (New York: Abingdon-Cokesbury, 1937)—DARB, 247ff.

10. Shailer Mathews (1863–1941), prof. at various ranks of rhetoric, history, political economy, Colby College, 1887–94, prof. NT University of Chicago, 1894–1906, prof. historical and comparative theology there, 1906–33, and dean there, 1908–33; editor of *The World Today*, 1903–11, and of *Biblical World*, 1913–20, active retirement; 1933–41; principal works: *The Gospel and the Modern Man* (New York: Macmillan, 1910), *The Faith of Modernism* (New York: Macmillan, 1924), *The Atonement and the Social Process* (New York: Macmillan, 1930), *The Growth of the Idea of God* (New York: Macmillan, 1931), *Immortality and the Cosmic Process* (Cambridge, MA: Harvard University Press, 1933), *New Faith for Old: An Autobiography* (New York: Macmillan, 1936)—DARB, 297ff.

claims. From its evangelical heritage, it affirmed a personal transcendent God, the authority of Christian experience, the authority of Scripture within Christian experience, the divinity of Christ, the need of personal redemption, and the importance of Christian missions.

The figures who made liberal Christianity compelling to millions of Americans were evangelical liberals who held together both heritages. In the nineteenth century, the major exemplar was Henry Ward Beecher; in the first half of the twentieth century, it was Harry Emerson Fosdick. To the evangelical liberals, there was no reason to choose between being modern and being gospel-centered. The very point of liberal theology was to hold these things together. At Union, when Bonhoeffer arrived there, the guardians of evangelical liberalism were Fosdick, Henry Sloane Coffin,[11] William Adams Brown,[12] and Pitney Van Dusen.[13] Harry Ward was an evangelical liberal too, although he had a very minimal theology, and politically he was a united front radical.

The second major theology usually belonged to the evangelical liberal mainstream, but it featured a distinct commitment to a post-Kantian philosophical system, personalist idealism. Founded by Borden Parker Bowne in the 1890s, the personalist school blended Descartes, Leibniz, Berkeley, Kant,

11. Henry Sloane Coffin (1877–1954), minister, Bedford Park Church, New York, 1900–05, assoc. prof. practical theology, Union Theological Seminary, New York, 1904–26, minister, Madison Avenue Presbyterian Church, New York, 1905–26, president, Union Seminary, 1926–45; active retirement 1945–54; principal works: *The Creed of Jesus* (New York: C. Scribner's Sons, 1907), *Some Christian Convictions: A Practical Restatement in Terms of Present-day Thinking* (New Haven: Yale University Press, 1915), *A More Christian Industrial Order* (New York: Macmillan, 1920), *The Meaning of the Cross* (New York: Macmillan, 1931), *Religion Yesterday and Today* (Nashville: Cokesbury,1940), *God Confronts Man in History* (New York: C. Scribner's Sons, 1947)—DARB, 104ff.

12. William Adams Brown (1865–1943), instr. and prof. systematic theology, Union Theological Seminary, New York, 1892–1930, prof. applied Christianity there, 1930–36; active retirement 1936–43; principal works: *Christian Theology in Outline* (New York: C. Scribner's Sons, 1906), *Modern Theology and the Preaching of the Gospel* (New York: C. Scribner's Sons, 1914), *Beliefs That Matter* (New York: C. Scribner's Sons, 1928), *The Church: Catholic and Protestant* (New York: C. Scribner's Sons, 1935), *A Teacher and His Times* (New York: Scribner, 1940), *Toward a United Church: Three Decades of Ecumenical Christianity* (New York: Scribner, 1946)—DARB, 71f.

13. Henry Pitney Van Dusen (1897–1975), at various ranks prof. systematic theology, Union Theological Seminary, New York, 1926–63, president there, 1945–63; active retirement, 1963–75; principal works: *The Plain Man Seeks for God* (New York: C. Scribner's Sons, 1933), *God in These Times* (London: Student Christian Movement, 1935), *World Christianity: Yesterday, Today and Tomorrow* (Nashville: Abingdon-Cokesbury, 1947), *Life's Meaning* (New York: Association Press, 1951), *One Great Ground of Hope* (Philadelphia: Westminster, 1961), *The Vindication of Liberal Theology* (New York: Scribner, 1963)—DARB, 481f.

Schleiermacher, and James; in its second generation it appropriated Hegel, Troeltsch, and the social gospel. Personalist idealism was a theory of the transcendent reality of personal spirit and the organic unity of nature in spirit. It taught that the soul is essentially active and is known immediately as the experience of consciousness. In the late nineteenth and early twentieth centuries the term "personality" had a golden status among American theologians, referring to the self as a center of experience. The leading personalists—Bowne, Edgar Brightman,[14] Albert Knudson, and Walter Muelder[15]—argued that personality is the single reality that cannot be explained by anything else.

The impact of personalist idealism registered far beyond its school, because virtually all liberals contended that spirit or personality holds primacy over the things of sense, even as many of them otherwise avoided metaphysical arguments. Fosdick, for example, was not a religious philosopher; he could not have taught a seminar on post-Kantian idealism. But his sermons conveyed a popular version of it to millions. He taught that the divine is present wherever goodness, beauty, truth, and love exist. Jesus was divine because he embodied these qualities fully. Divinity is the perfection of immanent love that every person is capable of mobilizing. Religions are true to the extent that they promote the flourishing of personality.

The third major type of American liberal theology, Chicago School empiricism, operated differently. Here the ideal of holding together the evangelical and Enlightenment traditions was abandoned. The other schools affirmed the continuity between modern and classical Christianity, but the Chicago School stressed that modernity is a revolution. If there was to be a modern theology, it had to rest on modern experience and tests of belief. The Chicago theologians Shailer Mathews, George Burman Foster,[16] Gerald Birney Smith,[17] Edward Scribner Ames,[18] and Shirley Jackson Case[19]—were committed

14. Edgar Sheffield Brightman (1884–1953), prof. philosophy, Nebraska Wesleyan University, 1912–15, prof. ethics and religion, Wesleyan University (CT), 1915–19, prof. philosophy Boston University, 1919–53; principal works: *Immortality in Post-Kantian Idealism* (Cambridge, MA: Harvard University Press, 1925), *The Problem of God* (New York: Abingdon, 1930), *Moral Laws* (New York: Abingdon, 1933), *Personality and Religion* (New York: Abingdon, 1934), *The Future of Christianity* (New York: Abingdon, 1937), *Persons and Values* (Boston: Boston University Press, 1952)—DARB, 68f.

15. Walter George Muelder (1907–2004).

16. George Burman Foster (1858–1919).

17. Gerald Birney Smith (1868–1929), ". . . defined Christianity almost entirely in terms of social concern," according to Sydney E. Ahlstrom, *A Religious History of the American People* (New Haven: Yale University Press, 1972)—DARB, 906f.

18. Edward Scribner Ames (1870–1958), prof. philosophy and education, Butler College, 1897–1900, at various ranks, prof. philosophy, University of Chicago, 1900–35, minister, Hyde Park (later

to historicism, pragmatism, and religious naturalism, and most of them also adopted radical empiricism.

All knowledge has an irreducibly historical character; every idea has a history that is the key to its meaning and truth. Concepts are habits of belief or rules of action, and ideas are true according to their practical usefulness. Ideas are like knives and forks, enabling useful action. William James and John Dewey were the chief influences on Chicago pragmatism; a bit later in its history, the Chicago School also made much of radical empiricism. Enlightenment empiricism studied experience, contending that sense data about things is all that we have in claiming to know anything. But James added that experience is relational. Instead of focusing on atomistic units of experience, empiricism needed to study experience as a flowing, immediate continuity. Life is a continuous flux or stream of experiences lacking distinct boundaries. By focusing on the relational flow of experience, the Chicago School practiced a form of process theology before this term existed.

When Bonhoeffer arrived at Union, America's leading theologian was D. C. Macintosh,[20] and its most powerful up-and-coming theologian was Henry Nelson Wieman. Macintosh had studied under Foster at Chicago before beginning his long career at Yale. He sought to make theology as scientific as possible. Macintosh argued that every science assumes the existence and knowability of its object. Chemistry assumes the existence of matter; psychology assumes the existence of states of consciousness; theology has the same right, as a working hypothesis, to assume *that* God is, without assuming *what* God is. Religious experience is the working material of theology, which describes the divine Object known through experience. Theology attends to that which is apprehended in religious experience.

University) Church of the Disciples, Chicago, 1900–40; editor of *The Scroll*, 1925–51; dean, Disciples Divinity House, 1927–45; active retirement, 1945–58; principal works: *The Psychology of Religious Experience* (Boston: Houghton Mifflin, 1910), *The Divinity of Christ* (Chicago: The New Christian Century Co., 1911), *The Higher Individualism* (Boston: Houghton Mifflin, 1915), *The New Orthodoxy* (Chicago: University of Chicago Press, 1918), *Religion* (New York: H. Holt & Co., 1929), *Letters to God and the Devil* (New York: Harper & Brothers, 1933)—DARB, 14ff.

19. Shirley Jackson Case (1872–1947), University of Chicago theologian who ". . . carried positivistic methods into scholarship on the New Testament and the early Church"—Ahlstrom, *A Religious History*, 906.

20. Douglas Clyde Macintosh (1877–1948) ". . . came to Yale from Canada and carried his pacifist refusal to bear arms in defense of the Constitution to the Supreme Court. He lost the case, and never became a U.S. citizen, but his defense of the reasonableness of Christianity won wide attention. God, for him, was an objective, verifiable reality; and the essentials of the Christian faith could be established quite apart from any historical evidence"—Ahlstrom, *A Religious History*, 906.

Macintosh reasoned that there ought to be a God to give spiritual meaning and moral direction to life. In that case, there may be a God, because science is compatible with the notion of an indwelling, divine mind at work in nature and history. That led to a tentative conclusion, that there must be a God if one is to have a morally healthy, rational existence. To put it concisely, with echoes of Kant and James: "We have a moral right to believe as we must in order to live as we ought."

Macintosh was deeply pious, and he had a complex theory of knowledge that he called realistic monism. Wieman was not as pious as Macintosh, but he had a similar pragmatic realism. Joining the Chicago faculty in 1927, Wieman admired his colleagues for pioneering an empirical, naturalistic, pragmatic approach to theology, but he could not fathom why they took so much interest in history, and he chided them for letting go of God's objective reality. History doesn't matter, because history doesn't prove anything. What matters is: What is it all about? In Wieman's view, liberal theology had become too sentimental; it shrank from defending God's existence; and it tried to make itself attractive by appealing to social concerns. That strategy was a loser; it drove the strong and intelligent types away from religion.

Wieman admonished that theology had to become tough-minded again. Religion is pointless without God, but science negates traditional ways of conceiving God's existence. Wieman argued that whatever else the word "God" may mean, at bottom it designates the Something upon which human life and the flourishing of the good are dependent. It cannot be doubted that such a Something exists. If there is a human good, it must have a source. The fact that human life happens proves the reality of the Something of supreme value on which life depends. Wieman made that the object of theology. He conceived God as a structured event and theology as the analysis of the total event of religious experience. For twenty years he was the Chicago answer to Barth, making theology more objective and empirical.

Imagine the cognitive dissonance for Bonhoeffer when he got here and discovered that this was where American theology was going. Where was the church in this theology? What happened to dogmatics? What happened to struggling with the scriptural text within a confessing community? It seemed to Bonhoeffer that at places like Union and Chicago, dogmatic theology had become subordinate to social ethics or practical theology. Then in December 1932, Niebuhr rocked the field with his icy, liberal-bashing book, *Moral Man and Immoral Society*, and American theology changed.

Niebuhr had very little idea of where he was heading theologically. He spoke vaguely of moving to the left politically and to the right theologically. In

1932 only his politics were clear—he had become a radical Christian Socialist. He spent the rest of the decade figuring out his theology, which he presented, magnificently, in *The Nature and Destiny of Man.* Then his politics changed again.

All of that is familiar to us, because Niebuhr has the Barth role in American theology. But Reinhold Niebuhr never came close to being a Barthian. He retained a thoroughly liberal view of authority and method in theology. He took for granted that reason and experience are the tests of religious truth. He taught that no external authority should establish or compel a religious belief; and that Christian Scripture and doctrine are pervaded by myth. He blasted Social Gospel idealism and pacifism, but he fully assumed the Social Gospel understanding of what social ethics should be about. He fashioned a neo-Reformationist theology of sin and redemption, but he was every bit as pragmatic, politicized, and social-ethical as his Social Gospel forerunners. If American theology was too pragmatic and social-ethical, as Bonhoeffer judged, one cannot exempt the American Barth from that judgment.

12

Contextualizing Dietrich Bonhoeffer: Nazism, the Churches, and the Question of Silence

Doris L. Bergen

The word most often used to describe the Christian response to the Holocaust and to Nazism in general is "silence."[1] In the vast theological, historical, and popular literature on the churches and National Socialism, silence has become the most serious charge leveled against Christianity.[2] Why did Christians not speak out? A litany of failures follows: examples abound of Christian individuals who "stood by," of institutions that "did nothing" to help persecuted Jews. But the churches did not keep silent, other observers insist. Indeed, for defenders of Christianity and most noticeably of Pius XII, countering the accusation of silence has become the principal way to make their case. The pope was not silent, they contend; nor by extension was Christianity.[3] As evidence they can point to the many Christian heroes and martyrs—and Dietrich Bonhoeffer features prominently on most such lists—and to the existence of Christian rescuers of Jews. In short, whether affirmed or negated, the "question of silence" has come not only to dominate but to define discussions of the churches under Nazism.

The preoccupation with silence has produced heated debates and piles of books, articles, and films of varying quality. It has also generated a remarkable body of scholarly work in several languages and academic disciplines. This essay

---

1. My profound thanks to Victoria Barnett, Guy C. Carter, and Clifford J. Green for their inspiration, assistance, and encouragement.

2. There are hundreds of books and articles with titles including the words "silence" and "churches," "Vatican," or "Christianity." A Google search in February 2013 for Pius XII and "silence" yielded about 859,000 hits.

3. See the many writings under titles such as Jenö Levai, *L'Église ne s'est pas tué: Dossier Hongrois 1940–1945* (Paris: Éditions du Seuil, 1966), and David Dalin, *A Righteous Gentile: Pope Pius XII and the Jews* (New York: Catholic League for Religious and Civil Rights, 2002).

builds on that research and revisits some sources from the 1930s and 1940s to suggest that, productive as the discourse around silence has been, it has limitations. What other ideas and frameworks have been, and can be, brought to the study of the churches and the Third Reich, in order to open new avenues of questioning and generate fresh insights? In the following sections I draw attention to three reconceptualizations, all of them evident in the literature and influenced by my reading of Bonhoeffer's words and life. The first section posits a different spectrum than the one usually applied to the churches under Nazism: rather than casting active resistance, even martyrdom, as the opposite of silence, what if we contrast silence with noise, that is, with loud, outspoken, Christian endorsements of Nazism? Section two shifts the focus from words and their absence (silence) to actions by asking not what Christians and church leaders said but what they did. The third part explores the stakes for the field of church history by asking what—and who—might be muffled or even silenced by the hegemonic discourse about silence?

Silence and Noise: A Different Polarity

Though not a Bonhoeffer scholar, I encounter him and his legacy through my work on Christianity, Nazi Germany, and the Holocaust. When I give a public talk, the questions I am most often asked are about Dietrich Bonhoeffer and Pius XII. With these questions, people focus on what many consider to be the opposite poles of Christian involvement with Nazism: success and failure, or put another way, martyrdom and silence. Bonhoeffer's injunction, from Proverbs 31:8, to "Open your mouth for the dumb," now translated as, "Speak out for those who cannot speak," is frequently invoked as a challenge to Christians who failed—and fail—to follow his example of active discipleship.[4]

Sometimes those who elevate Bonhoeffer as a model of Christian strength in contrast to Pius XII draw attention to the confessional divide. Protestantism, they imply, with its emphasis on the individual standing before God, proved more resilient than hierarchical, institutionalized Roman Catholicism. In other cases it is not the Lutheran Bonhoeffer but Catholic individuals, laypeople, and parish priests whose resistance and engagement stand out against the silence

---

4. See *Discipleship*, DBWE 4:237; DBWE 13:89, 217. Many lists of "Bonhoeffer quotes" include a sharper indictment: "Silence in the face of evil is itself evil. God will not hold us guiltless. Not to speak is to speak. Not to act is to act." See also Eric Metaxas, *Bonhoeffer: Pastor, Martyr, Prophet, Spy* (Nashville: Thomas Nelson, 2010), back flap. However, this formulation has not been found in Bonhoeffer's works. Possibly the words closest to it are those in his *Ethics* (DBWE 6:140): "The church confesses that it has looked on silently as the poor were exploited and robbed. . . . It has not condemned the slanderers for their wrongs and has thereby left the slandered to their fate."

of the Catholic hierarchy. Michael Phayer has done especially important work to demonstrate the differences between individual and institutional Catholic responses.[5]

History, it has often been pointed out, is lived looking forward but written looking back. From inside the situation Bonhoeffer saw things differently from the way they appear in hindsight. It was not the now-familiar dichotomy between his speech/resistance and the silence/failure of others that appeared significant to him. Instead, in his 1942 Christmas letter he leveled the charge of silence precisely against himself and his friends in the Confessing Church:

> We have been silent witnesses of evil deeds. We have become cunning and learned the arts of obfuscation and equivocal speech. Experience has rendered us suspicious of human beings, and often we have failed to speak with them a true and open word. Unbearable conflicts have worn us down or even made us cynical. Are we still of any use?[6]

Bonhoeffer wrote these words at the end of 1942, during the peak period of the killing of Jews, when tens of thousands were being murdered daily: at Chelmno, Belzec, Sobibor, Treblinka, and Auschwitz-Birkenau. It was at this time, too, that Pius XII issued his 1942 Christmas address, a text often cited as evidence that the pope did speak out for Jews.[7] Bonhoeffer's scathing self-criticism is a stark contrast to the detached reportage of the papal address, with its reference to the "hundreds of thousands of persons who, without any fault on their part, sometimes only because of their nationality or race, have been consigned to death or to a slow decline."[8] One can debate whether or not the pope's words constituted speaking out on behalf of Jews and argue about

---

5. Michael Phayer, *The Catholic Church and the Holocaust, 1930–1965* (Bloomington: Indiana University Press, 2000), and *Pius XII, the Holocaust and the Cold War* (Bloomington: Indiana University Press, 2008). A related point, about the difference between the Church hierarchy and parish priests, is implied in Kevin Spicer, *Resisting the Third Reich: The Catholic Clergy in Hitler's Berlin* (DeKalb: Northern Illinois University Press, 2004). Regarding Protestants, see Kyle Jantzen, *Faith and Fatherland: Parish Politics in Hitler's Germany* (Minneapolis: Fortress Press, 2008).

6. See "After Ten Years," *Letters and Papers from Prison*, DBWE 8:52.

7. An energetic argument for the impact of the 1942 message is in Margherita Marchione, *Pope Pius XII: Architect for Peace* (Mahwah, NJ: Paulist, 2000), 33, 50, 62, 148, 173. For discussion of that interpretation see Carol Rittner and John K. Roth, "Introduction: Calls for Help," in *Pope Pius XII and the Holocaust*, ed. Rittner and Roth (London: Continuum, 2002), 3–5.

8. *1942 Christmas Message of Pope Pius XII: With Text of the Holy Father's Prayer to the Immaculate Heart of Mary* (Washington, DC: National Catholic Welfare Conference, 1942).

whether Bonhoeffer's rejection of silence and his participation in the smuggling of a group of Jews, and converts from Judaism to Christianity, across the border into Switzerland make him worthy of the title "Righteous among the Nations." But it is crucial to acknowledge that focusing on these two positions alone omits a vast sweep of the range of Christian responses.

The opposite of silence, after all, is noise, and many Christians were loud in their enthusiasm for National Socialism. Consider, for example, the Protestant anti-Nazi Gertrud Staewen's memories of a May 1933 rally at the Tempelhof Field in Berlin: "I saw the huge masses with their flags, brightly lit in broad daylight, and heard this constant trumpeting of the fanfare. . . . And the Tempelhof Field was filled to the last place with jubilant, screaming people. Only our group sat there and wept. Everyone else was simply enraptured."[9] Given that more than 95 percent of Germans were baptized, church-tax-paying members of the Protestant and Catholic churches—and remained so throughout the twelve years of Hitler's rule—one has to assume that the vast majority of those raucous supporters were Christians, whether defined by tradition, culture, church membership, or self-identification.

Some Christians were more vociferous than others in their endorsement of National Socialism. On a June day in 1933, in a single ceremony, fifty couples were married at the Protestant Lazarus Church in Berlin. The brides, adorned with veils and flowers, glowed in their Sunday best. The grooms wore SS or Stormtrooper uniforms and sported Nazi Party badges. Such mass nuptials were a common sight in German cities that summer, as up to four hundred couples at a time stood before a pastor to pledge their troth. Most of these couples had already married in civil ceremonies, but in the spirit of national and religious revival that followed Hitler's rise to power in January 1933, they chose to have their vows blessed before God and their local congregations. For many Protestant clergymen and parishioners, these processions of newly-weds symbolized and embodied the marriage of true Christianity and the Nazi state.

The impresarios of the mass weddings—and the loudest proponents of a union between church and state in Hitler's Germany—came from the German Christian Faith Movement.[10] A group of clergy and laypeople, the "German

9. Quoted in Victoria J. Barnett, *For the Soul of the People: Protestant Protest against Hitler* (New York: Oxford University Press, 1992), 29. See also Manfred Gailus, *Protestantismus und Nationalsozialismus. Studien zur nationalsozialistischen Durchdringung des protestantischen Sozialmilieus in Berlin* (Cologne: Böhlau, 2001).

10. On the German Christian movement (*Glaubensbewegung "Deutsche Christen"*), see Doris L. Bergen, *Twisted Cross: The German Christian Movement in the Third Reich* (Chapel Hill: University of North Carolina Press, 1996).

Christians" sought to synthesize Nazism and Christianity, to purge Christianity of everything they deemed Jewish, and to transform the German Protestant church into an association based on "blood." By the late summer of 1933, "Germans Christians," riding a wave of enthusiasm for the Nazi revolution, had acquired key posts in the Protestant establishment—in national church governing bodies and university faculties of theology, as regional bishops, and on local church councils. Many kept those positions until 1945 and beyond. Calling themselves "Stormtroopers of Christ," the German Christians attacked every aspect of Christianity that was related to Judaism. They did so in public and at the top of their voices. Members rejected parts or all of the Old Testament, revised the New Testament, and denied that Jesus was a Jew. They refused to accept conversions from Judaism to Christianity as valid. A sign displayed in Westphalia in 1935 stated their position with crude clarity: "Baptism may be quite useful, but it doesn't straighten any noses."[11]

In early 1939, German Christians and likeminded Protestants founded the Institute for the Study and Eradication of Jewish Influence on German Church Life, a center of anti-Jewish theological scholarship and activism.[12] Headquartered in Eisenach, the Institute was under the academic leadership of Walter Grundmann, professor of New Testament and Folkish Theology at the University of Jena. A 1941 Institute publication described its work as essential to Christianity's survival: "Because in the course of historical development, corrupting Jewish influence has also been active in Christianity, the de-Judaization of Church and Christianity has become the inescapable and decisive duty of the church today; it is the requirement for the future of Christianity."[13]

As Susannah Heschel has demonstrated, the Institute was anything but quiet.[14] In keeping with its "de-Judaizing" mission, it disseminated new versions of Scripture, revised hymnals, liturgical guides, collections of devotions, and other materials, all purged of evidence of Christianity's Jewish roots. *Die Botschaft Gottes* ("The Message of God"), a compilation of the synoptic Gospels, appeared in December 1939. It avoided the word "Jew," opting instead to present Jesus in a historical and geographic vacuum and to depict Christianity as nothing but a collection of familiar sayings. Within six months, the Institute

11. Quoted in Doris L. Bergen, "Storm Troopers of Christ: The German Christian Movement and the Ecclesiastical Final Solution," in *Betrayal: German Churches and the Holocaust*, ed. Robert P. Ericksen and Susannah Heschel (Minneapolis: Fortress Press, 1999), 40.

12. *Institut zur Erforschung und Beseitigung des jüdischen Einflusses im deutschen kirchlichen Leben.*

13. Quoted in Bergen, *Twisted Cross*, 142.

14. Susannah Heschel, *The Aryan Jesus: Christian Theologians and the Bible in Nazi Germany* (Princeton: Princeton University Press, 2008).

boasted sales of two hundred thousand copies. A year later the new hymnal, *Grosser Gott, wir loben Dich!* ("Holy God, We Praise Thy Name") was released. It was the work of an Institute committee that reviewed over two thousand songs for "Jewish content, dogmatism, and tastelessness." The result included new material and familiar hymns from which words like "Hallelujah" and "Hosanna," along with references to the Old Testament and Jesus' Jewish lineage, had been expunged. The Institute organized conferences and gatherings for pastors, academic theologians, and other church people in various parts of Germany and engaged in outreach abroad. It maintained close ties with some Swedish Lutheran churchmen, and by 1942 had a branch office led by ethnic German Protestants in Romania. Funding came from individuals and groups in the "circle of supporters," central organs of the Protestant church, and regional Protestant church governments.

One need not reach to the German Christian Movement or the anti-Jewish Institute in Eisenach to find evidence of Christian "noise" in support of National Socialism. Whether it was Catholic priests who stumped for the Nazi Party in Bavaria in the early 1920s,[15] Superintendent Otto Dibelius' sermon in 1933 at the "Day of Potsdam,"[16] or the effusive telegrams Catholic bishops sent to Hitler every year for his birthday, including in April 1945, outspoken expressions of enthusiasm abounded. Perhaps it will suffice to quote just one more. In his pastoral letter of September 1, 1940, distributed to all Catholic military chaplains and through them to millions of Wehrmacht soldiers, Catholic Military Bishop Franz-Justus Rarkowski offered a Christian justification for the German invasions of the preceding year:

> The German people . . . have a clear conscience and they know who before God and History bears the responsibility for the gigantic struggle that is now raging. The German people know who recklessly released the dogs of war. They know that they themselves are waging a just war. . . . Our enemies wanted to turn us into

---

15. See Derek Hastings, *Catholicism and the Roots of Nazism: Religious Identity and National Socialism* (Oxford: Oxford University Press, 2010), 108–38.

16. On the Day of Potsdam see John S. Conway, *The Nazi Persecution of the Churches, 1933–45* (London: Weidenfeld & Nicolson, 1968), 19; Ulrich von Hehl, "Die Kirchen in der NS-Diktatur: Zwischen Anpassung, Selbstbehauptung und Widerstand," in *Deutschland, 1933–1945: Neue Studien zur nationalsozialistischen Herrschaft,* ed. Karl Dietrich Bracher, Manfred Funke, Hans-Adolf Jacobsen (Düsseldorf: Droste, 1992), 165; and Ulrich Schneider, *Bekennende Kirche zwischen "freudigem Ja" und antifaschistischem Widerstand* (Kassel: Brüder Grimm, 1986), 102–8. On Dibelius's address, see Anneliese Thimme, *Flucht in den Mythos: Die Deutschnationale Volkspartei und die Niederlage von 1918* (Göttingen: Vandenhoeck & Ruprecht, 1969), 63.

a people of slaves, and so there is no question for us on which side justice stands in this war and with it God's help. . . . Our enemies deceived themselves when they believed that the German people were weak and helpless. They had no idea of the power and self-sacrificing love of our people. They believed in the power of their money bags and the repressive force of the shameful and un-Christian Treaty of Versailles.[17]

Such words, spoken not in private or under duress, but openly and freely by Christians in positions of power, need to be viewed as a significant contrast to silence.

ACTIONS LOUDER THAN WORDS

Throughout the Nazi period the churches and church people were noisy, involved, and active. Rather than deploring their silence it seems appropriate to analyze what they said and did.[18] One starting point is the relationship between Nazism and Christianity. Were the Nazis Christians? Or were they anti-Christian? The answer, it seems to me, is "yes," they were both.[19] In fact the tension between those two positions is key to understanding the context in which Dietrich Bonhoeffer lived and worked. Fearful of the advance of secularization and sensitive to the charge from some elements within Nazism that Christianity was after all just disguised Judaism, many church leaders clamored to show that as Christians, they were loyal Germans, genuine Nazis, and committed anti-Semites. The churches in Germany were in a defensive posture vis-à-vis the National Socialist regime, and this defensiveness shaped their official responses, moving them to develop a pattern of behavior I call compensatory compliance. It was expressed in words but also in deeds.

Members of the German Christian movement were especially keen to defend themselves against neo-pagan charges that Christianity was antithetical to Nazism. They promoted their views through mass rallies, in newspapers, flyers, and scholarly works, as well as from the pulpit; lay members spread the word in schools and at local pubs. But the German Christians did more

17. Franz-Justus Rarkowski, "Hirtenschreiben," *Verordnungsblatt* 7 (September 1, 1940). My translation.

18. For a discussion of "Actions Louder Than Words"—using that same subtitle, in fact—pertaining to Bonhoeffer's actions to help Jews and converts from Judaism to Christianity, see Stephen R. Haynes, *The Bonhoeffer Legacy: Post-Holocaust Perspectives* (Minneapolis: Augsburg Fortress Press, 2006), xii–xv.

19. See Richard Steigmann-Gall, *The Holy Reich: Nazi Conceptions of Christianity, 1919–1945* (New York: Cambridge University Press, 2003).

than talk; they patronized one another's businesses, disrupted meetings of the Confessing Church, brawled with critical congregants, shouted down sermons and university lectures with which they disagreed, and barricaded church buildings.

In many congregations, the German Christians organized campaigns, including physical assault, against pastors, members of church councils, musicians, and parishioners who had Jewish ancestors, were married to Jews, or expressed empathy with the plight of Jews in Germany. Such attacks followed the lead of the Nazi government and Party elite. Every time there was a spike in official measures against Jews, or people defined as Jewish under German law, attacks by the German Christians surged, too. Thus the years 1933, 1935, 1938, and 1941, which brought the Nazi revolution, the Nuremberg Laws, the Kristallnacht pogrom, and the first deportations of Jews out of Germany to the east for killing, also saw renewed violence against Jews, Judaism, and Christians of Jewish descent in the words and deeds of German Christians.

The same patterns are apparent in the churches as a whole, Protestant and Catholic. In 1933 church leaders showed misgivings about National Socialism and about Hitler. But they set uncertainty aside in exchange for a claim to relevance. In the process they threw the Jews overboard. With passage of the Nuremberg Laws in 1935, Germans required so-called Aryan certificates to engage in many kinds of work and training programs: not only to join the Nazi Party or SS, but to enter a university, obtain a marriage license, or get a job. It was Christian clergy and their staff who provided the proof of baptism of at least two grandparents on which the definition of "Aryan" rested. Many parishes and congregations had to hire extra people to do the work required. The churches were not silent or passive at all on this point. To the contrary they were active, essential partners of the state and Party in creating a system in which the distinction between "Aryans" and "non-Aryans" was definitive.

In 1936, with the Spanish Civil War, German Catholic bishops explicitly made a deal with the regime: legitimation of Nazi measures in exchange for easing of pressure on church organizations. They promised to participate in the Nazi "crusade" against Communism in return for cessation of attacks on the church and especially on its clergy.[20] With the Kristallnacht pogrom in 1938, the defensive posture took another form. A handful of Protestant pastors preached against the violence against Jewish lives, Jewish property, and the sites of Jewish religious practice. Their colleagues and superiors isolated them

---

20. Beth Griech-Polelle, "The Impact of the Spanish Civil War on the German Roman Catholic Clergy," in *Antisemitism, Christian Ambivalence, and the Holocaust*, ed. Kevin P. Spicer (Bloomington: Indiana University Press, 2007), 121–35.

rather than risk showing Christianity to be, as its enemies charged, sympathetic to, or even a disguised form of, Judaism. This pattern of participation became a rut, and church leaders sought self-justification for their words and actions. They found it often in anti-Semitism. Bishop August Marahrens went to work the morning after Kristallnacht. The cathedral in Hanover stood adjacent to the still-smoldering synagogue. The bishop's secretary waited anxiously to hear how he would respond. He was not silent but immediately had something to say. "Back to the letter I was dictating," he told her.[21]

During the war, many regional churches and even local congregations issued proclamations refusing the sacraments and other rights of church membership to Christians of Jewish descent. No Nazi law required them to do so, nor was it only German Christians or the Catholic clergy—called by Kevin Spicer "brown priests"—who implemented such prohibitions.[22] Indeed, the *Erlass*, the infamous 1939 document that restricted the place of so-called Jewish Christians in certain regional Protestant churches, was penned by Heinz Brunotte, who started his career as a Confessing Church stalwart.[23]

Victor Klemperer's encounters with representatives of the Confessing Church show how their actions and words contributed to his isolation. Klemperer, a professor of French literature in Dresden, was the son of a rabbi and a convert to Protestant Christianity. Married to a gentile, he had served in the German army in the First World War, and identified fully with German culture. Under Nazi law, however, he counted as a Jew. In his detailed and insightful diary, one of the issues that preoccupied him was what he referred to as the *vox populi*. What did "ordinary Germans"—that is, the non-Jewish Germans around him, think of Jews? What did they make of Nazi anti-Jewish measures? How antisemitic were they?

At four points in his diary, in 1936, 1938, 1939, and 1941, Klemperer described an issue that arose about where he should pay his church taxes. Finally, in 1941, he met with Pastor Delekat of the Confessing Church, who told him that, unless there was a constraint on his conscience, he should "pay it to the Jewish community." Klemperer understood immediately what the pastor was saying. "You are afraid to be called a Jews' church?" he responded. "I am offended by that." Klemperer reported Delekat's answer: "We are under

21. As told to Hartmut Lehmann and recounted by him at the First Annual Powell-Heller Family Conference in Support of Holocaust Education, Pacific Lutheran University, November 2007.

22. Kevin Spicer, *Hitler's Priests: Catholic Clergy and National Socialism* (DeKalb: Northern Illinois University Press, 2008).

23. Jens Gundlach, *Heinz Brunotte: 1896–1984. Anpassung des Evangeliums an die NS-Diktatur. Eine biografische Studie* (Hanover: Luther, 2010).

surveillance, harassed . . . thinking of setting up special Bible evenings for the Jewish Christians."[24]

There were also more open ways in which churches and church people acted as agents of what Marion Kaplan has called the "social death" of Jews.[25] In 1939 a Protestant pastor in the Czech lands, by then under German control as the Protectorate of Bohemia and Moravia, wrote to the head of the local Jewish community. Give us your synagogue building, he urged; otherwise the Germans would seize it, and this way it would still be used as a house of worship. In his eyes, there was no future for Jews living among Christians.[26]

Germany's military chaplains provide another illustration of how Christians served the National Socialist system through deeds as well as words. The vocabulary of "silence" and "bystanders" suggests Christians on the outside looking in, reacting and responding to rather than participating in and constituting Nazi power. But military chaplains were engaged in concrete and particular ways. Indeed, it is not surprising that Bonhoeffer, with his commitment to ministry and also to confrontation—putting a spoke in the wheel—contemplated entering the chaplaincy.

Military chaplains epitomized the defensive position of the churches. Nazi authorities somewhat reluctantly accepted them in the new Wehrmacht, founded in 1935. But they faced restrictions on their activities that can only have been intended to curb their effectiveness. Such limits were most obvious during the early war years, when Germany's military seemed unstoppable. There were restrictions on the number of chaplains, on whether they could provide Christian burials for soldiers; even the so-called Uriah law. Chaplains also faced hostility from the men who taunted them that Jesus was a Jew, and that Christianity with its injunction to turn the other cheek was for the weak or for women.[27]

In response, the Wehrmacht chaplains redoubled their efforts to prove they were loyal and useful. They accompanied men condemned to death in the hours

---

24. Victor Klemperer, *I Will Bear Witness: A Diary of the Nazi Years*, vol. 1: *1933–1941*, trans. from German by Martin Chalmers (New York: Random House, 1998), 431.

25. Marion A. Kaplan, *Between Dignity and Despair: Jewish Life in Nazi Germany* (New York: Oxford University Press, 1998), esp. 5, 235–39. The insight stems from Orlando Patterson, *Slavery and Social Death: A Comparative Study* (Cambridge, MA: Harvard University Press, 1985).

26. Magda Veselská, "'Sie müssen sich als Jude dessen bewusst sein, welche Opfer zu tragen sind . . .' Handlungsspielräume der jüdischen Kultusgemeinden im Protektorat bis zum Ende der großen Deportationen," in *Alltag im Holocaust*, ed. Doris L. Bergen, Andrea Löw, and Anna Hájková (Munich: Oldenbourg, 2013).

27. See Doris L. Bergen, "German Military Chaplains in World War II and the Dilemmas of Legitimacy," *Church History* 70 (June 2001): 232–47.

before their executions and stood before the soldiers assembled to participate in or witness the firing squad. In this way they displayed support of a system that killed more than 20,000 of its own soldiers on charges that they had deserted, mutilated themselves, fraternized with the enemy, betrayed the Fatherland, or undermined the cause. Chaplains assembled statistics to try to demonstrate their usefulness in boosting morale and fighting power. For instance, in 1940, Protestant church officials put together an entire packet of materials—clippings about chaplains who had been decorated for bravery, protestations of loyalty to "Führer, Volk, und Vaterland," and excerpts from soldiers' letters—to try to prove to Hitler and the Reich Ministry for Church Affairs how useful and loyal the chaplains were.[28]

Robert Ericksen has been especially influential in showing how church leaders and university theologians were effective agents of legitimation for the Nazi regime.[29] Saul Friedländer too has analyzed German church leaders as elites who bridged the gap between the Nazi leadership and the rank and file, and served to legitimate National Socialism and its attacks on Jews. Victoria Barnett has produced a series of pathbreaking works that illuminate and complicate the myriad roles played in Nazi Germany and the Holocaust by church people of all kinds—Bonhoeffer, the Niemöllers, and other prominent figures in the Confessing Church, but also laywomen and men in and outside Germany.[30]

Less well documented or understood is an even more hands-on way that Christians participated in the Holocaust: as killers. Hilary Earl provides a chilling glimpse of the Einsatzgruppe leader who was an ordained Protestant pastor; another came from a distinguished family of Protestant theologians.[31]

28. See report on the meeting of September 12, 1940 on "Besprechung über Schrifttumsfragen," and the letter from the chancellery of the German Protestant church to Hitler; it was signed by Werner, Hymmen, Marahrens, and Schultz, Berlin-Charlottenburg, October 28, 1940. Bundesarchiv Potsdam, 51.01/23740. These materials have been relocated within the Bundesarchiv system (to Berlin-Lichterfelde) since I used them.

29. Robert P. Ericksen, *Theologians under Hitler: Gerhard Kittel, Paul Althaus and Emanuel Hirsch* (New Haven: Yale University Press, 1985), and *Complicity in the Holocaust: Churches and Universities in Nazi Germany* (New York: Cambridge University Press, 2012).

30. Victoria J. Barnett, *For the Soul of the People*; Barnett, *Bystanders: Conscience and Complicity during the Holocaust* (Westport, CT: Greenwood, 1999). In addition to her leading role in producing the definitive edition of Bonhoeffer's works, Barnett played a key part in making available in English two essential works: Wolfgang Gerlach, *And the Witnesses Were Silent: The Confessing Church and the Persecution of the Jews*, trans. and ed. Victoria J. Barnett (Lincoln: University of Nebraska Press, 2000); she also revised and edited the complete edition of Eberhard Bethge's *Dietrich Bonhoeffer: A Biography* (Minneapolis: Fortress Press, 2000).

Friedländer depicts Christian leaders from around Europe as enabling genocide in concrete ways: preaching hatred of Jews in Poland, turning away would-be converts from Judaism in Germany; and killing and inciting killers in Croatia and Hungary, where in 1944, Father Kun exhorted shooters of Jews, "In the name of Christ—fire!"[32] This treatment of the churches provides powerful ways to think about Christianity beyond the tired trope of silence—an insight that might also be applied to examinations of religion and genocide in other settings.[33]

Recognition of Christians as killers—not only enablers or facilitators—might also open up neglected aspects of the Holocaust. What roles did church leaders and Christians play in the second phase of the program to murder the disabled in Nazi Germany, the so-called 14f13 program? And what about forced abortions and infanticide committed against slave laborers and their babies in the last years of the war?[34] Many of those pregnancies were terminated and infants killed in hospitals run by the Catholic and Protestant churches: Is a systematic examination of their members and leaders possible? Daniel Goldhagen and others have contrasted the protests by Christian leaders against killings of disabled people in the so-called T-4 or "Euthanasia" program in 1941 with the "silence" of the Vatican and other Christian institutions regarding murder of Jews. But rather than a contrast, viewing programs of killing together may suggest patterns of responses and actions that are more of a piece.

Gerhard Weinberg has pointed out that Pius XII had information from reliable sources about at least five programs of killing that were organized and carried out in Nazi Germany or under Nazi German leadership: murders of the disabled beginning in 1939, Polish intellectuals in 1939, Serbian Orthodox

31. See discussion of Ernst Biberstein in Hilary Earl, *The Nuremberg SS-Einsatzgruppen Trial, 1945–1958* (New York: Cambridge University Press, 2009), 116–17, 122–24, and 293. Ordained in 1924, Biberstein served in 1942 as commander of *Einsatzkommando* 6 of *Einsatzgruppe* C. Martin Sandberger, another defendant in the same trial, was a lawyer but came from a family of Lutheran theologians. Bishop Theophil Wurm lobbied energetically on his behalf. Biberstein and Sandberger were condemned to death in 1948 but paroled in 1958. Earl, op. cit., 119, 270–71.

32. Saul Friedländer, *The Years of Extermination: Nazi Germany and the Jews, 1939–1945* (New York: HarperCollins, 2007), 641.

33. See Doris L. Bergen, "Religion and Genocide: A Historiographical Survey," in *The Historiography of Genocide*, ed. Dan Stone (Houndmills, UK and New York: Palgrave Macmillan, 2008), 194–227.

34. On forced abortions for slave workers, see Gabriella Hauch, "Zwangsarbeiterinnen und ihre Kinder. Zum Geschlecht der Zwangsarbeit in den Hermann Göring Werken/Linz, in *NS-Zwangsarbeit. Der Standort Linz der "Reichswerke Hermann Göring AG Berlin," 1938–1945*, ed. Oliver Rathkolb, vol. 1 (Vienna: Böhlau, 2001), 355–448.

Christians beginning in 1941, Jews starting that same year; and the newborn babies of slave laborers, many of them from Ukraine, in 1943 and after.[35] In each case the Vatican's response was to say as little as possible. And yet the pope was not incapable of taking action: in 1944 he wrote to British diplomats requesting that no "colored troops" be garrisoned in Rome after the Allied occupation.[36]

Focusing on deeds rather than words provides ways to look beyond issues of intention. Motive is important in law and central to moral philosophy but less central in history. Historians concern themselves with causes and consequences, and often the connections between them are unintended. I was reminded of the strange mismatch of actions, words, and intent when I read that already in 1938 someone prominent and powerful had urged Pius XI to excommunicate the Roman Catholic Adolf Hitler. It was Benito Mussolini.[37]

Other insights regarding intention and its absence are to be gained from a different source: Konrad Jarausch's collection of the letters of his father, a theologian and reserve officer who served with the Wehrmacht in Poland and the Soviet Union. A devout Christian, religious educator, and publicist, Konrad Jarausch Sr. was committed to serving his nation and the gospel. He studied the Bible daily and commented to his wife on a "nice essay by Bonhoeffer" that he read. By autumn 1941 a master sergeant, he was put in charge of the kitchen in a POW camp that held hundreds of thousands of dying, starving sick Soviet prisoners of war. The horrors he reported included incidents of cannibalism.[38] Sergeant Jarausch tried his best to keep order. His hand, he told his wife, became swollen from dealing out blows. And yet he felt solidarity with the Soviet prisoners and developed close relations with some of them. In his words, it was "already more murder than war." He died of typhoid in January 1942. Jarausch's son, also named Konrad Hugo Jarausch, concludes that his father's letters show us neither the "clean Wehrmacht" nor Nazified killers: "his fate demonstrates how annihilationist warfare could turn doing one's duty into becoming an accomplice of crime." Jarausch gave the collection of his father's letters the title

35. Gerhard L. Weinberg, "Pius XII in World War II," presentation at the University of Notre Dame, 2006; unpublished manuscript.

36. Pius XII quoted in Owen Chadwick, *Britain and the Vatican during the Second World War* (Cambridge: Cambridge University Press, 1986), 290.

37. Hubert Wolf, *Pope and Devil: The Vatican's Archives and the Third Reich*, trans. from German by Kenneth Kronenberg (Cambridge, MA and London: Belknap Press of Harvard University Press, 2010), 270.

38. Konrad Jarausch, *Reluctant Accomplice: A Wehrmacht Soldier's Letters from the Eastern Front* (Princeton: Princeton University Press, 2011), 324–25.

Reluctant Accomplice. This concept provides a valuable frame within which to analyze the actions of other church people, too.

DEAFENING SILENCE

It is not only criticism of the churches under National Socialism that focuses on the matter of silence. Expressions of guilt and statements of regret likewise point to silence as the essence of Christian failure. In August 1945, Bishop Marahrens expressed his sadness that "in the storm of persecution that fell over German Jewry, the church did not find the right word."[39] Fifty-two years later, Olivier de Berranger, bishop of Saint-Denis, read an apology on behalf of the bishops of France. Standing in front of a cattle car at Drancy, where tens of thousands of Jews had been held before being transported to the east to be killed, he deplored the "docility," the "conformism," and the silence of Christians in that time. "Today we confess that silence was a failure. . . . We beg God's forgiveness and ask the Jewish people to hear our words of repentance."[40]

Why, contrary to the evidence, has the notion of silence taken such hold? There is a lot at stake. Like the categorization of Christians as by definition "bystanders"—not perpetrators—it is more palatable than its alternatives. Better to be charged with sins of omission than crimes of commission; easier to apologize for failure to act than to admit active participation and partnership as facilitators, enablers, even beneficiaries and perpetrators of the persecution and killing of other people.

One thing covered over by the emphasis on silence is active involvement. Bonhoeffer's 1942 words about "silent witnesses of evil deeds" are echoed in the title of Wolfgang Gerlach's pathbreaking study: *And the Witnesses Were Silent: The Confessing Churches and the Persecution of the Jews.* Gerlach wrote his book in 1970, but it was not published in German until 1987.[41] One reason for the delay was Heinz Brunotte, whose role in writing the 1939 *Erlass*[42] had been revealed

---

39. Marahrens's *Wochenbrief* of August 15, 1945 quoted in Joachim Perels, "Die hannoversche Landeskirche im Nationalsozialismus 1935–1945. Kritik eines Selbstbilds," in *Bewahren ohne Bekennen? Die hannoversche Landeskirche im Nationalsozialismus,* ed. Heinrich W. Grosse, Hans Otte, and Joachim Perels (Hanover: Lutherisches Verlagshaus, 1996), 155. My translation; thanks to Guy Carter for this citation.

40. Patrick Henry, "The French Catholic Church's Apology," *The French Review* 72, no. 6 (May 1999): 1099–1105. Quotation (my translation) on p. 1099.

41. Wolfgang Gerlach, *Als die Zeugen Schwiegen. Bekennende Kirche und die Juden,* edited and translated by Victoria Barnett as *And the Witnesses Were Silent: The Confessing Church and the Persecution of the Jews* (Lincoln: University of Nebraska Press, 2000).

42. See above, note 23.

by Gerlach's research. Brunotte was tireless in his effort to prevent publication of Gerlach's book. Though Gerlach's title referred to silence, the content of his book spoke volumes about Christians who, like Brunotte and so many others, had been far from quiet, not as opponents but as proponents of Nazi ideas.

Somewhat paradoxically, another thing covered over by the fixation on silence is opposition, especially by people who did not pay with their lives. A poignant illustration of this point is the life and fate of Elisabeth Schmitz. A schoolteacher who resigned her position and gave up her career in 1938 because she could not serve a regime she considered criminal, Schmitz wrote a lengthy memorandum in 1935 for the Synod of the Confessing Church. In it she spoke out in no uncertain terms against Nazi persecution of Jews and Christian acquiescence to it. Schmitz duplicated her text and circulated several hundred copies, one of which came into Bonhoeffer's hands. The memorandum was not debated at the Synod, however, and for years its authorship was misattributed, most often to Marga Meusel, another woman associated with the Confessing Church.

When Schmitz died in 1977, only a handful of people attended her funeral. It took thirty years and the extraordinary engagement of the historian Manfred Gailus to bring attention to her and her protest.[43] Thanks to Gailus and the American filmmaker Steven D. Martin, she is now the subject of a documentary titled *Elisabeth of Berlin*.[44] That delay and the muted nature of her recognition even now reflect a sad truth about heroes under totalitarian rule. Crudely put: the best hero is a dead hero. Those who died can be held up as proof that speaking out put one in mortal peril: only rare individuals with superhuman courage or the mantle of martyrdom could be expected to embrace such terrible risks. Someone who dared to speak out yet lived—indeed, in the case of Elisabeth Schmitz, managed even to avoid incarceration—is an uncomfortable reminder, even a reproach, that perhaps it was possible to see, understand, and even protest Nazi crimes, including the assault on Jews. Viewed in this light, it is not surprising that Sophie Scholl, the Munich student executed for her role in the White Rose movement, is considered by many young Germans to be among the ten most important Germans of all time, whereas the women of the Rosenstrasse, who protested successfully for release of their German Jewish husbands in February 1943, remain virtually unknown.

43. Manfred Gailus, *Mir aber zerriss es das Herz. Der stille Widerstand der Elisabeth Schmitz* (Göttingen: Vandenhoeck & Ruprecht, 2010); also Gailus, ed., *Elisabeth Schmitz und ihre Denkschrift gegen die Judenverfolgung. Konturen einer vergessenen Biographie (1893–1977)* (Berlin: Wichern, 2008).

44. Steven D. Martin, *Elisabeth of Berlin*, 59 mins. (United States: Vital Visions, 2008).

Also obscured is the perception of those outside Christian circles, in particular the Jewish victims of Christian assault. They did not ask whether their aggressors were "real Christians." They knew only that they were out to destroy them. Witness the anguished cries of an "anonymous adolescent" in Łódź in August 1944:

> Is it not a shame to be a man on the same earth as the Ger-man? .
> . . Oh, God in Heaven, why didst thou create Germans to destroy
> humanity? . . . Why will you not punish, with all your wrath, those
> who are destroying us? Are we the sinners and they the righteous? Is
> that the truth? Surely you are intelligent enough to understand that
> it is not so, that we are not the sinners and they are not the Messiah![45]

Does the field of Bonhoeffer Studies need to pay more attention to history? I am not sure. Years ago when I was conducting research for my dissertation on the German Christian Movement, I used to regroup by reading the Bonhoeffer papers, then held in the Federal Archive in Koblenz. It is indeed tempting to reduce Bonhoeffer to the face of martyrdom just as it is to simplify the history of the Christian churches in the Nazi era to a lesson about the need to choose between two responses, silence and martyrdom. More useful—and more honest—is to try to look beyond those familiar assumptions to examine the complex web of institutions, forces, and events that surrounded Christians in the years after Hitler came to power. Perhaps history, like economics one of the dismal sciences, can be a useful corrective for theologians and others who have the privilege of seeing the Third Reich through the prism of Bonhoeffer's writings. To situate Bonhoeffer in the context of his times does not reduce his significance or weaken the challenge of his witness. But it may serve to remind us what was at stake.

45. Quoted in Friedländer, *The Years of Extermination*, 631.

13

Dietrich Bonhoeffer in History: Does Our Bonhoeffer Still Offend?

Robert P. Ericksen

Those of us who attended worship at Harlem's Abyssinian Baptist Church prior to the opening of the Conference, "Bonhoeffer for the Coming Generations,"[1] heard a powerful sermon in which the Rev. Dr. Marvin McMickle asked the question, "Does our gospel still offend?" He argued, of course, that it should, that the gospel of Christ should not simply make us feel comfortable. I will now steal his theme and ask, "Does our Bonhoeffer still offend?"

It is very tempting to get comfortable with Bonhoeffer. However, the German Protestant church in his day was not at all comfortable with him. Even the Confessing Church, that small rump group within the Protestant church, was not comfortable with Bonhoeffer. When he fled the *Kirchenkampf* (Church Struggle) for London in late 1933, he was asking himself what made him think that he was right and all his friends and colleagues, even in the Confessing Church, were wrong.[2] Bonhoeffer was a very lonely figure in the church, and we are denying history if we pretend that he was not.

The story of Wilhelm Niemöller can give us some insight into this issue. As a younger brother to Martin Niemöller, one of the most famous figures in the Protestant *Kirchenkampf*, he was active in his brother's cause throughout the Nazi era. He then spent his life after 1945 as a very important historian of the *Kirchenkampf*, but with a strong dose of historical denial. He developed an important archive in Bielefeld and he wrote the history of the church in that period. But he very explicitly wrote it as if the Confessing Church had been the only Protestant church. He refused to include the *Deutsche Christen* in his history, because they were simply wrong. He also refused to write about

---

1. Sunday, November 13, 2011.
2. Bonhoeffer, letter to Barth, October 24, 1933: DBWE 13:29.

127

the large middle section of the church, which sided neither with the *Deutsche Christen* or the Confessing Church, because they had said "nothing useful." Rather, he told the story of the Confessing Church as if that was the story of the Protestant church, even though, by his own figures, it represented only 20 percent of Protestants.[3]

It adds to our concern when we learn, only through others, that Wilhelm Niemöller himself had joined the Nazi Party as early as 1923. His brother Martin also voted for and welcomed the rise of Adolf Hitler to power, only changing his mind when he found the Nazi state impacting his sense of his role as a pastor. This is a more complicated story than we read in Wilhelm Niemöller's own version of the history. Not only was the Confessing Church a small minority, but we also eventually learned from Wolfgang Gerlach that Confessing Church leaders and members shared many or most of the anti-Semitic attitudes of the Nazi regime. Otto Dibelius, for example, happily announced in a 1928 Easter message to clergy in his region, "I have always considered myself an anti-Semite."[4]

We need to remind ourselves of these things. The Niemöllers, with their early support for Hitler, and Dibelius, with his self-confessed anti-Semitism, were leading figures in the Confessing Church. This church, its history carefully massaged by Wilhelm Niemöller and others for more than a generation, was often described in those early postwar decades as an opponent of the Nazi state. It is more accurate to say that Bonhoeffer and a few other radicals within the Confessing Church became opponents of the Nazi state. This group was referred to at the time as the "radical Niemöller wing" of the Confessing Church, after Martin Niemöller had learned to rue his early enthusiasm for the regime. The Confessing Church as a whole remained loyal to the Nazi state. Its founding document, the Barmen Declaration, openly stated, "Be not deceived by loose talk, as if we meant to *oppose* the unity of the German nation!"[5] Barmen, carefully crafted, tried to make sure that enthusiastic supporters of what was commonly called the "rebirth" of Germany under Hitler

---

3. See my treatment of these issues in Robert P. Ericksen, "Wilhelm Niemöller and the Historiography of the Kirchenkampf," in *Nationalprotestantische Mentalitäten in Deutschland—1870–1970*, ed. Manfred Gailus and Hartmut Lehmann (Göttingen: Vandenhoeck & Ruprecht, 2005), 433–52.

4. Wolfgang Gerlach, *And the Witnesses Were Silent: The Confessing Church and the Persecution of the Jews*, trans. and ed. Victoria J. Barnett (Lincoln: University of Nebraska Press, 2000), 14.

5. An English translation of the Barmen Declaration can be found in Arthur C. Cochrane, *The Church's Confession under Hitler* (Philadelphia: Westminster, 1962), 237–47. This comment is found in the opening, introductory section. A more recent translation by Douglas S. Bax is found in *Karl Barth: Theologian of Freedom*, ed. Clifford Green (Minneapolis: Fortress Press, 1991), 148–51.

could comfortably sign. The *Kirchenkampf* itself is now widely seen as having been a conflict *within* the church, far more theological than political.[6]

That leaves us with a radical Bonhoeffer, on the fringe and not within the center of his church. I received a strong hint of this in 1972, when I asked my landlady in Hamburg whether I could watch a television program on Bonhoeffer. She and her husband always tried to get me to come down from my attic apartment to watch television with them. In this case, however, she turned red in the face and said, "No. Werner would never allow that program to be on in this house. No doubt they will portray Bonhoeffer as a hero, but to us he was simply a traitor." These were people who went to church every Sunday. Twenty years earlier, Bishop Hans Meiser of Bavaria said the same thing, when he refused to attend a memorial for Bonhoeffer's execution at Flossenbürg. To Meiser, Bonhoeffer was not a hero but a traitor.

These people rejected Bonhoeffer for political reasons. It is also possible, of course, to reject Bonhoeffer for theological reasons, for the radical nature of what Eberhard Bethge called his "new theology" as developed in his letters from Tegel Prison. Both the political Bonhoeffer and the theological Bonhoeffer point back to my question of whether Bonhoeffer still offends.

Let me return for a moment to the theme of a *comfortable* church. It is a theme that resonates through history. The medieval church, for example, grew comfortable with the Inquisition and with burning alleged heretics and Jews at the stake. If we look at American Christians in the South before the Civil War, we know what they heard on Sunday mornings. They heard that God endorsed slavery, in fact, that God had created black people with all the best characteristics to serve as slaves to whites. Only now do we condemn the comfort with which that church fitted into its southern, slave-owning environment. If we look at Christian churches in Nazi Germany, we find pastors, bishops, theologians, and church newspapers praising Adolf Hitler, calling this a new birth for Germany, sending him telegrams on his birthday. Even Martin Niemöller was among those people for a while. As mentioned above, Wilhelm Niemöller had joined the Nazi Party already in 1923. Both brothers had fought in the right-wing *Freikorps*, a dramatic rejection of the Weimar Republic and its ideals of democracy.[7]

---

6. For an assessment of the historical treatment of this issue, see Robert P. Ericksen and Susannah Heschel, "The Churches and the Holocaust," in *The Historiography of the Holocaust*, ed. Dan Stone (London: Palgrave Macmillan, 2004), 296–318.

7. See biographies by James Bentley, *Martin Niemöller 1892–1984* (Oxford: Oxford University Press, 1984), and by Jürgen Schmidt, *Martin Niemöller im Kirchenkampf* (Hamburg: Leibniz, 1971).

One noteworthy thing about Bonhoeffer was that he never liked Hitler. That put him far outside the norm within his church.[8] When we ask what made Bonhoeffer so different, we get several answers. Reggie Williams has very convincingly told us about the influence of Harlem on Bonhoeffer.[9] We can add to that Bonhoeffer's personal experience of "internationalism"—in the United States, in England, and also in Italy, Spain, Sweden, Denmark, and Switzerland. Many nationalistic German theologians warned against international connections and international travel. Emanuel Hirsch and Paul Althaus, while Bonhoeffer was here at Union, warned church leaders against participating in ecumenism. They would be consorting with and aiding Germany's enemies while those enemies were refusing to confess the sins of the Versailles Treaty.[10]

Alongside these two factors—Harlem specifically and international travel in general—I would add one other important feature in Bonhoeffer's background. He and his family did not go to church! It seems that if you went to church in Weimar Germany, you breathed the air of God and country, you learned of God's special hopes and plans for justice for Germany, you heard criticism of the modern world and all its sins, and you became someone like Paul Althaus, who greeted the rise of Hitler as a "gift and miracle from God."[11] Bonhoeffer did not breathe that air. Rather, he grew up in a family that opposed Hitler, one that never succumbed to the charms of the Nazi ideology, and contributed two sons and two sons-in-law to the gallows set up by a bitter regime in its last days. It is also important, of course, that Bonhoeffer's twin sister married Gerhard Leibholz, a Jew by Nazi standards, and Bonhoeffer had other Christian friends of Jewish descent. All of these things placed Bonhoeffer well outside Bishop Hans Meiser's comfort zone.

Now let us look at Bonhoeffer's offensive theology. I will regress by mentioning an experience of mine five years ago. Steven Martin had just made a film based upon my book, *Theologians under Hitler*.[12] He invited about three dozen pastors, rabbis, and theologians from across the theological spectrum to

8. For my recent treatment of both churches and universities in their response to the Nazi state, see Robert P. Ericksen, *Complicity in the Holocaust: Churches and Universities in Nazi Germany* (Cambridge: Cambridge University Press, 2012).

9. See Chapter 16.

10. According to Althaus and Hirsch, "Germany's enemies from the World War under cover of peace are carrying on the war against the German Volk." See Robert P. Ericksen, *Theologians under Hitler: Gerhard Kittel, Paul Althaus and Emanuel Hirsch* (New Haven: Yale University Press, 1985), 143.

11. Paul Althaus, *Die deutsche Stunde der Kirche*, 3rd ed. (Göttingen: Vandenhoeck & Ruprecht, 1934), 5.

12. *Theologians under Hitler*, a film produced and directed by Steven Martin (vitalvisuals.com).

Nashville to discuss the book and the film. All of them condemned church leaders who had supported Hitler and the Nazis. However, several on the evangelical right began to argue that true, Bible-believing Christians like Dietrich Bonhoeffer were the ones who had recognized the evil in Adolf Hitler and stood up against it. I had a problem with that, because of the many Bible-believing Christians who thought that Hitler was a gift from God. Then I had a problem with those in the group who suggested that the Dietrich Bonhoeffers of today are those who stand up against abortion and declare it the Holocaust of our day. I disagree with that parallel. Furthermore, I later learned that one of the snipers who has murdered abortion doctors, James Kopp, specifically compared himself to Bonhoeffer—a radical Christian willing to use violence in a just cause.[13]

I suspect that most of us think that is an inappropriate claim upon Bonhoeffer. He certainly was willing to choose violence in an attempt to end Hitler's rule of Germany. Whether that can be compared to individuals murdering abortion doctors is at least questionable. More broadly we might question whether there really is a Bonhoeffer who gives inspiration but no offense to people across the entire spectrum of Christian belief. Let me cite a few passages from Bonhoeffer's "New Theology." For example, we have this passage in a letter to Eberhard Bethge on April 30, 1944:

> The foundations are being pulled out from under all that "Christianity" has previously been for us, and the only people among whom we might end up in terms of "religion" are "the last of the knights" or a few intellectually dishonest people. . . . Are we supposed to fall all over precisely this dubious lot of people in our zeal or disappointment or woe and try to peddle our wares to them? Or should we jump on a few unfortunates in their hour of weakness and commit, so to speak, religious rape?[14]

Are not these people in their vulnerability and stress exactly the targets of evangelical, witnessing Christians in the U.S. today? Are some or many

---

13. See various stories in the *New York Times*. There is also a popular history by Jon Wells, *Sniper: The True Story of Anti-Abortion Killer James Kopp* (New York: Wiley, 2008), but no scholarly treatment to my knowledge. I am indebted to Dr. Guy Carter for pointing out a passage in Bonhoeffer condemning abortion, and indicating concern about unrestricted birth control; see *Ethics*, DBWE 6:206–7 and also 24–25.

14. *Letters and Papers from Prison*, DBWE 8:363.

evangelicals among the "intellectually dishonest people" mentioned here? That might be the implication of Bonhoeffer's comment to Bethge on May 29, 1944:

> Weizsäcker's book on the *Weltbild der Physik* continues to preoccupy me a great deal. It has again brought home to me quite clearly that we shouldn't think of God as the stopgap for the incompleteness of our knowledge, because then—as is objectively inevitable—when the boundaries of knowledge are pushed ever further, God too is pushed further away and thus is ever on the retreat.[15]

Can this Bonhoeffer with his respect for modern physics be a model for those Christians who believe the Earth is 6,000 years old? To his thoughts on this connection between scientific knowledge and the human relationship to God, Bonhoeffer added in that letter of May 29, 1944:

> We should find God in what we know, not in what we don't know; God wants to be grasped by us not in unsolved questions but in those that have been solved. This is true of the relation between God and scientific knowledge, but it is also true of the universal human questions about death, suffering, and guilt. Today, even for these questions, there are human answers that can completely disregard God. Human beings cope with these questions practically without God and have done so throughout the ages, and it is simply not true that only Christianity would have a solution to them.[16]

In a letter of May 5, 1944, we get a comment that will sound strange to evangelical Christians:

> Hasn't the individualistic question of saving our personal souls almost faded away for most of us? Isn't it our impression that there are really more important things than this question . . . I know it sounds outrageous to say that, but after all, isn't it fundamentally biblical? Does the question of saving one's soul even come up in the Old Testament? Isn't God's righteousness and kingdom on earth the center of everything?[17]

---

15. Ibid., DBWE 8:405–6.
16. DBWE 8:406.
17. DBWE 8:372–73.

These thoughts on new forms for Christian understanding and the Christian message come under the phrase that Bonhoeffer used in these letters, "the world come of age." He recognized that Christians routinely fought against the modern world, but he had decided that this was an entirely false approach. In a letter to Bethge on June 8, 1944, he wrote,

> [I] consider the attack by Christian apologetics on the world's coming of age as, first of all, pointless, second, ignoble, and, third, unchristian. Pointless—because it appears to me like trying to put a person who has become an adult back into puberty, that is, to make people dependent on a lot of things on which they in fact no longer depend, to shove them into problems that in fact are no longer problems for them. Ignoble—because an attempt is being made here to exploit people's weaknesses for alien purposes to which they have not consented freely. Unchristian—because it confuses Christ with a particular stage of human religiousness, namely, with a human law.[18]

What do we do with these radical statements from 1944? I understand that evangelical Christians love Bonhoeffer's spiritual intensity in his early writings, and it is there. I also understand the desire of scholars to find consistency in Bonhoeffer, and I accept that much of his later thought can be reconciled to his earlier ideas. But I question any understanding of Bonhoeffer that ignores his roots in the Christian theology he studied in his early years—his acceptance of reason and modern science must be kept in mind here. I also question any understanding of Bonhoeffer that suggests the "New Theology" in his letters to Bethge can be downplayed or ignored.

Our desire to connect the early and late Bonhoeffer, our search for consistency in his ideas, should not allow us to deny that he changed and grew in important ways during his experience of the Third Reich! The crucible of the Nazi years intensified his grappling with Christian theology. It was a horrendous time. It tore people from their roots. It also exposed huge problems among Christians in Germany. They showed their willingness not only to accept but to be enthusiastic about Hitler's aggressive nationalism. Christians praised Hitler's brutal imposition of law and order, as they too carelessly accepted his feigned support for "positive Christianity" and traditional values. Christians showed relatively little empathy for fellow Christians of Jewish descent, and very little empathy for actual Jews. Too many Christians were far too willing to continue their stigmatization of Jews in Germany, to continue to

18. DBWE 8:427.

describe Jews as a threat to German values, even as Hitler intensified his brutal policies of persecution. Christians found too high a level of comfort in Nazi Germany. Bonhoeffer did not.

I respect Eberhard Bethge's response to these things. He argued that Bonhoeffer really did undergo a change in his attitude toward Jews between 1933 and 1945. In other words, he argued for discontinuity based on Bonhoeffer's experience.[19] Bethge is the one who pushed the Rhineland Synod to adopt a new statement on Christians and Jews—a statement that now is widely accepted and part of our "post-Auschwitz theology," though many in 1980 attacked it as heresy. Bethge is also the one who labeled Bonhoeffer's ideas written from Tegel Prison a "New Theology." I think we must take Bethge and Bonhoeffer seriously.

I would add one other thing, in particular response to Christiane Tietz's wonderful essay on Bonhoeffer's Christology:[20] It is very hard for some Christians to understand a Christology that is not something like this: "We know Christ and go to heaven. You don't know Christ, so you go to hell." Vatican II was Pope John XXIII's attempt to back away from this doctrine that there is only one truth, especially by removing the charge of deicide in Catholic doctrine and showing respect for Judaism as a religion. Since then John Paul II and Benedict XVI seem less convinced by Vatican II and more tempted to reestablish Catholicism as the one true Church.[21] I think many Christians who want to love Dietrich Bonhoeffer accept traditional Christology, not Bonhoeffer's version. We should be careful, as is Professor Tietz in this volume, to show the offense still to be found in Bonhoeffer's version of Christ for us today.

---

19. See, e.g., Bethge, "Dietrich Bonhoeffer and the Jews," in *Ethical Responsibility: Bonhoeffer's Legacy to the Churches*, ed. John D. Godsey and Geffrey B. Kelly (New York and Toronto: Edwin Mellen Press, 1981), esp. 74–75.

20. See Chapter 18.

21. See especially two documents issued by the Sacred Congregation for the Doctrine of the Faith: the 2000 declaration under Pope John Paul II, *Declaratio: De Iesu Christi atque Ecclesiae unicitate et universalitate salvifica. Dominus Iesus* . . . ("Declaration: On the Unicity and Salvific Universality of Jesus Christ and the Church" beginning with the words, "The Lord Jesus") drafted by then Prefect Joseph Cardinal Ratzinger; and the 2007 *Responsa ad quaestiones de aliquibus sententiis ad doctrinam de Ecclesia pertinentibus* ("Responses to Some Questions Regarding Certain Aspects of the Doctrine of the Church") under Pope Benedict XVI, drafted by Prefect William Cardinal Levada, *Acta Apostolicae Sedis—Commentarium Officiale*, ("Official Documents of the Holy See"), vol. XCII, no. 10 (promulgated 6 August 2000), 742–65, and vol. XCIX, no. 7 (promulgated 6 July 2007), 604–8, respectively.

14

Bonhoeffer and Coming to Terms with Protestant Complicity in the Holocaust

Matthew D. Hockenos

Many Bonhoeffer scholars exalt the prodigious influence Dietrich Bonhoeffer had on various post-1945 political and theological discourses in Germany and across the globe. This influence is rightly celebrated, for his theology and praxis have certainly enriched these discourses. It is therefore disappointing, although not entirely surprising, that in the immediate postwar years the more conservative leaders of the Evangelical Church in Germany (EKD) failed to draw on Bonhoeffer's insights on guilt and repentance as they drafted texts addressing Protestant accountability during the Third Reich. The reluctance of these older colleagues from the former Confessing Church to learn from Bonhoeffer's life, and to incorporate his thought, is unfortunate because it is clear that in many cases the confessions, statements, and declarations made by Protestants after the war would have benefited from Bonhoeffer's understanding of responsibility, discipleship, the costliness of grace, the universality of the church, and the place of the church in postwar reconstruction.

It is difficult to say with equal certainty how Bonhoeffer would have influenced the Protestant rethinking of the "Jewish Question" from 1945 to 1950 because he wrote so little on the topic. Yet, his actions in the German resistance and ecumenical efforts to save Jews may speak louder than his written texts. We know that from the very start Bonhoeffer opposed the Nazi regime and the German Christian Movement; that he spoke out forcefully and frequently against the attempt to introduce racial legislation into the church, which would have negatively affected baptized Jews; and that the Nazis executed him for aiding the resistance. What is not clear is his theological understanding of the place of Jews in Christian history. Bonhoeffer's only solo-authored text that directly addresses the "Jewish Question" is his April 1933 essay, "The Church and the Jewish Question," which, in one long paragraph, took an anti-Judaic and supersessionist theological stance. Given his role in the resistance and his opposition to Nazi racial policy, it is quite likely that his theological understanding of the "Jewish Question" would have evolved beyond what he expressed in 1933. How it would have evolved and to what extent is not known.[1]

While Bonhoeffer's position on the "Jewish Question" in 1945 is less clear, he showed remarkable clarity and foresight throughout the Nazi years in his unequivocal rejection of the accommodating position the church took in relation to the Nazi state. This position was not shared by the majority of his colleagues from the Confessing Church who survived the Nazi years. The postwar leaders of the EKD demonstrated more trepidation than courage, more equivocation than clarity, and more obstruction than determination when it came to addressing the church's share of responsibility for the policies of the Third Reich.

The flood of documents, images, news footage, and testimonials in the immediate postwar months depicting the horrors of the Holocaust spurred a small number of German clergymen, theologians, and church leaders to reflect on the churches' relationship to the Nazi state and its racial policies. This reflection led some churchmen to genuine feelings of remorse, confession, repentance, and a desire to implement reforms in the way the church related to the state to ensure that complicity with evil would not take place again. However, for most clergymen and church leaders, their nationalism, their conservative political outlook, their traditional Lutheranism, and their behavior during the Third Reich led them to take a conservative path in the immediate postwar years. The resulting discord between reform-minded churchmen such as Herman Diem, Adolf Freudenberg, Hans Iwand, and Martin Niemöller and conservative churchmen like bishops Theophil Wurm, Hans Mesier, and Otto Dibelius had its origin in the divisions that developed within the Confessing Church during the church struggle from 1933 to 1945.[2]

---

1. On Bonhoeffer and the issue of his anti-Judaism after 1933 see Stephen R. Haynes, *The Bonhoeffer Legacy: Post-Holocaust Perspectives* (Minneapolis: Fortress Press, 2006), and Victoria J. Barnett, "Dietrich Bonhoeffer's Relevance for Post-Holocaust Christian Theology," *Studies in Christian-Jewish Relations* 2, no. 1 (2007): 53–67.

2. See Gerhard Besier, Jörg Thierfelder, and Ralf Tyra, eds., *Kirche nach der Kapitulation*, 2 vols. (Stuttgart: Kohlhammer, 1989–90); Martin Greschat, ed., *Die Schuld der Kirche: Dokumente und Reflexionen zur Stuttgarter Schulderklärung vom 18./19. Oktober 1945* (Munich: Kaiser, 1982); Matthew D. Hockenos, *A Church Divided: German Protestants Confront the Nazi Past* (Bloomington: Indiana University Press, 2004).

However, with few exceptions, neither conservatives nor reformers in the postwar church leadership addressed the church's anti-Jewish biases. Even among the more progressive-minded confessing churchmen, few made a connection between Protestant complacency toward and complicity in Hitler's policy of extermination and the church's teaching about Jews. They vaguely acknowledged that the church could have done more during the Nazi period, but insisted that the church itself had nothing to do with Nazi racial policy or the Holocaust.

According to the postwar EKD leadership council, which consisted of both reformers and conservatives from the former Confessing Church, the church was not guilty of spreading a hateful message regarding Jews but rather it was guilty for not "witnessing more courageously, for not praying more faithfully, for not believing more joyously, and for not loving more ardently," as they stated in October 1945 in their Stuttgart Declaration of Guilt.[3] At Martin Niemöller's insistence, the following sentence was added to the declaration: "With great pain do we say: through us has endless suffering (*unendliches Leid*) been brought to many peoples and countries." It was the only sentence in the declaration to acknowledge concretely the misery Germans caused throughout Europe. In fact, before mentioning German guilt, the declaration spoke of German suffering. Adolf Freudenberg, a pastor in the Confessing Church, the husband of a Jewish woman, and director of the Committee for Refugees of the World Council of Churches (WCC) in Geneva, wrote in a letter to Hans Asmussen, the president of the EKD Church Office and a principal author of the Stuttgart Declaration, that it was a "crying shame" that the little word "Jews" was missing from the statement.[4]

There were statements by the Ecclesiastical-Theological Society of Württemberg under the direction of Hermann Diem and the Westphalian Provincial Synod that reproached the church for sitting idly by while Jews were murdered.[5] But the Stuttgart Declaration of Guilt was as far as the conservative churchmen in the EKD leadership were willing to go. Their reluctance to

---

3. The Stuttgart Declaration of Guilt is reprinted in Hockenos, op. cit., 187, and discussed in chapter 4. For more on the Stuttgart Declaration see John S. Conway, "How Shall Nations Repent? The Stuttgart Declaration of Guilt, October 1945," *Journal of Ecclesiastical History* 38, no. 4 (October 1987): 596–622; and Gerhard Besier and Gerhard Sauter, eds., *Wie Christen ihre Schuld bekennen: Die Stuttgarter Erklärung 1945* (Göttingen: Vandenhoeck & Ruprecht, 1985).

4. Hartmut Schmidt, "First EKD Confession of Guilt over Crimes Against Jews," *EKD Bulletin* (February 2000) in http://www.ekd.de/english/1693.html accessed February 22, 2012.

5. Wolfgang Gerlach, *And the Witnesses Were Silent: The Confessing Church and the Persecution of the Jews*, trans. and ed. Victoria J. Barnett (Lincoln: University of Nebraska Press, 2000), 227–28.

state concretely the sins of the German church and nation was in part due to their desire to placate an unrepentant populace. Angry letters from parishioners poured in, complaining that the church confessed *too much* at Stuttgart and that the real guilty party was the Allies, who had destroyed their cities and their homes. In postwar statements, conservatives emphasized the forgiving God, his grace, and mercy. They assured their pastorate and parishioners that suffering was the first stage of a two-stage process. The second stage would be marked by God's mercy and a period of renewal.

Bishop Wurm—a staunch opponent of Hitler's persecution of the Confessing Church and the church's elder statesman in the immediate postwar years—was representative of many conservative Protestant church leaders. For Bishop Wurm, the urgent task at hand was providing for and defending everyday Germans, who he believed were victims of victors' revenge. When he did mention Jewish wartime suffering it was often to liken it to German postwar suffering. He let the wider world know where his sympathies lay in an open letter to Christians in England, which was broadcast by BBC radio in January 1946. To the consternation of many, he stated: "To pack the German people into a still more narrow space, to cut off as far as possible the material basis of their very existence, is no different, in essentials, from Hitler's plan to stamp out the existence of the Jewish race."[6] For Wurm, the attempt to systematically exterminate the Jews of Europe was exclusively the work of Hitler and the Nazi regime, not the German people and certainly not the Protestant church. Thus, in his view, there was no need to rethink Protestant attitudes toward Jews or the church's relationship to politics.

Dietrich Bonhoeffer's overt opposition to the Nazi regime and his theological statements addressing guilt, the centrality of confession, and the costliness of grace, all suggest that he would have been squarely aligned with, and probably a leading voice among, the reformers in the postwar church. What many conservative Lutherans seemed to be seeking after the war for themselves and the German people was what Bonhoeffer called "cheap grace" in *Discipleship*. "Cheap grace," he wrote, "is that grace that we bestow on ourselves. . . . Like ravens we have gathered around the carcass of cheap grace."[7] In Bonhoeffer's understanding of Luther's doctrine of justification, forgiveness was neither cheap nor unconditional. Grace required true discipleship, and true discipleship was hard work; it was costly. In *Discipleship* Bonhoeffer offered a

---

6. Bishop Wurm's letter is reprinted in Stewart W. Herman, *The Rebirth of the German Church* (New York: Harper & Brothers, 1946), 275–79, here, 278. Also see chapter 5, "The Guilt of the Others: Bishop Wurm's Letter to English Christians," in Hockenos, op. cit.

7. *Discipleship*, DBWE 4:44, 53.

poignant critique of those conservative church leaders and pastors who assured fellow Christians of God's forgiveness but failed to emphasize confession, repentance, and reform. Bonhoeffer maintained that

> [f]orgiveness can only be preached within the church-community of saints, where repentance also is being preached; where the gospel is not separated from the proclamation of the law; and where sins are not only and unconditionally forgiven, but where they are also retained. For it is the will of our Lord himself not to give what is holy, the gospel, to dogs, but to preach it only under the safeguard of the call for repentance. A church-community that does not call sin sin will likewise be unable to find faith when it wants to grant forgiveness of sin. . . . It is not enough to lament the general sinfulness of human beings. . . . Rather specific sins have to be named, punished, and sentenced.[8]

Bonhoeffer's insistence on the confession and repentance of concrete sins was articulated most eloquently in his essay "Guilt, Justification, Renewal," where he provided concrete examples of how the church was guilty of violating the Ten Commandments. He goes much further than the Stuttgart Declaration of Guilt when he writes:

> The church confesses its timidity, its deviations, its dangerous concessions. . . . It has often withheld the compassion that it owes to the despised and the rejected. The church was mute when it should have cried out, because the blood of the innocent cried out to heaven. It did not resist to the death the falling away from faith and is guilty of the godlessness of the masses.[9]

Bonhoeffer's confession of guilt, written long before the true horrors of the Holocaust were apparent, was unflinching in its condemnation of the church's witness under Nazism.

In August 1947 in Darmstadt, the Council of Brethren in the EKD (*Bruderrat*), which was different from the EKD Council because it consisted of the reform-minded churchmen, initiated a new stage in the Protestant church's coming to terms with the past. They issued their statement "Concerning the Political Course of Our People." This statement, whose principal author was

---

8. Ibid., 269–70.

9. *Ethics*, DBWE 6:138.

Hans Iwand, forcefully addressed the ways in which the Protestant church and the German nation had strayed in their political aims and actions from the gospel's message of "reconciliation of the world with God in Christ."[10] They condemned the church's defense of a strong centralized government at home, the use of military force abroad, and the reliance on all that was "old and conventional." They acknowledged that they were blind "to the cause of the poor and unprivileged as a Christian cause." Many of the themes addressed in this political confession clearly overlapped with Bonhoeffer's political liberalism and view of the church as a force for peace and reconciliation. Conservative Lutherans as well as some churchmen in the Soviet Zone of Occupation vehemently condemned the statement for what they saw as its radical and pro-Marxist political message. Despite the reformers' rebuke of conservatism and Protestant timidity in the face of Nazism, they neglected to mention the church's failure to see the cause of the Jews as a Christian cause.

When and how would the German church account for its silence on the persecution and mass murder of Europe's Jews? Responding to the growing pressure from within Germany and wider ecumenical circles for an answer to this searing question, the Council of Brethren, meeting again in Darmstadt, finally broke its silence in April 1948 with their statement, "A Message Concerning the Jewish Question." Over the objections of Bishop Wurm and other conservatives, the *Bruderrat* stated upfront that "Christians helped to bring about all the injustices and suffering inflicted upon the Jews," and that Christians had a duty to reexamine their beliefs regarding Jews and Judaism.[11] They concluded that the church's adoption of the racial anti-Semitism prevalent in secular society under the Nazis was to blame for its lack of opposition to the Nazis' Jewish policy—*not the church's own anti-Judaic traditions.* Although the Brethren Council's message strongly condemned racial anti-Semitism, it nevertheless perpetuated the church's anti-Judaic teaching by continuing to adhere to a traditional supersessionist belief that Jews were cursed for rejecting Christ and were replaced by Christians as God's chosen people. The statement described Jews as "erring brothers," and described the fate of the Jews as "a silent sermon" and "God's constant warning" to Christians that those who mock the Lord will suffer his wrath. Good Christians will remind Jews "that the promises

10. The *Bruderrat*'s statement "Concerning the Political Course of Our People" is reprinted in Hockenos, 193f., and analyzed in chapter 6. Also see Dorthee Buchhaas-Birkholz, ed., *"Zum politischen Weg unseres Volkes": Politische Leitbilder und Vorstellungen im deutschen Protestantismus 1945–1952, Eine Dokumentation* (Düsseldorf: Droste, 1989).

11. The *Bruderrat*'s "Message Concerning the Jewish Question" is reprinted in Hockenos, 195–97, and discussed in chapter 7.

of the Old Testament are fulfilled in Jesus Christ." The *Bruderrat*'s blending of anti-Judaic theology with strong criticism of racial anti-Semitism indicates that even these reform-oriented churchmen understood Christian complicity in the Holocaust as unrelated to Christian doctrine on Jews. The Council of Brethren was not alone; even the Protestant Federation of France and the World Council of Churches, although well intentioned and less insensitive in their anti-Judaism, took similar approaches in their statements on the "Jewish Question" in 1948.[12]

The *Bruderrat*'s "Message Concerning the Jewish Question" has much in common with the paragraph in Bonhoeffer's 1933 "The Church and the Jewish Question," which articulates the Christian approach to the Jews. Both texts strongly defend the place of Christians of Jewish descent in the church and thereby reject racial criteria for membership in the church. But both also repeat the centuries-old claims that unbaptized Jews suffer because they are cursed by God and that the suffering will end when they submit to baptism. "The Church of Christ," Bonhoeffer wrote in 1933, "has never lost sight of the thought that the 'chosen people,' which hung the redeemer of the world on the cross, must endure the curse for its action in long-drawn-out suffering."[13] He expressed his hope that one day Jews will convert when he writes: "But the history of suffering of this people that God loved and punished will end in the final homecoming of the people Israel to its God. And this homecoming will take place in Israel's conversion to Christ."[14] It is important to remember the context within which these statements were made. This one infamous paragraph appeared in an essay the purpose of which was not to disparage Jews but rather to remind the church that it "has an unconditional obligation to the victims of any ordering of society, even if they do not belong to the Christian community,"—a clear reference to Jews who had not converted. He also urged the church to actively resist the Nazi state's attempt to exclude baptized Jews from the church and its attempt to ban the church's mission to the Jews. Bonhoeffer considered these actions by the state to be "an attack on the nature of the church and its proclamation."[15]

As far as we know, Bonhoeffer never formally repudiated the anti-Judaic rhetoric in his April 1933 essay. During the next ten years until his arrest in April 1943 he remained an ardent foe of the Nazis, a constant critic of the

---

12. World Council of Churches, *The Relationship of the Church to the Jewish People: Collection of Statements* (Geneva: WCC, 1964), 1–11 and 12–18.

13. DBWE 12:367.

14. Ibid., 367.

15. Ibid., 366.

church's willingness to compromise with the state, and an advocate of the ecumenical movement. Through the help of his sister Christine's husband, Hans von Dohnanyi, Bonhoeffer became acquainted with Admiral Wilhelm Canaris and his deputy General Hans Oster, leaders of the resistance in the Army High Command. Bonhoeffer became a military intelligence secret agent under their command and used this position to travel to Switzerland, Norway, Sweden, and Italy, where he kept his ecumenical and political contacts informed about the resistance to Hitler from within Germany. With his Swiss contacts, Bonhoeffer was able to help make travel of the "Operation 7" group to Switzerland possible, and to include Charlotte Friedenthal in their number.[16]

It was around this time that he also completed his text, "Guilt, Justification, Renewal," for his *Ethics* manuscript, in which he describes one by one how the church was guilty of breaking all of the Ten Commandments. He is quite explicit when he gets to the Fifth Commandment about the church's guilt for the murder of Jews. "The church," he states, "confesses that it has witnessed the arbitrary use of brutal force, the suffering in body and soul of countless innocent people, that it has witnessed oppression, hatred, and murder without raising its voice for the victims and without finding ways of rushing to help them. It has become guilty of the lives of the weakest and most defenseless brothers and sisters of Jesus Christ."[17] In short, the church was guilty of not just neglecting to "[bind] up the wounds of the victims" but more importantly for failing "to seize the wheel," of the Nazi machine that was crushing the victims in the first place.[18] While the offensive passage in his 1933 essay cannot be excused and we cannot be certain that his own thinking on the "Jewish Question" would have been dramatically different from that articulated by the *Bruderrat* in 1948, Bonhoeffer's witness on behalf of Jews far exceeded that of nearly all of his colleagues in the Niemöller wing of the Confessing Church, and this would likely have influenced his theology.

The intransigence of the *Bruderrat* on the "Jewish Question" is particularly discouraging because they were certainly aware of a very different and singular approach to the "Jewish Question" that emerged from an ecumenical and interreligious conference in Seelisberg, Switzerland in 1947, officially called "The International Emergency Conference on Anti-Semitism." In Seelisberg a group of European and American Catholics and Protestants, in consultation

---

16. Eberhard Bethge, *Dietrich Bonhoeffer* (Minneapolis: Fortress Press, 2000), 817. "Operation 7" involved transporting fourteen Jews to Switzerland under cover of their working for the Abwehr. Charlotte Friedenthal was a Jewish Christian who worked for the Confessing Church.

17. DBWE 6:139.

18. DBWE 12:365.

with Jewish participants, issued an "Address to the Churches" that repudiated the churches' anti-Semitism, anti-Judaism, and Christian triumphalism.[19] They acknowledged that Christian teaching on Jews, not the gospel itself, but rather "misleading presentations of the Gospel . . . contributed to the rise of anti-Semitism."[20] In ten points, the authors of the statement recommended ways to amend some common teaching practices in the churches that have led to animosity toward Jews. "Avoid presenting the Passion in such a way as to bring the odium of the killing of Jesus upon Jews alone." "Avoid promoting the superstitious notion that the Jewish people is reprobate, accursed, reserved for a destiny of suffering"—these are just two examples. They also made practical suggestions as well, such as introducing into the churches' teaching a "more sympathetic and more profound study of biblical and post-biblical history of the Jewish people, as well as of the Jewish problem." [21]

More than twenty prominent Jewish leaders and scholars were among the sixty-five participants at the conference in Seelisberg, including French historian Jules Isaac, whose text, *Jesus and Israel*, greatly influenced the participants. Regrettably none of the major leaders of the postwar church were in attendance—not even Martin Niemöller. As the vice-president of the EKD council and the head of its department for relations with foreign churches, Niemöller spent the postwar years crisscrossing Germany lecturing on the topic of German guilt, and he had returned to Germany in the spring of 1947 after a three-month speaking tour in the United States. But neither Niemöller nor his colleagues from the former Confessing Church issued a statement acknowledging with such forthrightness the role that the churches played in fostering contempt for Jews as that expressed by the Christians at Seelisberg.

Although supersessionist theology and missionary thinking permeated the EKD in the immediate postwar years, later events including the founding of the State of Israel, recurrent acts of anti-Semitism, and the dogged fact that the Holocaust was not going away galvanized some pastors and theologians into questioning traditional church doctrine on supersessionism and the relationship between Jews and Christians. Only after the profound political and theological shock of these events had had time to sink in were some reformist pastors and theologians prepared to abandon their former stance.

19. The Seelisberg "Address" is reprinted on the Jewish-Christian Relations website, http://www .jcrelations.net. Also see Christian Rutishauser, "The 1947 Seelisberg Conference: The Foundation of the Jewish-Christian Dialogue," *Studies in Christian-Jewish Relations* 2, no. 2 (2007): 34–53 and Victoria J. Barnett, "Seelisberg: An Appreciation," *Studies in Christian-Jewish Relations* 2, no. 2 (2007): 54–57.

20. Rutishauser, "The 1947 Seelisberg Conference," 41.

21. Ibid., 44.

Urged by clerics and laity dissatisfied with the Brethren Council's long-winded and anti-Judaic theological statement, the Protestant church issued its first *official* statement on the Jewish question at its 1950 synod in Berlin-Weissensee. In stark contrast to the *Bruderrat*'s 1948 statement, in eight brief sentences the Berlin-Weissensee statement explicitly rejected supersessionism when it renounced the traditional claim that Christians had replaced or superseded Jews as God's chosen people.[22] It also called on Christians to combat anti-Semitism, and even urged Christian congregations to protect Jewish cemeteries in the wake of a rash of cemetery desecrations. Critics of the statement rightly object to the EKD's tactless rhetoric about the eventual "triumph of Jesus Christ" as well as the claim that the church's guilt lay in its "silence" during the Holocaust. A more forthright statement would have acknowledged the active role that the church played through its teaching of contempt for Jews and Judaism.

In its rejection of supersessionism, however, this statement went beyond Bonhoeffer's position in 1933. One can only speculate that, given his demonstrated willingness to challenge and rethink many aspects of traditional Lutheranism during his life and his opposition to Nazi racial policy toward Jews, he would have been a part of this monumental shift in thinking about the Jews at Berlin-Weissensee in 1950. Perhaps he would even have been present at the Seelisberg Conference on anti-Semitism three years earlier.

---

22. The Berlin-Weissensee statement is reprinted in Hockenos, 199, and analyzed in chapter 8.

PART II

Emerging Issues of Interpretation

15

D. New Research in Text and Context

Reading Discipleship and Ethics Together: Implications for Ethics and Public Life

Florian Schmitz

From the beginning, people who have researched the life and work of Dietrich Bonhoeffer have taken a particular interest in his theological development as well as in the question about the unity of his work. Different as the answers may be that have been given to these questions, there is still general agreement on one matter: many researchers have compared *Discipleship* and *Ethics* and concluded that, with his decision in support of the conspiracy, Bonhoeffer retreated from *essential* theological concepts in his *Discipleship* period in three main respects: first, by developing a broader vision of the reconciliation between Christ and the world; second, by rejecting *Discipleship*'s "realm-thinking" or "spatial-thinking"; third, by explicating the relationship of the disciples to the world according to Bonhoeffer's *Discipleship* as distinct from his view of the world in *Ethics*.[1]

I will discuss the place of *Discipleship* in the Bonhoeffer corpus as a whole, and thus provide an impetus for discussing possible answers to the question of its coherence. My thesis is that Bonhoeffer's work is much less inconsistent, including on the level of logical content, than has been assumed up to now.

---

1. See especially Hanfried Müller, *Von der Kirche zur Welt. Ein Beitrag zur Beziehung des Wortes Gottes auf die Societas in Dietrich Bonhoeffers theologischer Entwicklung*, 2nd ed. (Leipzig: Koehler & Amelang, 1966); Rainer Mayer, *Christuswirklichkeit. Grundlagen, Entwicklung und Konsequenzen der Theologie Dietrich Bonhoeffers,* 2nd ed., Arbeiten zur Theologie, Series II, vol. 15 (Stuttgart: Calwer, 1980); Ernst Feil, *Die Theologie Dietrich Bonhoeffers. Hermeneutik—Christologie—Weltverständnis*, 2nd ed. Studien zur systematischen Theologie und Ethik, vol. 45 (Berlin: LIT, 2005). English translation: *The Theology of Dietrich Bonhoeffer*, trans. Martin Rumscheidt (Philadelphia: Fortress Press, 1985).

This especially applies to Bonhoeffer's book *Discipleship*. I have come to this conclusion in the course of my doctoral thesis on *Discipleship* in the theology of Dietrich Bonhoeffer,[2] which contains extensive evidence and arguments on the subject.[3] My approach is to read *Discipleship* and the fragments of *Ethics* comparatively, or, as my title proposes, to read *Discipleship* and *Ethics* together. In doing so, I will be guided by the three previously mentioned points, in which the theology of *Discipleship* seems to differ crucially from the theology of *Ethics*.

THE EXPANDED VISION OF THE CHRIST-REALITY

The central dogmatic assumption in *Ethics*, upon which Bonhoeffer justifies everything else, lies with the claim that God reconciled himself with the *whole* world in Jesus Christ. No one is excluded from this reconciliation through Christ. The entire reality of the world is enclosed by the reality of Jesus Christ, and this does not depend on whether the world "recognizes it or not."[4]

With regard to the concept of *reality* in *Discipleship*, one notices that the terminology of *Ethics* is not yet present, since Bonhoeffer does not mention "Christ-reality"; neither does he mention "reality of God" nor "reality of the world" in *Discipleship*. However, that does not imply that the underlying understanding of the concept of *reality* differs from that in *Ethics*. Instead, just as in *Ethics*, the reconciliation of God in Christ is presented in *Discipleship* as a universal and ontologically relevant act which is fulfilled in the entire world: "It is true that all human beings as such are 'with' Christ as a consequence of the incarnation."[5] What happened to Jesus Christ "happened to all of us."[6] "Wherever his human body is, there all flesh is being accepted."[7] Just as the reality of sin encloses all of mankind, the reality of the reconciliation encloses the entire world.

What Bonhoeffer describes in *Ethics* as the concept of "*Christ-reality*" is described by him in substance in *Discipleship* by asserting that the immediacy of all human relationships is abolished through Christ, the mediator. Christ stands "between son and father, between husband and wife, between individual and

2. Ph.D. dissertation, University of Kassel, 2010.

3. Florian Schmitz, *Nachfolge. Zur Theologie Dietrich Bonhoeffers*, Forschungen zur Systematischen und Ökumenischen Theologie, vol. 138 (Göttingen: Vandenhoeck & Ruprecht, 2013).

4. *Ethics*, DBWE 6:65.

5. *Discipleship*, DBWE 4:217.

6. Ibid., 4:255.

7. Ibid., 4:214.

nation, whether they can recognize him or not."[8] "Ever since Jesus, there are no longer . . . unmediated relationships. . . . Immediacy is delusion."[9] Outside the reality of Christ, the mediator, there is no true reality.

This leads to the second point, which concerns so-called "spatial-thinking" or "realm-thinking."

Two-Realm-Thinking: Bonhoeffer's Radical Critique

The theory that the *whole* world is borne by Christ is expressed by Bonhoeffer in *Ethics* through the metaphor of space. "Hence there are not two realms, but only the one realm of the Christ-reality" (DBWE 6:58). Therefore, it is not the case that the world is divided into two realms, "one divine, holy, supernatural, and Christian; the other worldly, profane, natural, and unchristian" (DBWE 6:56). From a theological point of view, it is thus *only* possible to speak of one world that is divided into two realms at the *expense* of the Christ-reality. For the world, that means in effect that since Christ there has been "no real worldliness outside the reality of Jesus Christ" (DBWE 6:61), whether it believes it or not. For Christians, that means in effect that since Christ there has been "no real Christian existence outside the reality of the world" (ibid.).

While Bonhoeffer severely criticizes "spatial thinking" in *Ethics*, he seems to represent such thinking in *Discipleship*. "The 'ekklesia' of Christ," he writes at the beginning of the chapter "The Saints," "still lives in the midst of the world. But it already has been made into one body. It is a territory with an authority of its own, a space set apart."[10] How do we deal with this finding? It is out of the question that Bonhoeffer supposed two distinct spaces of reality when he spoke about church as "realm" in *Discipleship* because he expected only one reality in *Discipleship*: the reality of Christ, the mediator. What is his space-metaphor in *Discipleship* aiming at, though? When Bonhoeffer writes about church as a distinct realm in *Discipleship*, two different aspects are considered—and there is no difference from *Ethics*.

First, believers not only belong to Christ, to his body, in the power of his incarnation (meaning in a universal-ontic sense), but they are justified by God. What God did in Christ for the whole world, God did for them. As the justified, they belong to the body of Christ, the "realm of holiness in the midst of the world" (DBWE 4:253), not just as an empirical space (cf. DBWE 6:63f.), but

8. Ibid., 4:95.
9. Ibid., 4:95.
10. DBWE 4:253; the original German reads "ein Raum für sich," DBW 4:269.

rather in the sense of the reconciliation-reality of Christ, which already encloses the whole world.

2. Furthermore, Bonhoeffer expresses the *visibility* of the church through the "space" or "realm" metaphor.[11] Insofar as the church is *visible* in the world *as the body of Christ*, he identifies it as a "realm" in *Discipleship*. The church-community is *visible* in the world: through its proclamation (that is, "the church-community that gathers around word and sacrament"), through its order (that is, through its ministries), and through the daily life of its members (that is, through its concrete actions in and for the world[12]). *That* is how church becomes visible. If it were not visible as church, it would sink to the level of the world, it would be equal to the world. Then, however, it would not be what it is according to Bonhoeffer: the living Christ himself.

This interpretation does not contradict *Ethics* but is rather confirmed there: By discarding the "realm-thinking" in *Ethics*, Bonhoeffer acknowledges it at the same time: "It is clear from this that where the church is to be described as a visible church-community of God on earth, spatial images cannot be avoided" (DBWE 6:62). So, in a way that confirms the former usage, Bonhoeffer adds at this point, in a rare footnote: "See *Discipleship*."[13] This leads to the third aspect.

THE RELATION OF CHRISTIANS TO THE WORLD

If one wants to describe the relation of Christians to the world in *Ethics*, one particular concept is most suitable: the concept of *responsibility*. As Christ is the Lord of the whole world, the moral responsibility of Christians is not restricted to their own isolated realm, but rather applies to all people. The Christian is responsible for the world. It is the essential character of the Christian church that "it is there for others," as the famous statement in *Letters and Papers from Prison* claims (DBWE 8:503). The first and most essential act for Christians of this "being there for others" entails proclaiming the all-embracing reconciliation of God in action and word. "This means not being separated from the world, but calling the world into the community of the Body of Christ to which the world in truth already belongs" (DBWE 6:67).

In *contrast* to that, the relationship to the world in *Discipleship* is perceived in the literature as being more negative: The actions of the believers have

---

11. It is no coincidence that Bonhoeffer titles two chapters of the book "The Visible Church-Community"!

12. Cf. DBWE 4:225–52.

13. Cf. *Ethics*, DBWE 6:62, n. 1.

hardly any positive aspects, but are defined through their separation from the world. Wherever Bonhoeffer takes positive aspects into consideration, they are restricted to the actions within the church-communities. The world is "ripe to be demolished" (DBWE 4:239). With regard to these and to other similar statements by Bonhoeffer, one reckons that in *Discipleship* the view of the world is widely negative and not targeted at reconciliation.

No doubt, Bonhoeffer's view of the world is more negative in *Discipleship* than it is in *Ethics*. Nevertheless, I claim that *Discipleship* contains a moral imperative that is open to the world and that the obedience of the disciples is not restricted to the church-community. To illustrate this claim at least to some extent, I will cite a central passage from *Discipleship*:

> Inasmuch as we participate in Christ, the incarnate one, we also have a part in all of humanity, which is borne with him. Since we know ourselves to be accepted and borne within the humanity of Jesus, our new humanity now also consists in bearing the troubles and the sins of *all* others. The incarnate one transforms his disciples into brothers of *all* human beings. The "philanthropy" (Titus 3:4) of God that became evident in the incarnation of Christ justifies the love of Christians for *every* human being on earth as a brother or sister.[14]

Conclusion: Some Hermeneutical Implications for Ethics and Public Life Today

Discipleship and *Ethics* do not differ from each other as far as the essential Christological assumptions are concerned. The idea that God reconciled himself with the whole world in Christ leads to a rejection of two realms of reality in both books, *Discipleship* and *Ethics*. For *Discipleship* it is valid that the church will keep pure through unconditional devotion to the world that is loved by God on the one hand, and through segregation from the sinful and anti-Christian world on the other hand. Christians need to be there for the world—*and* Christians need to differ from the world. In *Ethics*, this dialectic is not repealed, but Bonhoeffer now stresses more clearly than in *Discipleship* that "even the lost and condemned world is being drawn ceaselessly into the event of Christ" (DBWE 6:66).

With regard to these determinations of Christology and the understanding of the world that have already been unfolded in *Discipleship*, Bonhoeffer does

---

14. DBWE 4:285; italics mine.

not develop any new *basic* ideas in *Ethics*. Contrary to the time of *Discipleship* though, he presents them *now* against the background of being certain that even the highest virtues may not reveal "the huge masquerade of evil" (DBWE 8:38) of "the tyrannical despiser of humanity" (DBWE 6:85). With his decision pro conspiracy, Bonhoeffer finds himself in a situation in which the possibility of not becoming guilty and of remaining pure is no longer available.

It is the concept of *faith* that changes with this experience. Whoever burdens himself or herself with guilt through a free and responsible deed, without regarding one's own life, and thus shares in God's suffering in the world, will have a faith that consists only of surrendering entirely to God while hoping for his mercy. It is in this sense that the important alienation from *Discipleship*, even though expressed in a cautious way, should be understood. Bonhoeffer writes on July 21, 1944, in a letter to Eberhard Bethge: "I thought I myself could learn to have faith by trying to live something like a saintly life. I suppose I wrote *Discipleship* at the end of this path. Today I clearly see the dangers of the book, though I still stand by it" (DBWE 8:486). What could Bonhoeffer have meant with these "dangers"? In my opinion, it is nothing but *the resolve to remain pure from guilt, no matter what evil is loose in the world and demands a decision on behalf of the oppressed.*

As a result of this, it can be said that Bonhoeffer develops contextual theology by getting involved in new situations, and by questioning, updating, and continually developing sovereign theological convictions that pervade his entire work.

Consequently, one needs to differentiate within the theology of Bonhoeffer between *basic assumptions* on the one hand and *updates of these basic assumptions* on the other hand. It can be said that *Discipleship* and *Ethics* are updates of these unchangeable basic assumptions depending on their specific manner and their having emerged out of very different historical situations. The same applies, by the way, to Bonhoeffer's considerations concerning a "religionless Christianity" and a "non-religious interpretation of the Bible."[15]   To my mind, many studies of the reception of Bonhoeffer's theology have been primarily concerned with these updates and have thus highlighted more strongly the moment of discontinuity while reading *Discipleship* and *Ethics*: *Discipleship* as the position of the evil world and the pure church-community, *Ethics* as the position of the reconciled world and the church-community, which acts responsibly and which does not want to remain pure, but rather takes on guilt.

---

15. See DBWE 8:361–482.

An adequate hermeneutics, however, must pay attention to what is beneath these updates and consider the theological foundations of Bonhoeffer's work, which have always been the same. To avoid misunderstanding: it was Bonhoeffer's tremendous ability to update his theology which contributed to his worldwide fame. Nevertheless, as this is about updates that were the result of a specific and unrepeatable historical situation, we cannot just repeat these updates by simply restating the same contents. How could Bonhoeffer's responses possibly be our responses, if his questions are not our questions? However, it is worth dealing with Bonhoeffer's basic assumptions—and this I have tried to show—and then to reach the force of these theological basic assumptions and to make use of them for one's own present time and life. It will then be possible to grasp not the updated answer, but *the way of thinking that leads Bonhoeffer to his answers*.

With regard to Bonhoeffer, one may now ask: How do we enter a dialogue with other people, maybe with people of a different faith or of another religion, maybe with Muslims, presuming that the whole world is reconciled with God? How do we address the world today as a reconciled one? Or: Do we Christians live as if there were two realms of reality in the world, living perhaps as if the church-community does not have to differ from the world—as if it is not its own realm? In which situation would it be useful to recognize church as a space for itself and in which situations would it be necessary to remind the church that it is not an isolated institution of piety? Finally, instead of evoking and repeating Bonhoeffer's statement again and again that "[t]he church is church only when it is there for others" (DBWE 8:503), one could rather ask: What happens if the church is *only* there for others, and not also for itself? Both, a form of Protestantism that is only there for itself, as well as one that is only there for others could mean the *self-secularization of Protestantism*, as Wolfgang Huber argues.[16] Being there for others certainly does not mean forgetting that the church needs to be there for its Lord as well, for Jesus Christ.

---

16. See Wolfgang Huber, *Kirche in der Zeitenwende. Gesellschaftlicher Wandel und Erneuerung der Kirche* (Gütersloh: Gütersloher Verlagshaus, 1998), 31.

16

Dietrich Bonhoeffer, the Harlem Renaissance, and the Black Christ

Reggie L. Williams

Dietrich Bonhoeffer was raised in an educated, wealthy German family. His father was a psychiatrist at the University in Berlin, where the brilliant young Dietrich would later become a popular lecturer. But as soon as he had delivered his inaugural lecture at the university, he spent some time in New York, as a Sloane Fellow at Union Theological Seminary. The Sloane Fellowship annually invited three international students to come and study at Union, and during the 1930–31 academic year, Dietrich Bonhoeffer was granted one.

Spring 1931 was the second semester of Bonhoeffer's Sloane Fellowship year. That spring he took a course with Reinhold Niebuhr titled "Ethical Viewpoints in Modern Literature."[1] In his end-of-the-year summary to the Church Federation Office in Germany, he described that course in the following way: "In a lecture course by Dr. Niebuhr, the social and Christian problem was discussed in the context of modern American literature. That was extremely informative. I learned much from my own experiences in Harlem."[2]

That class was one in a collection of courses he took that spring, in a course schedule that reflected an interest in a different engagement with theology than he had in the fall. His altered course schedule was not the only change between the semesters. In the fall, he didn't have much positive to say about his academic experience at all. For example, in December of his fall semester, he wrote these words to his church superintendent about his experience in America thus far:

> [T]here is no theology here. Although I am basically taking classes
> and lectures in dogmatics and philosophy of religion, the impression
> is overwhelmingly negative. They talk a blue streak without the

1. Bonhoeffer, *Barcelona, Berlin, New York: 1928–1931*, DBWE 10:318.
2. Ibid.

slightest substantive foundation and with no evidence of any criteria. The students—on the average twenty-five to thirty years old—are completely clueless. . . .[3]

But his description of his second-semester courses was very different. The difference indicated a noticeable interest in the social performance of theology, in Christian ethics. It is a difference that, I am arguing, was in part influenced by the experiences he was having in Harlem. In my view, his description of Niebuhr's class, along with the other very positive language he used to describe classes in that second semester with Ward and Webber, indicate a turning for Bonhoeffer that may tell us something of the personal significance of that time in New York for him, and his Christian development. What was this learning that he was referring to in Harlem? We may begin to discern an answer to that question by paying attention to what was going on in Harlem at the time of his Sloane Fellowship year.

Bonhoeffer was studying at Union Seminary during the Harlem Renaissance. That meant that all of his descriptions of his involvement in African American life in 1930–31 were occurring at this critical moment in African American history. He turned twenty-four years old in February of that school year; thus, in addition to that time being very influential in the course of African American history, the young Bonhoeffer was also experiencing this critical moment while he was yet impressionable.

In New York, the Harlem Renaissance consisted of the formation of a "New Negro," with regard to perspectives on politics and the economy, in addition to the creation of a culture that was to be a public declaration of an authentic black self-perception. From the late nineteenth century, until roughly 1935,[4] Harlem, New York, was the destination of choice for large masses of the nonwhite world. It involved the migration of thousands from among the African diaspora, from rural spaces like southern farm fields, or the Caribbean, to urban and metropolitan areas. The time period can also be understood as the urbanization of black life, when old pejorative perceptions of black people were exchanged for the sophisticated, educated, cultured, urban black. Additionally, this self-perception worked to animate a seedling of a theology of civil disobedience. It was an interim moment with a nascent social theology, post–Civil War and pre–Civil Rights, that expressed the already-present black definition of Christ the suffering servant, for the reclaiming

---

3. Ibid., 265.

4. Shamoon Zamir, *The Cambridge Companion to W. E. B. Du Bois*, Cambridge Companions to American Studies (Cambridge and New York: Cambridge University Press, 2008), 265.

of African American humanity and self-worth. Yet, during the Harlem Renaissance, this theology also included a theologically informed engagement with social and political expectations, by reclaiming Christ in the face of human suffering. As a movement, the Harlem Renaissance is generally understood to have involved at least two stages, beginning around the time of the First World War, and lasting into the mid-1930s, well into the global Great Depression that was ravishing Harlem during Bonhoeffer's fellowship year.

Bonhoeffer's practice of an incarnational ethic, with his notion of Christ as an empathetic vicarious representative (*Stellvertreter*), had been a working part of his theology since his first dissertation, and it equipped him to enter into the evolving Harlem world as an engaged learner, even a participant, through his relationship with his African American friend, Frank Fisher. His theological practice of incarnational ethics equipped him for that encounter, helping him to see the concrete needs for justice as they were perceived by the people within the communities gathered in Harlem, during his time there in 1930–31. That incarnational practice thickened his interpretation of the way of Jesus, and equipped him for the prophetic stance that he took in the Confessing Church.

His desire for a pastorate in poor communities prior to the church struggle,[5] his unique position early on as perhaps the only German theologian to argue that the Jewish question was, for Christians in Germany, *the* Christian problem,[6] indeed a *status confessionis* for the church;[7] his insistence on the importance of solidarity with those in suffering,[8] and his claim, in his 1933 Christology lectures, that proletarian Christians separate Christ from the constructs in which the bourgeois church and its religion have confined him,[9] can all be recognized as inspired by his Harlem-world experiences 1930–31.

This essay will look at one aspect of his exposure to the Harlem Renaissance, his theological encounter with the race divide. I will examine this encounter by paying particular attention to Bonhoeffer's interaction with Countee Cullen's 1929 poem "The Black Christ" as a critical engagement with the race divide in American Christianity. His exposure to the critical engagement with postcolonial Christianity, by virtue of his time in Harlem,

5. Bonhoeffer, *Berlin: 1932–1933*, DBWE 12:22.

6. Eberhard Bethge, *Dietrich Bonhoeffer: A Biography*, rev. ed. Victoria J. Barnett (Minneapolis: Fortress Press, 2000), 325–26.

7. Bonhoeffer, *Berlin: 1932–1933*, DBWE 12:371.

8. This is representative of his efforts in poor Germany, and his advocacy for Jewish Christians. Cf. Bonhoeffer, *London: 1933–1935*, DBWE 13:22.

9. Bonhoeffer, *Berlin: 1932–1933*, DBWE 12:306.

was a vital piece of Bonhoeffer's later, politically inflected Christian witness in Germany.

The Harlem Renaissance community gave to Bonhoeffer a unique perspective on the modern racialized understanding of humanity, and its corresponding white Jesus, existing within American Christianity. That insight allowed him to see the harmful distortions that occur with Christianity when it becomes blended with oppressive power structures. In Harlem he caught some of what that community saw operating within the dominant, white, Christian worldview. From there he observed a worldview nurturing a racial imagination that was in itself a diseased practice of Christian discipleship. Historically, the theology of that discipleship worked to legitimate white supremacy as the accepted God-given norm, manipulating whites and blacks to accept the story of the world it described, and proselytizing them to be its obedient disciples. But in the Harlem Renaissance community, as Cullen's poem indicates, Bonhoeffer was exposed to a theological critique of race from within, as he put it, "this rather hidden perspective."[10] That perspective gave him insights into the theological ability of an oppressed group to deflect the proselytizing influence of popular, harmful ideology.

A lengthier engagement with Bonhoeffer's experience in Harlem is forthcoming,[11] that will unpack further important pieces of this time in Harlem for the young Bonhoeffer. Among the important pieces that I engage in a full-length treatment are three tropes that one can see in his writing and advocacy as a result of his Sloane Fellowship year: his interpretation of W. E. B Du Bois' notions of "the veil" and "the color-line," and their respective roles in the further development of his interpretation of Martin Luther's notion of the *theologia crucis*.

Briefly, in his end-of-the-year report to the Church Federation Office, written at the end of his spring semester 1931, Bonhoeffer borrowed from Du Bois, a prominent Harlem Renaissance intellectual, to describe some of what he learned during his brief sojourn as a Sloane Fellow. When he mentioned the "rather hidden perspective" of the African American community, Bonhoeffer was referencing Du Bois' description of the "veiled corner" from his book, *Darkwater: Voices from Within the Veil*, published in 1920:

> I have seen the human drama from a veiled corner, where all the outer tragedy and comedy have reproduced themselves in

---

10. Bonhoeffer, *Barcelona, Berlin, New York: 1928–1931*, DBWE 10:314.

11. Reggie Williams, *Bonhoeffer's Black Jesus: Harlem Renaissance Theology and an Ethic of Resistance* (Waco, TX: Baylor University Press, forthcoming).

microcosm from within. From this inner torment of souls, the human scene without has interpreted itself to me in unusual and even illuminating ways.[12]

For Du Bois, the veiled corner was a perspective that was hidden from the white majority. It was the border of the modern hope for utopia, where the white narrative of hope and human advancement tortures nonwhites. By referencing it, Du Bois indicated that his social and theological analysis in *Darkwater* would come from outside of the one-world narrative of white supremacy. The hidden perspective affords a truer representation of the dominant streams of consciousness on both sides of the black/white global power divide than what is offered by the one-history-fits-all, white supremacist worldview.

As he continued his descriptions of that year, Bonhoeffer demonstrated further familiarity with Du Bois's use of the veil imagery with at least one direct reference to it: "Here one gets to see something of the real face of America, something that is hidden *behind the veil* of words in the American constitution saying that "all men are created equal."[13] This explicit reference to "the veil" was borrowed from Du Bois's seminal work *The Souls of Black Folk*, published in 1903, as a foundation for what we see in his sequel *Darkwater*. In addition to a device that provides a hidden perspective, the veil is a construct that describes racialization; it is the forced attribution of racial identity by white folks upon black bodies that works like a projector screen. Du Bois argued that real black selves are hidden "behind the veil." That is also the reason for what Du Bois described as double consciousness; blacks know themselves as whites see them, in addition to their knowledge of their real black selves. In *Souls*, Du Bois described "double consciousness" and "the veil" as hermeneutical keys to the interpretation of the black/white encounter. This framework is vital to understand his theological critique of race.

Du Bois claimed that the problem of the twentieth century was the problem of the color line. The color line is an authority scheme that belts the planet, subjugating people of color to brutal whites-only power structures. It is reinforced by an abstract theology that gives theological support to a socially constructed humanity that places white European males in an ascendant position, and relegates concrete social interaction with others to the column of *adiaphora*, or things indifferent. In Harlem, Bonhoeffer became familiar with this racialized religious power scheme. He described reading literature

12. W. E. B. Du Bois, *Darkwater: Voices from Within the Veil*, Dover Thrift Editions (Mineola, NY: Dover, 1999), ix.

13. Bonhoeffer, *Barcelona, Berlin, New York: 1928–1931*, DBWE 10:321.

by prominent Harlem Renaissance intellectuals, even writing an essay on their work that is now lost to us.[14] Those same works were without a doubt familiar to the community of Christians, and his pastor Adam Clayton Powell Sr., at Abyssinian Baptist Church, where Bonhoeffer was a lay leader. Within that community Bonhoeffer gained the ability to see that the color line is a Christian problem, and most importantly for what he was to face at home, to see how the color line passed through Germany in the form of *die Judenfrage*, the Jewish question.

We see his engagement with the color line in Germany, at the very beginning of the church struggle. Bonhoeffer quickly rebuked his colleagues in the Pastor's Emergency League for their willingness to ignore what he saw was the heart of the problem with the Nazi Christians—their racism. Early in the church struggle, the majority of his colleagues viewed their conflict with the Nazi-sympathizing German Christians much the same way that Martin Niemöller did; they resisted government intrusion in church affairs, while remaining loyal to the Nazi government, and viewed the Jewish question as adiaphora.[15] The Jewish question was, for Niemöller, not a church issue. But it was *the* church issue for Bonhoeffer. Indeed, it was for Bonhoeffer a *status confessionis* for the church. He rebuked his colleagues for their inability to see that the privileges of the "Aryans only" power structure in the church, that they were willing to accept, fundamentally changed the nature of Christian discipleship:

> The German Christians' demands destroy the substance of the ministry by making certain members of the Christian community into members with lesser rights, second-class Christians. The rest, . . . those who remain privileged members, should prefer to stand by those with lesser rights rather than to benefit from a privileged status in the church. They must see their own true service, which they can still perform for their church, in resigning from this *office of pastor as a privilege*, which is what it has now become.[16]

Early in the struggle, Bonhoeffer stood alone in his opposition to what he described as "fatal privilege,"[17] having come to recognize the color line that

---

14. DBWE 12:95.

15. Bethge, *Dietrich Bonhoeffer*, 306.

16. DBWE 12:430–31.

17. Bethge, *Dietrich Bonhoeffer*, 306.

he saw from the "hidden perspective" of oppressed blacks in Harlem, passing through Germany in the shape of the Jewish question.

These two pieces, his interaction with the hermeneutical key of the black experience in America, and his criticism of the color line in Germany, are important to the further development of his understanding of Luther's *theologia crucis*. This development is vital to our understanding of Bonhoeffer after New York 1930–31. His language about the hiddenness of God was deepened, from a primary emphasis on Christ's hiddenness, and our acceptance of grace bestowed upon Christians who are indifferent to the Bible—Christ hidden in the world in the lives of Christians who cannot be distinguished from non-Christians[18]—to an emphasis on concrete obedience to Christ's commandments, and dependence on costly grace. His insistence on costly grace was the fruit of this development; it is the result of an emphasis on the revelation of Christ who is, not hidden in our likeness to the world, which became understood as cheap grace.[19] He came to insist on our solidarity with outcasts, where Christ is *hidden in suffering*.

A more significant treatment of Bonhoeffer's experience in Harlem must include analysis of the ministry of Powell Sr. and Abyssinian Baptist Church during the Great Depression regarding these tropes that Bonhoeffer experienced in Harlem.[20] Here I will simply argue that it is the Christ "hidden in suffering" that Bonhoeffer came to see within the hidden perspective of Harlem, by exposure to the latent critique of the problem of race during the Harlem Renaissance. He wrote home regularly describing what he was learning about the "race problem"[21] in America. He was learning about the race-based division within American Christianity at a time when the notion of race was being critically analyzed in the proliferation of literature, music, theatre, and art by African American artists and intellectuals. He may have even personally met some of the prominent literary shapers of the Harlem Renaissance.

In November 1930, Frank Fisher brought his German friend with him to visit his alma mater Howard College, now called Howard University, in Washington, D.C. At the time of their visit, Alain Locke, the author whose monumental book *The New Negro* named the movement, was a very well-known faculty member of the college, and the chair of its philosophy department. Dr. Locke and Dr. W. E. B. Du Bois are still recognized as the two foremost intellectual architects of the New Negro Movement. Of that visit

18. DBWE 10:353.

19. See "Christ and Peace," DBWE 12:260.

20. Cf. Williams, *Bonhoeffer's Black Jesus*.

21. Bonhoeffer, *Barcelona, Berlin, New York: 1928–1931*, DBWE 10:321.

to Howard with Fisher, Bonhoeffer claimed "I was introduced not only to the leaders of the young Negro movement at Howard College in Washington, but also in Harlem, the Negro quarter in New York."[22] We know that he read some of Locke's and Du Bois' work, along with other prominent Harlem Renaissance intellectuals, in Niebuhr's spring course, and that he wrote an essay on the works of Harlem Renaissance writers, many of whom he was voraciously studying, even apart from assigned reading.[23] He also learned about the very public dispute between Booker T. Washington and Du Bois over the role that blacks must embrace for themselves in a white racist society. Washington's perspective was understood by some to be an "Old Negro" type of black accommodation of white supremacy. From the perspective of a number of Harlem Renaissance intellectuals, Washington represented an assimilated white racist perspective of black people—one that was absorbed into a black self-perception and formed an internalized mandate for an inferior black existence. Du Bois had a different perspective. Bonhoeffer would have read the following when he read Du Bois' book *Souls of Black Folk*: "Mr. Washington represents in thought the old attitude of adjustment and submission. . . . Mr. Washington's program practically accepts the alleged inferiority of the Negro races."[24]

Du Bois, and his students, rejected Washington's model of black engagement with white racism. Rather than "adjustment and submission," Du Bois' model can be described as a resistance model of engagement with racism. The resistance model seems to have been attractive to the young Bonhoeffer. Regarding the conflict between Du Bois and Washington, Bonhoeffer said the following: "B. T. Washington preaches the gospel of working, with regard to the white people separate like the fingers and one like the hand."[25] This is a reference to Washington's famous Atlanta Compromise speech delivered in 1895, in which he encouraged blacks to accommodate a white racist worldview by accepting segregation, and their second-class citizenship, for the advancement of humankind. Bonhoeffer continued. "Du Bois criticizes Washington sharply, accuses W. to agree with the statement of the inferiority of the black race. More race-proud!"[26]

His emphasis on Du Bois' race-pride sounds as though he is affirming it. That is not surprising given what he came to learn about the reception of Washington's perspective within the communities of young participants in

22. Ibid., 314.
23. DBWE 12:95.
24. W. E. B. Du Bois, *The Souls of Black Folk* (London: Penguin, 1989), 43.
25. DBWE 10:421.
26. Ibid.

the Renaissance, among whom he was gathering friendships. Indeed, some interpreted black leaders who succumbed to this submission-to-racism perspective to be pawns of white racist leadership.[27] Within the black community, at Abyssinian Baptist, in classes at Union, and on campus at Howard, Bonhoeffer would have learned that this perspective was particularly problematic for younger blacks. It was not only a social worldview; it housed a theological justification of racial inferiority that was leading young blacks away from Christianity because, as Bonhoeffer observed them to reason, it "made their fathers meek in the face of their incomparably harsh fate."[28] Christianity was, in their opinion, an opiate.

We can see their theological critique of opiate religion in Cullen's "The Black Christ," which Bonhoeffer referred to by name. Cullen was Du Bois' son-in-law, and Bonhoeffer read his poetry in that spring-semester course with Niebuhr.[29] He was the "young Negro poet" and his "black Christ" that Bonhoeffer refers to eight years later when commenting on the racial condition of American Christianity in his 1939 essay "Protestantism without Reformation":

> For American Christendom *the racial issue* has been a real problem from the beginning. . . . The young, forward-looking generation of Negroes are turning away from the faith of their elders because they view its strong eschatological orientation as an obstacle to the progress of their race and rights. This is one of the dangerous signs of the church's guilt in past centuries and a grave problem for the future. The fact that today the "black Christ" of a young Negro poet is pitted against the "white Christ" reveals a destructive rift [*Zerstörung*] within the church of Jesus Christ. . . . Many white Christians through influential organizations do whatever they can to improve the relations between the races, and . . . discerning Negroes recognize the serious difficulties. But today the general picture of the church in the United States is still one of racial fragmentation. Blacks

---

27. C. Eric Lincoln and Lawrence H. Mamiya, *The Black Church in the African-American Experience* (Durham, NC: Duke University Press, 1990), 15.

28. DBWE 10:315.

29. DBWE 10:421–22. Bonhoeffer lists Cullen's *Copper Sun* among the readings for February 18, 1931, and comments that his poetry, and that of Langston Hughes, "is often very passionate and satiric in its accusation against the suppression of their race" (ibid., 422). *Copper Sun* was published in 1927 and *The Black Christ and Other Poems* in 1929.

and whites come separately to word and sacrament. They have no common worship.[30]

The "strong eschatological orientation" Bonhoeffer referred to was the opiate features of oppressive religion that were being rejected by the younger blacks. Cullen's "Black Christ" was indicative of that rejecting process.

It was a rejecting process performed in the context of a critical analysis of race and religion that was unique to the Harlem Renaissance. The Black Christ is representative of the connection that Harlem Renaissance intellectuals were making between the suffering of black people and the suffering of Jesus. Cullen's poem is one of a number of Harlem Renaissance lynching parables written by black intellectuals of the Renaissance that placed Christ in the lived experience of race-terror, as a "colored" victim, to provide a theological critique of race and African American suffering in a white supremacist society. Their efforts can also be understood by what womanist ethicist Emilie Townes suggests as a distinction between suffering and pain. Townes references Audre Lorde when she describes suffering as cycles of inescapable, unscrutinized pain.[31] Yet, similar to what Du Bois describes as lifting the veil, when pain is highlighted, it becomes something different. It gets extracted from the undetermined, vicious, inescapable cycles, and becomes an experience that is recognized, named, and can be used for transformation. Hence, our responsibility in the face of human suffering is to resist it, by moving from suffering to pain. Pain, as Townes describes it, is a constituent of the struggle against injustice. We may interpret the goal of the lynching parables in this light. They represent critical theological analyses by Harlem Renaissance intellectuals, of religion and black suffering, in an effort to move from suffering to pain.

Du Bois also wrote numerous lynching parables. One in particular placed a Jewish Jesus in Waco, Texas, to be encountered by pious Christian whites who were aghast at his "colored" appearance to the point that he is lynched.[32] "Jesus Christ in Texas" represented the color line as an ironic, Christological tragedy; in a white-centered world, the Son of God becomes a frightening disruption,

---

30. Bonhoeffer, *Theological Education Underground: 1937–1949*, DBWE 15:456–57. See editor's footnote 48: "*The Black Christ and Other Poems* is the title of a collection of poetry by the black poet Countee Cullen (cf. DBWE 10:315, note 31). [See also Bonhoeffer's reading notes on 'Negro Literature,' DBWE 10:421–22, and the editor's introduction to DBWE 10:30–31–VB]."

31. See Emilie Townes, "Living in the New Jerusalem," in Emilie Maureen Townes, *A Troubling in My Soul: Womanist Perspectives on Evil and Suffering* (Maryknoll, NY: Orbis, 1993), 78–91.

32. See "Jesus Christ in Texas," in Du Bois, *Darkwater*, 70–77.

simply one more inhabitant of the racialized communities that are intimately familiar with white Christian scorn. They are the people Howard Thurman described as "the disinherited," until white Christians come to recognize Christ's natural, physical identification with the subjugated and disinherited, who comprise the populations on the unfavorable side of the color line.

That Cullen's poem is also this kind of critical engagement with race is indicated by the audience to whom Cullen dedicates it: "Hopefully dedicated to white America."[33] In the poem, the historical Jesus becomes the first lynched victim of an evil mob, in a succession of lynched victims that includes African Americans:

How Calvary in Palestine,
Extending down to me and mine,
Was but the first leaf in a line,
Of trees on which a Man should swing
World without end, in suffering.[34]

The poem consists of three main characters, a Job-like pious Christian mother, and her two young-adult sons who function in a role that resembles Job's accusatory friends. Both of these young men, the younger one named Jim, and the older unnamed brother, wrestle with questions of theodicy; since his childhood, Jim has doubted the existence of God because of white cruelty and innocent suffering:

"A man was lynched last night."
"Why?" Jim would ask, his eyes star-bright.
"A white man struck him; he showed fight.
Maybe God thinks such things are right."
"Maybe God never thinks at all—
Of us," and Jim would clench his small,
Hard fingers tight into a ball.
"Likely there ain't no God at all . . .
God could not be if he deemed right,
The grief that ever met our sight."[35]

---

33. Countee Cullen, *The Black Christ & Other Poems*, 1st ed. (New York and London: Harper & Brothers, 1929), 67.

34. Ibid., 69.

35. Ibid., 77–78.

Initially, this language used in conversation about God is problematic for the older brother. He is introduced as being friendly towards the religion of his mother. But we soon learn of his growing concern for the safety of his smart, handsome younger brother. That concern leads to bitter words of fear and anguish over the role of God in black suffering: Why is it dangerous for Jim, the younger brother, to exist as an intelligent, handsome, and self-confident black man? This gets to the theological critique in Cullen's depiction of race. It is the problem of discipleship and obedience within the racialized structure of Christianity, and a vital insight on the intersection of race, religion, and oppression, in white power structures. This perspective would have proven enlightening for Bonhoeffer. From this viewpoint, he saw white Christians turn Christ into the representative of white cultural longing, and a fetish of idealized humanity. That Christ was not a guide for daily interaction with one's real neighbor, not one who has commanded that we must do unto others as we would have them do to us; he had become a policeman on the borders of white racial identity, and a theological justification for dehumanizing real people in the name of an ideal Christian community. Discipleship had become training in hatred. That was the white Christ that Bonhoeffer was referring to in his letters home that year. That Christ was the source of the cheap grace active within the fatal privilege[36] he was protesting in the church struggle, and was also the repellant within the Christianity that he noticed younger blacks turning away from in Harlem.

Jim represents this youthful resistance model of race critique within the Harlem Renaissance: proud, intelligent, good-looking, and no longer silent. He strikes an assaultive white racist man, resulting in his death-by-lynching at the hands of an angry white mob, at his home, in front of his mother and brother. At this, his elder brother is devastated. The elder brother's emotional state is exaggerated by the sight of his mother on her knees in prayer to a white Christ:

> "Call on him now," I mocked, "and try
> Your faith against His deed, while I
> With intent equally as sane,
> Searching a motive for this pain,
> Will hold a little stone on high
> And seek of it a reason why.
> Which, stone or God, will first reply . . . ?
> What has He done for you who spent
> A bleeding life for His content?

36. Bethge, DB-ER, 306.

Or is white Christ, too, distraught
By these dark skins His Father wrought?[37]

The white Christ is the artificial Jesus of the socially constructed humanity that places white European males in ascendant status. He frames the structure that is the scale of racial hierarchy. And as the divine representative of white supremacy, the white Christ is not an advocate of this family's well-being. He only hurts, humiliates, and kills them. But here is the heart of Cullen's critique: the religion of the pious, black Christian mother has nothing to do with the religious representation of white supremacy. She is not praying to a white Christ. The Christ she worships betrays the lethal nature of the mixture of race-terror and Christianity that white-racist Christians force society to drink. That mixture is lethal for victims and perpetrators alike. Her faith in Christ extracts him from that lethal concoction, and disassociates him from the structures that fail to acknowledge his life in solidarity with the oppressed. Her Jesus is very different from the Christ who is co-opted by forces that turn him into a weapon wielded against marginalized people, in a world built on a Manichaean interpretation of humanity. With her, Jesus becomes a contradiction to the way in which white racist Christians construct society. Her Jesus cannot be found in the domination and race-based privileges of racialized communities; she knows that Christ is hidden from racists in and among their victims, with those whom Bonhoeffer in his *Ethics* would later describe as "the poorest of our brothers and sisters."[38] Indeed, Christ was hidden even from her own son, who did not know that Jesus was there, among them, until he came to recognize him in his brother's suffering. *That* is the poem's admonition to us. Only at *that* recognition did the elder brother come to know Christ, and to proclaim him as the "form immaculately born, betrayed a thousand times each morn, as many times each night denied, surrendered, tortured, crucified!"[39] Cullen's black Christ exists in solidarity with this suffering black family. Indeed, he is one of them. Understanding Jesus in this way, as one who is intimately participating in the lives of suffering and marginalized people, has significant implications for Christian discipleship.

Christ entering into the suffering of the outcasts and marginalized is a theme that resonates with Bonhoeffer's Christology. When he returns to Germany, we see that Bonhoeffer not only agreed with this Christological theme as the mode of Christ's existence in the world, but also as the ethical

---

37. Cullen, *Black Christ*, 103, 105.

38. Dietrich Bonhoeffer, *Ethics*, DBWE 6:253.

39. Cullen, *Black Christ*, 108.

imperative for real Christian discipleship. It is this form of Christ-centered Christianity that Bonhoeffer saw expressed with zeal at Abyssinian Baptist:

> I heard the gospel preached in the Negro churches. . . . Here one really could still hear someone talk in a Christian sense about sin and grace and the love of God and ultimate hope, albeit in a form different from that to which we are accustomed. *In contrast to the often lecture-like character of the "white" sermon, the "black Christ" is preached with captivating passion and vividness.*[40]

The captivating passion of the black Christ was invigorating, and a source through which Bonhoeffer came to identify with African Americans, in the spirituals he loved so much that spoke of grace in suffering, and in their theology. One Sunday, during that Spring Semester of 1931, one of Bonhoeffer's fellow students, Myles Horton, observed Bonhoeffer returning to his seminary lodging from Abyssinian Baptist, where he had become a lay leader with his friend Frank Fisher, after teaching Sunday School that day. Bonhoeffer lingered for a time, excited to talk about that day at church. To Horton's surprise, Bonhoeffer was quite emotional; this was out of character for Bonhoeffer's typically logical, unemotive temperament. Horton remembered Bonhoeffer claiming that "the only time he had experienced true religion in the United States" was in black churches, and he "was convinced that it was only among blacks who were oppressed that there could be any real religion in this country."[41] As Horton recalled: "Perhaps that Sunday afternoon . . . I witnessed a beginning of his identification with the oppressed which played a role in the decision that led to his death."[42] Indeed, Horton was right. Bonhoeffer's identification with the resistance model of Christ who knew and accepted suffering in America, placed him in solidarity with the outcast and the marginalized in Germany. It led him to drink the full measure of the cup of Christ's suffering, as described by the lynching parables of the Harlem Renaissance, at the gallows at Flossenbürg concentration camp, in the early morning hours of April 9, 1945.

---

40. DBWE 10:315, italics mine.
41. DBWE 10:31, editor's introduction.
42. DBWE 10:31.

17

Church for Others: Bonhoeffer, Paul, and the Critique of Empire

Brigitte Kahl

What is Christianity? It's the Holy Spirit. What is the Holy Spirit? It's an egalitarian community of believers who are linked by love for each other and who only have their own freedom and responsibility to do it. In this sense the Holy Spirit is here now. And down there on Wall Street, there are pagans who are worshipping blasphemous idols.[1]

A non-Christian talking strangely but powerfully Christian—when I heard Slavoj Žižek speak to the Occupy-movement in October 2011 down at Wall Street, all of a sudden I couldn't help hearing another voice in the no-mike chorus of mouth-to-mouth communication, the voice of a Christian who at one point in his life and from a prison cell, started to talk strangely and powerfully non-Christian: Dietrich Bonhoeffer. So there was Žižek, the unruly philosopher-celebrity performing this epiclesis of the Holy Spirit on the "*ek-klesia*" of those called outdoors at Zuccotti Park. I kept wondering whether he perhaps embraced a piece of something that Bonhoeffer as a state prisoner on death row anticipated with an enigmatic clarity that has kept confusing us until today: in a completely nonreligious environment, exemplary of the world come of age, the old and arcane words of Christianity one day would start to make sense again and in new ways.

---

1. Slavoj Žižek, addressing Occupy Wall Street at Liberty Plaza, New York, on October 9, 2011; http://www.versobooks.com/blogs/736http:/. During the night of November 14, after this paper was delivered at the Union Seminary conference, the protestors at Zuccotti Park in lower Manhattan were raided by the police and their encampment broken up. This created a crisis for Union Seminary since about twenty Union students were working as protest chaplains among those encamped in Zuccotti Park.

There is another voice, however, who speaks through both Bonhoeffer and Žižek: the voice of Paul. Žižek, like Giorgio Agamben, Alain Badiou—and the Jewish philosopher Jacob Taubes before them—is one of those who from a non-Christian perspective have recently worked extensively on the apostle, with a sense of reverent impiety and urgency that makes the Paul of the philosophers at the moment often more captivating than the Paul of the theologians. But what about Bonhoeffer's Pauline affiliations? We are more inclined to link him to the First Testament, or to the Sermon on the Mount and other gospel passages, as both Samuel Wells and Wolfgang Huber have so persuasively outlined.[2] What I will try to show is that Bonhoeffer's Tegel prison-notes on nonreligious interpretation, on "religionless Christianity" and the "church for others," are intensely steeped in Paul as well.

Here is my thesis: Bonhoeffer's wrestling with religion and nonreligion, church and unchurched in a world come of age, is only decodable through the deep grammar of Paul's justification theology; it contains the nuclear version of a complete rethinking of justification by faith as the theological core of Protestantism. In particular Bonhoeffer, with striking clear-sightedness, anticipates (and maybe also inspires) two decisive developments in Pauline studies of a much later day: first, the "New Perspective" turn to Paul as the theologian of a religiously transgressive and pluriform inclusivity that is no longer framed in an anti-Judaistic key;[3] secondly, the more recent move of empire-critical and postcolonial Pauline interpretation toward a critique of Roman imperial religion and the body politics of empire, an approach that has been pioneered by the likes of Dieter Georgi, Elsa Tamez, Robert Jewett, Neil Elliott, Richard Horsley—and again, Jacob Taubes.[4]

In the famous letter dated April 30, 1944, Bonhoeffer writes programmatically to Eberhard Bethge: "The Pauline question whether *peritome*, circumcision, is a condition for justification is today, in my opinion, the

---

2. See Epilogue, pp. 219–36 and Chapter 1, p. 8.

3. James D. G. Dunn, *The New Perspective on Paul: Collected Essays*, WUNT 185 (Tübingen: Mohr Siebeck, 2005); for a more comprehensive introduction to current paradigm shifts in the study of Paul see Magnus Zetterholm, *Approaches to Paul: A Student's Guide to Recent Scholarship* (Minneapolis: Fortress Press, 2009)

4. Still convenient as an introduction to the empire-critical work of Georgi and others are the essays collected in Richard A. Horsley, ed., *Paul and Empire: Religion and Power in Roman Imperial Society* (Harrisburg, PA: Trinity Press International, 1997); Elsa Tamez, *The Amnesty of Grace: Justification by Faith from a Latin American Perspective* (Nashville: Abingdon, 1993); Neil Elliott, *Liberating Paul: The Justice of God and the Politics of the Apostle* (Maryknoll, NY: Orbis, 1994); Jacob Taubes, *The Political Theology of Paul* (Stanford, CA: Stanford University Press, 2004); Robert Jewett, *Romans: A Commentary*, Hermeneia (Minneapolis: Fortress Press, 2007).

question of whether religion is a condition of salvation."[5] In the same letter he asks the question "What is Christianity?" with a new sense of urgency.[6] For the first time the terms "religionless Christians" and "religionless Christianity" come up. And Bonhoeffer anchors them in Paul and his signature debate on circumcision, treating the contemporary question of religion or nonreligion as identical to Paul's question of circumcision and foreskin. This is a remarkable statement. It requires us to read Bonhoeffer's construct of religion and religionlessness in a Pauline key throughout, even when Paul isn't explicitly mentioned.

"Christians and Pagans/Gentiles"

The poem "Christians and Pagans," from summer 1944, might assist us in a more in-depth exploration of the "Pauline" Bonhoeffer. It is a well-known text that summarizes in a nutshell the Christological core of Bonhoeffer's critique of religion and the turn to a "church for others." While this is more or less acknowledged in scholarship, the scriptural basis for Bonhoeffer's argument is widely obscured, namely Paul. This eclipse of the biblical frame of reference might be partly linked to the common translation of the German "Christen und Heiden" as "Christians and *Pagans*." Bonhoeffer's *Heiden*, in German a somewhat archaic term, are clearly rooted in the Luther Bible where they are the equivalent of the Greek *ethne*, especially in the Pauline phrase *Ioudaioi kai ethne*: Jews and *Gentiles*. In almost all standard translations, *Gentiles* is the English equivalent for the Greek *ethne* and the German *Heiden*. This is of some importance, as the term *Gentiles* (rather than *pagans*) is needed to take us specifically to all those places where Paul talks about circumcision (= Jews) and foreskin (= Gentiles). The clash between circumcision and foreskin indisputably is the core conflict of his Gentile mission and the "real life context" that gives birth to the entire theology of justification by faith, and eventually Christianity.[7] Bonhoeffer, as we have seen, explicitly links his thoughts on religion and nonreligion to Paul's wrestling with the circumcision question, the *Heiden/Gentile* issue. His poem on "Christen und Heiden" therefore arguably should be titled "Christians and Gentiles."

---

5. *Letters and Papers from Prison*, DBWE 8:365–66.

6. ". . . what is Christianity, or who is Christ actually for us today?" *Letters and Papers from Prison*, DBWE 8:362.

7. Cf. Gal. 2:15-21 in the context of Gal. 2:1-14; Rom. 3:21-31 in the context of Romans 1–3; Acts 15:1.

In order to bridge the gap between translation and original even further, I'll use a very raw and imperfect interlinear English translation to get us as close to the German text as possible, as we take a look at the poem itself.[8]

Christians and Gentiles / *Christen und Heiden*

Humans go to God in their need
Menschen gehen zu Gott in ihrer Not
Pleading for help, asking for good fortune and bread
Flehen um Hilfe, bitten um Glück und Brot,
For salvation from sickness, guilt (or debt) and death
Um Errettung aus Krankheit, Schuld und Tod
All do so, all, Christians and Gentiles
So tun sie alle, alle, Christen und Heiden.

As we can observe already in the first stanza, the poem is steeped in the thoroughly Pauline terminology of "humans" (*anthropoi*) and "all"—(*pantes*):[9] Humans in need go to God and ask for help, bread, good fortune, salvation from sickness, guilt, and death. *All* of them do that, *all*—Bonhoeffer repeats this twice!—Christians and Gentiles alike.

If we bracket the second stanza for a moment, we can see that in the third stanza, this movement is reversed. *God* in return goes to *all* humans in their need:

God goes to all humans in their need
Gott geht zu allen Menschen in ihrer Not
Feeds body and soul (or spirit) with his bread
Sättigt den Leib und die Seele mit Seinem Brot
For Christians and Gentiles he dies the death on a cross
Stirbt für Christen und Heiden den Kreuzestod
And forgives both of them.
Und vergibt ihnen beiden.

Again *all* humans and their need are at stake. God feeds their body and soul/spirit with his all-inclusive bread. God dies for *Christians and Gentiles* alike the death on the cross—and forgives *both of them*. The Christ event is focal

---

8. Compare the translation by Nancy Lukens in *Letters and Papers from Prison*, DBWE 8:460–61.

9. E.g., Rom. 3:9, 22, 23, 28.

in this all-comprising transformation, and we easily can see how Bonhoeffer's theology of the cross is linked to the Reformation *particula exclusiva*: by God's grace alone, through Christ alone, and thus by faith alone humans are forgiven, justified, set right in their relation to God. In this point Bonhoeffer, Paul, and the established Lutheran interpretation would be in full agreement.

But there is a second point where Bonhoeffer, as I believe, is much more in agreement with Paul than Paul's Protestant interpreters usually are. If the scriptural base (the *sola scriptura*) of all this is to be taken seriously, God's grace according to Paul puts *Christians and Gentiles* alike into a very uneasy commonality. As we have seen in the first stanza, Christians, the church, all that we would define as the *proper* religion, all of a sudden appear on the same path to God as those who have the allegedly *wrong* religion or no religion at all: the *Gentiles/Heiden*. *All* of them want the strong god, the *deus ex machina*[10] to compensate for human weakness, vulnerability, misery, or just to fulfill human desire and the dream of prosperity. This all-inclusive *all* in itself is deeply offensive to any Christian identity-construct that perpetually draws its self-righteousness from an inferior, unrighteous Other, like the notorious "work-righteous" and law-obsessed "Jew" in standard Christian, and particularly Protestant interpretation.[11]

CHURCH FOR/WITH OTHERS: PAUL AND BONHOEFFER AT ZUCCOTTI PARK

Are *we* then no longer better than *them*? What about "Christ alone," a clear criterion for upholding *our* faith-righteousness over and against the unrighteousness of others? Bonhoeffer sharpens the question, rather than easing any of the outrage it evokes. It is precisely and in particular the *Christ event* of incarnation, crucifixion, and redemption that requires *us* to accept our solidarity with *them*, who we had thought were the sinners, the outsiders, the non-us: Jews, Catholics, heretics, Muslims, unbelievers. . . . God goes to *all* humans in their need, including ourselves. God doesn't die for Christians in particular, nor *against* anybody, but for Christians *and* Gentiles, forgiving them both alike. Bonhoeffer here seems to paraphrase and reassemble Paul's most famous justification statement in Rom. 3:27-30, which is usually is cut off in the middle

---

10. See Bonhoeffer's criticism of that concept, *Letters and Papers from Prison*, DBWE 8:366, 450, 479.

11. For an exploration of Self-Other binaries as obscuring Paul's theology of justification by faith, see Brigitte Kahl, "Galatians and the 'Orientalism' of Justification by Faith: Paul among Jews and Muslims," in *The Colonized Apostle: Paul through Postcolonial Eyes*, ed. Christopher D. Stanley (Minneapolis: Fortress Press, 2011), 206–22.

of the sentence: *For we hold that a person is justified by faith apart from works of the law. . . .* This is the familiar part—justification through Christ, by faith (and grace) *alone*, which means without works.[12] But Paul's statement, like Bonhoeffer's, doesn't end here; it hasn't even reached its climax yet, rather it goes on: . . . *Or is God the God of the Jews alone? Not also the God of the Gentiles? Yes, of the Gentiles also, since God is One, who will justify the circumcised on the ground of faith and the uncircumcised through that same faith.*[13]

The god, who is God not of the Jews alone, nor of the Christians, for that matter—this is what Bonhoeffer hears when he writes "Christen und Heiden." It echoes the Pauline "church *with* others," a church of circumcised and uncircumcised, religiously acceptable and unacceptable ones, *together* rather than in mutual exclusion. *Justification without works for Bonhoeffer, as for Paul, aims at a transformed relationship between the Christian Self and its religious or nonreligious Other.* It implies constantly wrestling with this unbearable diversity of Self and Other, One and Different, and the conflicts this uneasy commonality of not-sameness creates, stubbornly refusing to move toward uniformity and an erasure of difference, rather seeking reconciliation through "bearing one another's burdens"[14] in mutuality and solidarity. This kind of unity that holds Self and Other in an egalitarian pluriformity of love, without suppressing difference, for Paul is the only way that expresses the Oneness of God and the Oneness in Christ adequately in the new messianic age: *For God is ONE.*[15]

I believe that some of the very concrete difficulties and conflicts that Paul's messianic approach to community building and transformation must have created were present as well down at Zuccotti Park in Fall 2011. Indeed the task to establish and practice a new kind of unity that does not *erase* differences but is *constituted* by differences is a key question for any social justice movement today. Would Paul, the tentmaker, have pitched his tent among the tent-dwellers at Wall Street? And Bonhoeffer, Hitler's state prisoner? Paul, by the way, never called his new type of community "Christian"—the term is completely absent from his vocabulary—rather he talks about Jews and Gentiles, *we* and *they* being together and transformed *in Christ*. Is this maybe the

---

12. Romans 3:28; as is well known, Martin Luther in his translation added the "alone" that is not contained in the Greek text.

13. Romans 3:29-30.

14. Galatians 6:2; for a more sustained rereading of Galatians along these lines see Brigitte Kahl, *Galatians Re-imagined: Reading with the Eyes of the Vanquished* (Minneapolis: Fortress Press, 2010), 245–89.

15. Romans 3:30; cf. Gal. 3:28.

point where Bonhoeffer and Paul could start debating with each other about religionless Christianity and the "Church with/for Others"?

One more word about Protestant anti-Judaism: "The Jews" (in contradistinction to Gentiles) are the defining religious Self for Paul. When Bonhoeffer titles his poem "Christians and Gentiles," for Paul's "Jews" he substitutes "Christians" as the defining and dominant Self of western civilization since Constantine. This is a strong move away from the dominant anti-Judaism of the mainstream Protestant matrix. It both preserves and transforms the most agonizing provocation of Paul's justification theology: God as "magic marker" of a superior religious Self over and against its inferior religious (or nonreligious) Other becomes erased. Justification theology is the Pauline deconstruction of Christian (or any other) supersessionism with regard to an inferior Jewish, or any other religious or nonreligious Other. It took twenty more years until, in the 1960s, another Lutheran, Krister Stendahl, made these things more explicit and reframed the whole Pauline controversy from *Jews versus Christians* to *Jews together with Gentiles*.[16] In a move that already had been anticipated by Bonhoeffer in his prison cell, the commonality, rather than the antagonism, of Self and Other was retrieved as defining element in Paul's perception of the Christ-event. The subsequent emergence of the so-called *New Perspective* on Paul was the first large-scale post-Holocaust attempt to deal with the complicity of Protestantism in German anti-Judaism and anti-Semitism by redrafting the Pauline paradigm; it has profoundly changed Pauline studies since then, mostly without any awareness of its Bonhoefferian roots.

In the meantime, empire-critical and postcolonial studies have started to read Paul's border-transgressing intervention into the fabric of religion and Self not just within the framework of Judaism but against the backdrop of the Roman Empire as well. Robert Jewett's magisterial *Hermeneia* Commentary on Romans for the first time interprets "works of the law" not primarily with regard to Jewish Torah but Roman *Nomos*, that is, as the principle of hierarchical divisions in the competition for honor, status, and privilege. Paul's subversive community building from this perspective is an anti-imperial counter-strategy that connects the politically subjugated and economically defeated in a new type of horizontal mutuality and solidarity "from below," rejecting the mutual competitiveness and combativeness imposed from "above."[17] This brings me to my last point: the critique of empire.

16. See Krister Stendahl, "The Apostle Paul and the Introspective Conscience of the West," *Harvard Theological Review* 56 (1963): 199–215; also Stendahl, *Paul Among Jews and Gentiles* (Philadelphia: Fortress Press, 1976).

17. Robert Jewett, *Romans: A Commentary*, Hermeneia (Minneapolis: Fortress Press, 2007).

The Other God and the God(s) of Empire: A Reimagination

We haven't read the second stanza of Bonhoeffer's poem on Christians and Gentiles yet.

> Humans go to God in their need
> *Menschen gehen zu Gott in Seiner Not*
> Find him poor, stigmatized, homeless and without bread
> *Finden ihn arm, geschmäht, ohne Obdach und Brot*
> See him devoured by sin, weakness and death
> *Sehn in verschlungen von Sünde, Schwachheit und Tod*
> Christians stand with God in his suffering.
> *Christen stehen bei Gott in seinem Leiden.*

Humans go to God in his need, find him poor, stigmatized, homeless, hungry, see him devoured by sin, weakness, death. Christians stand with God in his suffering. What Bonhoeffer evokes here is an *Other* God than the God both Christians and non-Christians usually envision and worship: a God who is Other and with the suffering Others, rather than the Ourselves. This for Bonhoeffer is the God that Christians only can encounter and recognize as God in their solidarity with the suffering of fellow-humans.

Bonhoeffer's evocation of the *Other* God implies a total reversal of "seeing"—an *apocalypsis* in the genuine sense of this term, as an *unveiling* of God's essence in contradistinction to what we thought we knew about God and what we imagined God to be. This *reimagination* prompts us to look at images, images of Paul's world, Bonhoeffer's world, and ours in their interaction with the biblical text. One image that might help us bridge the gap between these worlds and assist our critical reimagination is the *Gemma Augustea*, a small piece of jewelry from the first century CE. We are going to look at its upper part first.

This section of the image depicts the world from above. It shows Caesar Augustus posing as Jupiter/Zeus, holding a huge scepter in his left arm and the small *lituus* of the augurs in the other hand, at his feet the eagle that is both the sign of the Roman legions and of the supreme world god. Goddess Roma/Livia is sitting next to him, and a celestial sign combining the sun disc and the imperial Capricorn is hovering between the two of them. From behind, Jupiter Augustus is crowned by *Oikoumene.* The mural crown she wears symbolizes the entirety of cities and civilization throughout the inhabited world, whereas the oak-leafed crown she extends to the emperor-God designates Augustus as the *savior* of civilization and humanity. It is clear that his universal power, that includes also Sea/*Okeanos* and Earth/*Gaia* to the right, rests on military might—*Nike/Victory* appears in the left corner, two young men (one of them probably Tiberius) return from military campaigns, and the ground is littered with the armor of defeated enemies. The image is meant to communicate *euangelion,* good news about global salvation, fertility, and well-being in harmony with the divine law and order. It is the image of religion tied to world power and total victory: imperial religion.[18]

18. The concept of imperial religion or emperor worship that traditionally has been somewhat underestimated in its relevance for the interpretation of New Testament texts has recently received renewed attention among New Testament and classical scholars and is at the center of much controversy; cf. e.g., Justin K. Hardin, *Galatians and the Imperial Cult: A Critical Analysis of the First-Century Social Context of Paul's Letter* (WUNT 2/237, Tübingen: Mohr Siebeck, 2008); Michael Peppard, *The Son of God in the Roman World: Divine Sonship in Its Social and Political Context* (Oxford: Oxford University

At Paul's time, all other established religions and deities have to acknowledge the divine supremacy of God Caesar. This includes the Jewish God (though for him some noteworthy exemptions were in place). Paul disturbs this consensus by proclaiming a different *euangelion*, a gospel that contests the worldwide worship of power by claiming sole allegiance to the Jewish God who revealed his divinity at a Roman cross—and by making the heresy and idolatry of imperial religion *Anathema*: a status confessionis, we might say.[19]

This is, I believe, what links him and Bonhoeffer at the core. What Paul and Bonhoeffer saw, more sharply and critically than most of their fellow-believers, was the world in the grip of an almost irresistible religion of power. Both Paul and Bonhoeffer witnessed how faith, worship, and interaction with the neighbor were permeated and hijacked by imperial religion and the God of power—the emperor/supreme God/world ruler in the first century ce, or the *Führer* who promised that tomorrow the Aryan master race would own the world two thousand years later. Both Bonhoeffer and Paul were exposed to particularly massive and abusive forms of emperor worship or "Führerkult" that left not many places or communities in established religion—including Judaism at Paul's time and Protestantism during the Third Reich—really immune and intact. And both responded with an exodus out of imperial religion into an all-inclusive communality from below that embraced the *Anathema* of any religion of power: the crucified, weak, vulnerable.

Press, 2011), esp. 31–49; Jeffrey Brodd and Jonathan L. Reed, eds., *Rome and Religion: A Cross-Disciplinary Dialogue on the Imperial Cult* (Atlanta: Society of Biblical Literature, 2011).

19. On this see Kahl, *Galatians Re-Imagined*, 129–67.

This is the complete picture of the *Gemma Augustea*, the indispensable underside that comes with the glorious and beautiful upperside of world rule and the all-powerful God: human beings defeated, enslaved, abused, dehumanized, downtrodden—the rebellious, godless, undeserving *barbarians* of Greco-Roman civilization. Imperial religion, the worship of empire of any kind, channels the gaze of its followers to the above, the above of Self-fulfillment, salvation, prosperity—away from the below of the Others. Both Bonhoeffer and Paul refused to see God and the human Other in the likeness of the imperial idol above, but rather became exposed to the reality below with their own bodies: imprisonment, punishment, execution. They knew about the misery of those who sat in their cells, their feet or hands shackled like the barbarian couple underneath a Roman trophy on the *Gemma*, awaiting execution. The humiliation of those begging for mercy in vain like the bearded man on his knees, being forced into submission and betrayal by torture and abuse. The pain of those being dragged by their hair to submit themselves to the conquerors—or to board a train bound for Auschwitz.

This is the point where the veil, the blinding cover, is removed and an *apocalypsis* happens, a flash of new seeing. What Bonhoeffer and Paul have in common is this unsettling theological core vision: the god on the upperside that is so imposingly and beautifully portrayed on the *Gemma Augustea*, the world god of power, the god of the war machine—*deus ex machina*—is NOT God at all, but the beast, a monstrosity that shapes all humans in the images of the monstrous. Rather God resides on the underside, tied to a trophy, the cross-shaped sign of imperial victory, dying there for all of us who are deformed in our humanity by being both victims and perpetrators in this universal monstrosity, the all-powerful system of imperial idolatry. There, on the underside of a skyscraping deification of power, on the dark side of all glossy religions of self-worship where the evicted and executed *Other* God dwells, the church with the *Other* and for others is born.

18

E. New Theological Issues and Interpretation

Bonhoeffer's Strong Christology in the Context of Religious Pluralism

Christiane Tietz

Bonhoeffer's circumstances were different from ours. Most people in the western world at that time were Christians. In Germany, almost everybody belonged to the Protestant or the Roman Catholic church. Jews lived in Germany too—half a million at the beginning of the Third Reich, distressingly almost none at its end. In Bonhoeffer's time, *Islam*, *Buddhism*, and *Hinduism* were religions of people living far away from Germany.

Our circumstances are different from Bonhoeffer's.[1] A high percentage of people in the western world still belongs to one of the Christian denominations (in Germany around 62 percent, in the United States 76 percent). Nevertheless *religious pluralism* is the signature of today.[2] Through the mass media, other countries with different religious traditions are present in our living rooms every day; movies and books introduce us to their thinking; we travel to countries that have been shaped by different religious cultures—and enjoy how colorful and various they are. While all this somehow has the character of observing something interesting from a distance, the fact that many people of other faiths have immigrated into former "Christian countries" has changed

---

1. See David H. Jensen, "Religionless Christianity and Vulnerable Discipleship: The Interfaith Promise of Bonhoeffer's Theology," *Journal of Ecumenical Studies* 38 (2001): 151–67, 151.

2. See Christoph Schwöbel, "Religiöser Pluralismus als Signatur unserer Lebenswelt," in Schwöbel, *Christlicher Glaube im Pluralismus: Studien zu einer Theologie der Kultur* (Tübingen: Mohr Siebeck, 2003), 1–24.

our societies. In New York City for example, the population nowadays is comprised of 169 different religions and denominations—not to mention the large numbers of agnostics and atheists.

Two issues arise from this new situation of religious pluralism. On the one hand, intense interreligious dialogue about our different traditions and about how we want to live together becomes necessary. On the other hand, our own homogenous view of the world is questioned, our assumption that it is natural to be *Christian*. The new situation raises the question of truth: Is my religious tradition the only true one or are other religious traditions true as well?

Different answers to the question of truth in a setting of religious pluralism are on the market: Some argue *agnostically* that we just don't know the answer, only God knows, therefore we have to qualify our own faith. Others argue *exclusively*, that only Christianity is true and all other religions are false. Some argue *inclusively*, that there is some truth in other religions, but Jesus Christ is the highest form of truth and only in him is comprehensive salvation possible. Finally, some hold the *pluralistic* view that all religions, or at least all the world religions, are true. All these concepts develop a *theology of religions*, a theological approach to the phenomenon of the plurality of religions.[3] Yet there are also scholars who criticize such a theology of religions as an impossible attempt to achieve a metatheory. It ignores that we already belong to a certain religious tradition, which means that we cannot abstract from our concrete religious worldview and take up a bird's-eye view in which we judge from outside about the truth of religions.[4]

Bonhoeffer developed neither an elaborated "theology of religions," nor a detailed discussion on how to deal with the plurality of religions. But the theme of other religions and the relation of Christianity to them is nevertheless present in his thinking. And his Christology contains a Christian perspective on religious pluralism. In the first part of this article, I will discuss Bonhoeffer's own awareness of other religions. In the second part I will develop his Christology in the context of religious pluralism.

---

3. Cf. as introductions in German Christian Danz, *Einführung in die Theologie der Religionen* (Wien: LIT, 2005); Ulrich H. J. Körtner, ed., *Theologie der Religionen: Positionen und Perspektiven evangelischer Theologie* (Neukirchen: Neukirchener, 2005); and Reinhold Bernhardt, *Ende des Dialogs?: Die Begegnung der Religionen und ihre theologische Reflexion* (Zürich: TVZ, 2005).

4. So Klaus von Stosch, "Komparative Theologie—ein Ausweg aus dem Grunddilemma jeder Theologie der Religionen?," *Zeitschrift für Katholische Theologie* 124 (2002): 294–311.

I. Bonhoeffer's Own Awareness of Other Religions

Bonhoeffer was of course aware of the existence of other, non-Judeo-Christian religions.[5] He sometimes referred to *Islam*. When he visited North Africa in 1924, after a very short glance at Islam, he tried to grasp essential elements of Islam and quickly compared Islam and Judaism: "In Islam, everyday life and religion are not separated at all. . . . To a great degree this is due to their strong and overt pride in their race. This same trait is exhibited by the Jews and the Arabs."[6] He continued, comparing world religions not carefully but in broad strokes: "Both Islamic and Israelite piety must, of course, be expressly law-oriented. This is the case because the national and cultic moments are so heavily mingled that they coalesce, so to speak. It is the only way that their sharp separation from other races and religions can be achieved. A religion that would be a world religion, like Christianity or Buddhism, can't be a religion of law at all."[7]

In his *Ethics*, Bonhoeffer argued in a similar schematic manner that only in the West (*Abendland*), on the basis of Christianity and Reformation, technical development was possible. Only the "liberation of reason for dominance over creation," which took place in the western world, led to the "triumph of technology."[8] Wherever *oriental countries* import modern technology, it "remains completely in the service of belief in God and the building of Islamic community."[9]

Bonhoeffer's schematic and typological view on Islam represents the type of religious studies existing at that time. In Bonhoeffer's library one can find religious studies books, for example, of Helmut von Glasenapp, Friedrich Heiler, Gerardus van der Leeuw, Rudolf Otto, and Johannes Verweyen.[10] Heiler, famous for his book on prayer,[11] worked with *typologies* (e.g., naïve

---

5. I will not analyze Bonhoeffer's view on Judaism, because there have been several studies about that already.

6. DBWE 9:118. He continued: "The Arab stands apart from every person of a different race as a person stands apart from an animal. Mohammed is the prophet of the Arabian tribes. This is why the tendency to propagandize is now totally absent, as in the past when they didn't attempt to evangelize Christians but simply did away with them as non-Arabs, i.e., unbelievers." And he described some folkloristic singing of the Koran on the streets.

7. DBWE 9:118. He confessed: "It would really be interesting to study Islam on its own soil, but it really is very difficult to gain access in some way to the cultic aspects."

8. DBWE 6:117.

9. Ibid., 117.

10. Others are P. Feldkeller and P. Hofmann.

11. Friedrich Heiler, *Das Gebet: Eine religionsgeschichtliche und religionspsychologische Untersuchung* (Munich: Ernst Reinhardt, 1918).

prayer of the primitives, mystical prayer, and prophetic prayer) under which he *subsumed* different religious phenomena. Van der Leeuw, quite similarly, searched for universal structures in religious thinking[12] that help *classify* religious phenomena.[13] Otto started with the idea of a general religious a priori and developed a concept of *the holy*, which he understood as present in the core of all religions.[14] All these authors represent a type of religious studies which, since it uses general terms that are developed from a western framework, and aim at homogenizing the religious variety through a certain typology,[15] is today considered problematic.

Bonhoeffer uses this general, typological perspective quite often. He describes "the desire in *all religions* to have the *spirit* become visible in the *sacrament*"[16]—here he uses *Christian* categories (spirit, sacrament) to analyze all religions, including religions that may not have those categories at all. He also compares *Christianity* with all other religions and diagnoses big differences:[17] In his lectures in Barcelona, he argues that all other religions conceive revelation as revelation of new ideas or new moral imperatives that are part of the general truth, but not as revelation in historical facts as Christianity does: ". . . God's revelation in Christ is revelation in concealment, secrecy, all other so-called revelation is revelation in openness."[18] In *Letters and Papers from Prison*, he

12. So Willem Hofstee, "Art. Leeuw," in RGG[4] 5:174.

13. So Johann Figl, ed., *Handbuch Religionswissenschaft: Religionen und ihre zentralen Themen* (Innsbruck/Wien/Göttingen: Tyrolia/Vandenhoeck & Ruprecht, 2003), 25.

14. Rudolf Otto, *Das Heilige: Über das Irrationale in der Idee des Göttlichen und sein Verhältnis zum Rationalen* (Breslau: Trewendt und Granier, 1917).

15. Understood as self-description of religious science of that time [Joachim] Wach, "Art. Religionswissenschaft," in RGG[2] 4:1954–59.

16. DBWE 8:107 (my emphases).

17. As in DBWE 4:183f.: Jesus "could not consider isolating himself aristocratically with his disciples and transmitting to them in the manner of great founders of religions the doctrines of higher knowledge and more perfect way of life separated from the mass of the people."

18. DBWE 10:465. Krötke, who is referring to this, continues: "Bonhoeffer's theology is . . . a critique of religion, because in his opinion the religions show a tendency away from the concretely near mystery of God in history. Insofar as the religions . . . do not permit God to come near in the concrete sense, they miss the reality of God by veering off instead into the most plausible and likewise fanciful conceptions about God. Quite opposed to this is faith in God on the basis of God's own revelation as a God-given capacity of the human person to allow God to approach." Wolf Krötke, "Die Bedeutung von 'Gottes Geheimnis' für Dietrich Bonhoeffers Verständnis der Religionen und der Religionslosigkeit," in Krötke, *Barmen—Barth—Bonhoeffer: Beiträge zu einer zeitgemäßen christozentrischen Theologie* (Bielefeld: Luther-Verlag, 2009), 333–55, esp. 348. Krötke continues: "The world of religions brings into clear focus the other aspect of the truth of God's revelation, that the human person is related to a mystery that has something to do with him and out of which he lives. The religions are all orientated to the presence of

speaks of "the crucial distinction between Christianity and *all religions* [in regard to the suffering, not omnipotent Christ]. Human religiosity directs people in need to the power of God in the world, God as *deus ex machina*."[19]

From these examples we can see that Bonhoeffer does not have a very differentiated awareness of religious phenomena;[20] he compares other religions to Christianity by using categories from his own tradition, and by quite promptly judging that the other religions don't fulfill these categories. He looks at them from a Christian angle. Sometimes his descriptions of other religions sound almost naïve. Very simplifying, for example, is Bonhoeffer's picture of the religions of India, which he painted in 1932: India is a fertile, sunny world, in which the hand only has to reach out for fruits. Because physical life is so easy the soul lives in free devotion, breathes in unity with the rhythm of life, and recognizes itself in all that lives. In Bonhoeffer's judgment, it is this awe of the holiness of life that leads to the concept of nonviolence and to the aim of giving up oneself.[21]

But did Bonhoeffer not at least have a strong and concrete interest in the Indian religions? Did he not three times make plans to travel to India?[22]

this mystery. Since the religions are as such and by the same token a work of the sinful human being, they live in the tendency to make sure that God comes into view as the highest possibility of this world" (ibid., 349f.)—Editors' translation.

19. DBWE 8:479. See also DBWE 8:480: "'Christians stand by God in God's own pain'—that distinguishes Christians from heathens. 'Could you not stay awake with me one hour?' Jesus asks in Gethsemane. That is the opposite of everything a religious person expects from God." Some greater differentiations can be found in DBWE 8:501, where he distinguishes Christianity from the oriental religions which paint their Gods "in animal forms as the monstrous, the chaotic, the remote, the terrifying," from philosophical concepts of religion that conceive God as "the absolute, the metaphysical, the infinite," and from the Greek religion and its "God-human form of the human being in itself."

20. In *Sanctorum Communio*, Bonhoeffer refers to studies of the sociology of religion and of philosophy of religion (Emil Durkheim, Friedrich Heiler, Georg Simmel, Max Weber), which analyze the communal character of religions in a typological manner (see DBWE 1:131–33, n. 23). But he is also aware that a "collective basis and a corresponding motivation for empirical community formation can be demonstrated only in concrete religions, since *the general concept of religion does not contain specifically social impulses*. Only observation of the concrete characteristics of the religions can discern their possible affinity to community" (DBWE 1:133, n. 23). Thus Bonhoeffer is aware that one needs to have a look at concrete religions to understand their impulses towards community.

21. See DBWE 11:250. This romantic picture is quite astonishing, because only four months before, Bonhoeffer, in a sermon, had described the current hunger crisis in India of millions starving as a "most gruesome reality" (DBWE 11:404).

22. Three times, Bonhoeffer had plans to travel to India. *In 1928* his grandmother encouraged him "to get to know the counterpoint of the world of the east; I am thinking of India, Buddha and his world" (DB-ER, 105); Bethge traces this interest back to "a vague, generalized thirst for new experience that impelled him to seek contact with a different intellectual world," but maybe also to some interest in

There are lots of documents that prove Bonhoeffer wanted to study Gandhi's concept of opposition to the colonial government, his way of following the Sermon on the Mount,[23] and the community life supporting this:[24] In 1934, Bonhoeffer writes in a letter: "there [in India] could be important things to be learned,"[25] and the context shows that he was thinking especially of how to be in opposition to government.[26] In Fanø he states: "Must we be put to shame by non-Christian peoples in the East? Shall we desert the individuals who are risking their lives for this message [of peace]?"[27] Bell, when writing to Gandhi in the same year introducing Bonhoeffer, explained: "He wants to study community life as well as methods of training."[28]

But what about *Hindu spirituality*? It's common in Bonhoeffer scholarship to assume that this was another reason for Bonhoeffer's interest in India.[29] Yet, there are quotes of Bonhoeffer that point in a different direction because they indicate that Bonhoeffer hoped to find in India a new type of *Christianity*. Bonhoeffer writes: "I am becoming more convinced every day that in the West Christianity is approaching its end—at least in its present form, and its present interpretation."[30] Therefore he wants "to get to the Far East"[31]—to find a different form of Christianity there. From India he expects to find the solution to solve the "great dying out of Christianity."[32] He reminds himself: "Christianity did in fact come from the East originally, but it has become so westernized and so permeated by civilized thought that, as we can now see, it is

Gandhi already (ibid., translation altered); *in 1931/32* (see DBWE 10:272, 294; DBWE 11:55; DBWE 12:67, 71); and *in 1934* (see DBWE 13:81, 136, 152, 154, 184, 217; and DB-ER, 406ff.). While at Union, he observed the development in India (see DBWE 10:431f.). He owned some studies in Indian religiosity; see Dietrich Meyer, *Nachlaß Dietrich Bonhoeffer. Ein Verzeichnis. Archiv—Sammlung—Bibliothek* (Munich: Chr. Kaiser, 1987), 223–25.

23. See Andrews's letter to Bonhoeffer, DBWE 13:137.

24. See DBWE 13:152, where Bonhoeffer stresses that he would love to go to Gandhi directly.

25. Ibid.

26. See also DBWE 13:184, where Bonhoeffer emphasizes as well that he wants to go to Gandhi because he hopes to learn from him what "opposition" is.

27. DBWE 13:309.

28. DBWE 13:225. Gandhi responded by inviting Bonhoeffer, see DBWE 13:229f. (The answer addresses only financial aspects and issues of organizing the trip, where to stay, etc.)

29. See, e.g., Reinhold Mokrosch, "'Stationen auf dem Weg zur Freiheit.' Wie mir bei meinen Bonhoeffer-Vorlesungen in Indien der Sinn des Gedichts neu aufging," in *Dietrich Bonhoeffers Christentum: Festschrift für Christian Gremmels*, ed. Florian Schmitz and Christiane Tietz (Gütersloh: Gütersloher, 2011), 386–98, 390f.

30. DBWE 13:81.

31. Ibid.

32. DBWE 11:55.

almost lost to us."[33] Bonhoeffer wonders if the *gospel* can be found in India, with other words and other deeds.[34] And he adds: "If we cannot see in our personal life that Christ has been here, then we want at least to see it in India . . ."[35] These quotes seem to show that Bonhoeffer also had an interest in Indian *Christianity* and in Indian interpretations of the *Christian gospel*.

But could this be possible? What was the situation of Christianity in India at that time? It is quite astonishing to learn that at that time *Christian Ashrams* were of some importance in India. Small groups of Christian men and/or women, some practicing celibacy, lived together and tried to live as conscious Christians in their special cultural context.[36] In these Ashrams, they had regular prayer times and meditation, held church services together, tried to organize their daily lives on a communal basis, and took their common religious praxis as basis for their social and political engagement. Interestingly, most of the Christian Ashrams were founded in the twenties and thirties of the twentieth century, by Protestants who were related to the independence movement and who had intense contacts with Gandhi and Tagore.[37] It's surprising how close the character of those Ashrams comes to Bonhoeffer's own ideas of Christian community and to his interest in Christian communities in England at the same time.

Could Bonhoeffer have known of Christianity in India? To be sure! The first evidence can be found in Bonhoeffer's travel to the United States in 1930. His traveling companion on the ship was Dr. Lucas, a president of a college in Lahore. What kind of college was that? When you do some Internet research you find out that Dr. Lucas was the president of the Forman Christian College in Lahore, now Pakistan,[38] founded in the 1830s. Today the community room of the college is named after Bonhoeffer's companion, Dr. Lucas, who actually was the first person to invite Bonhoeffer to India.

Bonhoeffer could also have known of Christian Ashrams in India because he met Charles Freer Andrews at several ecumenical meetings.[39] Andrews was

---

33. DBWE 13:152.

34. DBWE 11:55: "Is our time over? Has the gospel been given to another people, perhaps proclaimed with *completely* different words and actions? How do you see the eternal nature of Christianity in light of the world situation and our own way of living?"

35. DBWE 11:55.

36. See Hans-Peter Müller, "Art. Ashrams, christliche," in RGG[4] 1:811.

37. See ibid.

38. See http://www.fccollege.edu.pk/.

39. In Cambridge 1931, DB-ER, 194; in Geneva 1932, DB-ER, 249; in Gland 1932, DB-ER, 252, where the situation in India was a topic too.

an Anglican minister and one of Gandhi's closest friends. At those ecumenical conferences, Andrews asked the World Alliance for Promoting Friendship among the Churches to include the *East-Asian Christians* much more strongly than before.[40] Andrews himself was strongly committed to interreligious dialogue, while remaining a Christian.[41]

While these two contacts provide evidence that Bonhoeffer knew of the Indian Christians and their Indian type of Christian spirituality, Bethge mentions that Bonhoeffer during his last months in England studied books of Jack Winslow, and calls Winslow "an expert of Asian spiritual exercises."[42] Actually Winslow's books are books about Christian Indian spirituality. Bonhoeffer owned Winslow's book on the Christian Ashram that he founded: *Christa Seva Sangha* ("Christ Service Society"). Winslow describes the aim of the Ashram as twofold: "a life of common service and equal fellowship for Indians and Europeans; and the development of Indian ways for the expression in India of Christian life and worship."[43]

I do not wish to say that Bonhoeffer was only interested in *Christian* communal life in India. He obviously was interested in Gandhi and his way of lived opposition, and his way of interpreting the Sermon on the Mount. But there is evidence, from Bonhoeffer's letters and from his contacts, that he was also interested in the type of Christianity and Christian community life to be found in India. This fits with the observation that even when speaking of people of other faiths in India, Bonhoeffer does it from a Christian—and precisely from an inclusivist's—perspective. This becomes clear when we read in a letter: "[in India] there's more Christianity in their 'heathenism' than in the whole of our Reich Church."[44]

II. BONHOEFFER'S STRONG CHRISTOLOGY AS A STARTING POINT FOR A CHRISTIAN PERSPECTIVE ON RELIGIOUS PLURALISM

No doubt, Bonhoeffer has a *strong Christology*, which means that Christology is the *cantus firmus* of all his thinking. Christ is in the center of his Christian worldview.[45] One quote from *Ethics* might be enough to verify this: "The

---

40. Cf. DB-ER, 250.

41. Cf. Daniel O'Connor, "Art. Andrews," RGG⁴ 1:473.

42. DB-ER, 407.

43. Jack C. Winslow, *Christa Seva Sangha* (London: The Society for the Propagation of the Gospel in Foreign Parts, 1930), 10.

44. DBWE 13:152.

45. There are some articles that use other theological themes of Bonhoeffer for a Christian theology in the context of religious pluralism: John de Gruchy uses Bonhoeffer's concept of the religious "other" as a

place where the questions about the reality of God and about the reality of the world are answered at the same time is characterized solely by the name: Jesus Christ. . . . From now on we cannot speak rightly of either God or the world without speaking of Jesus Christ."[46] The quote makes clear that when Christians discuss who God is or how the world and its manifold phenomena have to be understood, they point to Christ.

There are scholars in today's academy who argue that such a Christ-centeredness is a hindrance for interreligious dialogue. Whoever wants to enter into interreligious dialogue, they claim, has to weaken the Christian exclusiveness of Christ.[47] Yet if we would minimize Bonhoeffer's emphasis on Christ in order to use his theology in interreligious dialogue, we would lose the center and heart of his theology. Furthermore, there is good reason not to try to approach religious pluralism from a neutral perspective, but from the religious tradition that one belongs to. It is here that religious pluralism is challenging and the encounter of religions is interesting. And third: from a Christian perspective, it would not be satisfying and would be contrary to Bonhoeffer's emphasis on the comprehensiveness of the Christian faith to say: Christ has only to do with Christians, Christ has nothing to do with people from other religions. Therefore I will ask: Does Bonhoeffer's Christology itself contain constructive impulses in the situation of religious pluralism? I will do this by starting with the assumption that Bonhoeffer's *method* to look at the world come of age, which can't be religious anymore, can be used similarly when approaching a world of religious pluralism.[48]

Bonhoeffer's openness for the world come of age which will soon be religionless had two reasons. *On the one hand*, he *observes* the world of his

starting point, for example, in "God's Desire for a Community of Human Beings: Religious Pluralism from the Perspective of Bonhoeffer's Legacy," in *Religion im Erbe: Dietrich Bonhoeffer und die Zukunftsfähigkeit des Christentums*, ed. Christian Gremmels and Wolfgang Huber (Gütersloh: Chr. Kaiser, 2002), 147–63, esp. 149ff. For a similar approach see Jensen, "Religionless Christianity and Vulnerable Discipleship." Christoph Schwöbel, "'Religion' and 'Religionlessness' in *Letters and Papers from Prison*: A Perspective for Religious Pluralism?" in *Mysteries in the Theology of Dietrich Bonhoeffer: A Copenhagen Bonhoeffer Symposium*, ed. Kirsten Busch Nielsen, Ulrik Nissen, and Christiane Tietz (Göttingen: Vandenhoeck & Ruprecht, 2007), 159–84, uses several aspects of Bonhoeffer's concept of a nonreligious Christianity. See also Ralf K. Wüstenberg, "Religionless Christianity and Religious Pluralism: Dietrich Bonhoeffer 'Revisited,'" *Journal of Theology for Southern Africa* 131 (2008): 4–15, esp. 13, who takes Bonhoeffer's "concept of life" as starting point. Krötke, "Die Bedeutung von 'Gottes Geheimnis,'" ibid., discusses the notion of mystery in the same perspective.

46. DBWE 6:54.

47. For a summary of these arguments, see Klaus von Stosch, *Komparative Theologie als Wegweiser in der Welt der Religionen* (Paderborn: Schöning, 2012), 42ff.

day without prejudices: in many respects, the world gets along without any reference to God. *On the other hand*, he *argues Christologically*: Because of the cross of Jesus Christ on which God consented "to be pushed out of the world"[49] the world come of age is accepted by God—and therefore it should be accepted by us as well. Yet the theologian's task still is to understand the world come of age "better . . . than it understands itself, namely from the gospel and from Christ."[50]

The same approach can be taken for the world of religious pluralism. We have already *observed* that the world of today is a world of religious pluralism.[51] Not in the sense that individuals are themselves pluralists but in the sense that differently convicted people exist. Can we also find any Christological insight in Bonhoeffer that helps us comprehend this situation of religious pluralism better, namely from the gospel and from Christ? It is interesting that at this point, there is no need to go "beyond Bonhoeffer." It's enough to look more carefully at what he has already considered.

When writing his *Ethics*, Bonhoeffer actually wanted to address the relationship between Christianity and the other religions. This is not well known, because it is part of his *notes* for the preparation of his *Ethics*. In these notes, Bonhoeffer makes it clear that he considered the chapter "Ethics as Formation" as dealing with the question of "Christianity and the other religions."[52] What is the content of that chapter? In the chapter "Ethics as Formation," Bonhoeffer describes the meaning of Jesus Christ through the phrase "*Ecce homo*—behold, what a human being."[53] He unfolds what God's becoming human in Jesus Christ and Christ's crucifixion and resurrection mean for humanity: "behold God become human"[54]—"behold the *one whom God has*

---

48. It would not be correct to say that our world of religious pluralism is identical with the world come of age, which lives without the religious God; in many religious forms of today, even in Christianity, the religious God, the almighty *deus ex machina* (see DBWE 8:366, 450, 479), is still present.

49. DBWE 8:479.

50. DBWE 8:431.

51. Bonhoeffer did not deduce a general anthropological theory from his observation that the world is getting along without God, for example the theory that human beings as such do not need God (as some critics of religion concluded). He simply stuck to the historical observation. Accordingly, we do not need to deduce a general anthropological theory from our observation that today there exists a variety of vital religions. There is no need to argue that the recurrence of religion in its plurality proves that human beings have to be religious because this is part of their nature. Again, it is enough—and much more fair to atheists—to simply describe the current situation.

52. Dietrich Bonhoeffer, *Zettelnotizen für eine "Ethik,"* ed. Ilse Tödt (Gütersloh: Chr. Kaiser/ Gütersloher Verlagshaus, 1993), 46 (my translation).

53. DBWE 6:82.

judged"[55]—"see the Risen One."[56] Because of Bonhoeffer's note for preparing the *Ethics*, it is legitimate to read these Christological theses as a description of the relationship of Christianity and the other religions.

For Bonhoeffer, the fact that God became human in Jesus Christ shows that God loves real human beings. "What we find repulsive in their opposition to God, what we shrink back from with pain and hostility . . . , this is for God the ground of unfathomable love. . . . While we distinguish between pious and godless, good and evil, noble and base, God loves real people without distinction. God has no patience with our dividing the world and humanity according to our standards and imposing ourselves as judges over them."[57] What does this mean? As God in Jesus Christ loves all human beings, we should stop sorting human beings into groups of pious and godless, etc. We should not sort and judge other *religious people*. This, of course, does not mean to say that all *religions* are equally pious or good or noble. Not to judge the person does not necessarily include a positive judgment on everything the other thinks or does. That is not what *God's love* means. That God loves us does not mean that God acknowledges our goodness or our piety. God's love addresses the person, yet God's love is not a sanctification of the person's convictions or deeds.

Jesus Christ also is the crucified in whom God executed the judgment on himself. All human beings are included in this event.[58] All human beings, no matter which religion they belong to, are now "judged and reconciled by God."[59] This includes a judgment about all religions as an attempt to reach God by one's own effort and to get to God without Christ.[60] Already in a lecture in Barcelona, Bonhoeffer argued that *all religions* are a human path to God.[61] Human beings can't reach God on that path, because "human beings remain human beings, and that means sinners" on that path. Thus "their religion is part of their flesh," "of their desire . . . for their own ego"[62] and therefore stands

54. DBWE 6:84.

55. DBWE 6:88.

56. DBWE 6:91.

57. DBWE 6:84.

58. See DBWE 6:88.

59. DBWE 6:88.

60. See DBWE 6:94: People who are conformed to the crucified "demonstrate in their lives that before God nothing can stand except in judgment and in grace."

61. See DBWE 10:357f.

62. DBWE 10:484. See also DBWE 2:58: "The natural human being has a *cor corvum in se*. Natural religion . . . remains flesh and seeks after flesh. If revelation is to come to human beings, they need to be changed entirely. Faith itself must be created in them. . . . All that pertains to personal appropriation of the fact of Christ is not *a priori*, but God's contingent action on human beings."

under God's judgment. Christ instead is God's path "from eternity into time."[63] Even Christendom stands under God's judgment; it is religion as well.[64] All religions take place in the penultimate, judged by Christ the ultimate.[65]

At the same time, religions, taking place in the penultimate, should be claimed "once again for the ultimate."[66] Bonhoeffer develops this aspect through the idea of an "unconscious Christianity."[67] He considers people of other faiths as Christians—and thus claims other religions for the ultimate of Christ—if they do what is the command of Christ in this situation. Similar to Bonhoeffer's explanation of his interest in India ("there's more Christianity in their 'heathenism' than in the whole Reich Church"), he argues in his *Ethics*: "The human and the good . . . should be claimed for Jesus Christ."[68] When doing this, Christ remains the criterion for what is to be counted as "human" and as "good."

To sum up, the cross means: All human beings, no matter to which religion they belong, are judged and reconciled in Christ. All *religions* are judged as human *paths to God*, and at the same time, *the human and the good which are in correspondence to Christ* should be claimed for Christ.

63. DBWE 10:484.

64. DBWE 10:357f. See also DBWE 8:362f.: "'Christianity' has always been a form (perhaps the true form) of 'religion.'"

65. So Schwöbel, "'Religion' and 'Religionlessness,'" ibid., 183: "Witnessing to the gift of salvation in this exclusiveness includes its comprehensive inclusiveness for the world. . . . For Christians, this includes the liberating insight that the ultimate status of the deities of other religions, quasi-religions and of other spiritual paths to the ultimate goal is denied and they are firmly placed in the realm of the penultimate."

66. DBWE 6:169.

67. Bonhoeffer refers to this concept that you somehow are a Christian but are not aware of it, briefly in one letter from prison, in relation to his "theological theme" and to the distinction between *fides directa* and *fides reflexa* (cf. DBWE 8:489), but he describes it at length in the words of Christoph in his *Fiction from Tegel Prison* as people who don't go to church but have the right ethical behavior, because they still live from Christianity, without knowing it: "That's because without knowing it and certainly without talking about it, in truth they still base their lives on Christianity, an unconscious Christianity'" (DBWE 7:111). Bonhoeffer's poem "Christians and Heathens" could be included here as well. While all human beings go to God in their pain and ask for help, only Christians (here probably including also the unconscious ones) participate in God's suffering, but Christ has died for all, no matter to which religion they belong (DBWE 8:460f.).

68. Bonhoeffer continues (in relation to those shaped by a Christian tradition): ". . . especially where, as an unconscious remnant, they represent a previous bond to the ultimate. It may often seem more serious to address such people simply as non-Christians and urge them to confess their unbelief. But it would be more Christian to claim as Christians precisely such persons who no longer dare to call themselves Christians, and to help them with much patience to move toward confessing Christ" (DBWE 6:169f.). Bonhoeffer also made a marginal notation at the end of the manuscript: "unconscious Christianity" (see ibid., n. 111).

All human beings are judged by God, but all are also included in the event of renewal. Jesus Christ finally is the risen one. In him the "new human being has been created."[69] Bonhoeffer stresses that this is true for all humanity: "In Christ the form of humanity was created anew. What was at stake was not a matter of place, time, climate, race, individual, society, religion [!] or taste. . . . What happened to Christ happened to humanity."[70] The only difference between Christians and people from other religions lies in this, that "only a part of humanity recognizes the form of its savior."[71]

Bonhoeffer continues by saying that when we speak of the formation of the world in Christ, we can only "address humanity in the light of its true form, which belongs to it, which it has already received, but which it has not grasped and accepted, namely the form of Jesus Christ which is its own." In other words, every human being, no matter what religion he or she belongs to, is a member of humanity that has "already received" that new form of Christ, but those belonging to another religion have not "grasped and accepted . . . the form"[72] which is properly their own. Accordingly, all religious efforts of human beings are now taking place in the one Christ-reality, even if they are not aware of it. Therefore Bonhoeffer does not see the others as people who do their religious practice far away from God; they do their prayers, rites, and community life in the realm of the Christ-reality.

But is this not some sort of infringement, making demands on other religions that they will surely reject, because they do not wish to be considered as unconscious Christians or as living in the Christ-reality?

III. The Hermeneutical Premise of Bonhoeffer's Strong Christology

Yes, at first sight, Bonhoeffer's Christological statements seem to be an infringement and to make strange claims on foreign religions. But one has to keep in mind how Bonhoeffer wants his Christological statements to be understood. They do not contain general truth, which can be demonstrated in an abstract, bird's-eye perspective. Their truth can only be recognized in faith, from "within," by those who already are Christians. This is one of the basic insights of *Sanctorum Communio* and of *Act and Being*. The correct response to revelation in the Christ-event is faith. Only Christian faith understands this

---

69. DBWE 6:91.

70. DBWE 6:96.

71. DBWE 6:96.

72. DBWE 6:98.

event coming "'from outside' adequately."[73] For faith does not try to deduce the correctness of the truth claim of revelation, but rather submits to revelation.[74] Everything that has been said in the second part of this chapter is true only from the perspective of Christian faith.

What does this mean? This Christological perspective on the world of religion cannot be presented to other religions as if it would be possible to recognize its truth from the outside, from the perspective of other religions. Christians cannot approach people from other religious traditions demanding that they recognize the Christian truth. Christians can be witness to their own faith, and they might also from time to time invite others to participate in that faith; but this participation would mean stepping inside Christianity, would mean becoming a Christian; and this we cannot expect of people faithful to their own religious convictions.

That the whole world is reconciled in Christ is the Christian perspective—and if Christians believe in Christ as the Lord of the whole world, they cannot leave other human beings out of the Christ-reality. But they cannot expect that people of other religions see it similarly—because without being a Christian believer this is impossible.

A second insight follows from Bonhoeffer's hermeneutical perspective and his emphasis on faith. From the outside, on the level of reflection and phenomenological analysis, Christians are religious people like all the others; and the Christian community, the church, "viewed from the outside,"[75] is a religious community similar to other religious communities. That I *have* faith in Christ, that the church *is* "God's church,"[76] the community of those who believe in Christ and are formed by Christ as the revelation of God,[77] cannot be demonstrated from the outside. "God alone knows whether I have believed; this is not accessible to my reflection. Faith rests in itself as *actus directus* . . ."[78] *"The church . . . logically establishes its own foundation in itself;* like all [!] revelations, it can be judged only by itself. What is to be found is presupposed. Knowledge and acknowledgment of its reality must exist before one can speak about the church."[79]

---

73. DBWE 2:89.

74. See, e.g., *Sanctorum Communio*, DBWE 1:202; *The Young Bonhoeffer*, DBWE 9:500, and *Ecumenical, Academic, and Pastoral Work: 1931–1932*, DBWE 11:260.

75. DBWE 1:126.

76. Ibid.

77. Cf. DBWE 6:93.

78. DBWE 2:128.

79. DBWE 1:127.

From this follows, that the truth of a religion cannot be conceived through comparing religious phenomena. The truth of a religion cannot be judged from outside, it can only be experienced from within, by accepting that truth claim. And it is impossible to argue: My religion is true and yours is not, because I am not able to say something about the truth of the religion of the other from outside.

IV. Practical Consequences for Interreligious Encounter from Bonhoeffer's Christology

In conclusion, Bonhoeffer's strong Christology can be summarized in three theses as follows:

a) I cannot consider myself as a better believer in God than people of other faith traditions. If Christians are aware that only through Christ they are able to stand before God, then they neither idolize themselves nor have contempt for other human beings.[80] Christians cannot "lift themselves above other people or establish themselves as models because they recognize themselves as the greatest of all sinners."[81]

Consequently, Christians cannot consider other religious communities as less close to God than the church but also not as close as or as closer than the church. All these judgments would be comparisons of religious communities from the outside. Of course you can compare religious communities from the outside (e.g., size, aim, rites, etc.), but this comparison does not touch the reality of God; only faith from within a community does.

b) If Christ is the one who is there for others, no matter who the other is, the same should be true for Christians. Christians should be there for others, "even if they do not belong to the Christian community."[82]

c) From a Christian perspective, the other religions take place in the Christ-reality, just as Christianity itself does. Therefore Christians should not be afraid of encountering other religions. No religion belongs to an evil world, for all religions participate in the Christ-reality.[83] Encountering religious people from other religions can include learning[84] from them, being questioned by

---

80. Cf. DBWE 6:94.

81. DBWE 6:95.

82. DBWE 12:365.

83. ". . . it is just the 'evil world' that is reconciled in Christ to God and has its ultimate and true reality not in the devil but, again, in Christ. The world is not divided between Christ and the devil; it is completely the world of Christ, whether it recognizes this or not. . . . The dark, evil world may not be surrendered to the devil, but [must] be claimed for the one who won it by coming in the flesh, by the death and resurrection of Christ" (DBWE 6:65).

them—and questioning them: learning, where they unfold the human and the good; being questioned by them, because they may understand the human and the good better than Christians do; and questioning them, where they contain elements that the Christian cannot understand as human and good.[85] One important result of this is that Christians can work together with people from other faiths to turn the world into a more human place.

84. See Krötke, ibid., 351: Christian faith ". . . judges human ways of life as they actually present themselves according to whether they equip the human person for bearing living witness to God's truth or not."

85. DBWE 6:90, for example, where they adore success or where those who failed hate the successful; and Jesus' "concern is neither success nor failure but willing acceptance of the judgment of God."

19

Bonhoeffer from the Perspective of Intellectual History

Michael P. DeJonge

HISTORY AND THEOLOGY

I find it appropriate that a panel on "Bonhoeffer the theologian" follows a panel on "Bonhoeffer and the historians" because theological and historical inquiries converge in the figure of Bonhoeffer in fascinating ways. Academic interest in Bonhoeffer has tended to come from people we might broadly characterize as theologians: constructive thinkers who approach Bonhoeffer with present-day ethical, theological, political, or ecclesiological concerns in mind. Comparatively speaking, there has been little scholarship taking intellectual historical approaches to Bonhoeffer. By "intellectual historical," here I mean the kind of scholarly approach that foregrounds, to the degree that it is possible, Bonhoeffer's own issues and questions rather than those of the present day.[1] I think there can be and must be a mutually beneficial relationship between constructive theological and intellectual historical work on Bonhoeffer. They need each other. Here is what I mean.

On the one hand, intellectual historical work on Bonhoeffer needs constructive theological work. This is because, as historians have pointed out, Bonhoeffer was a marginal figure in his own time. His reputation has been made postmortem and by theologians. Some historians, lamenting that the theologians' image of Bonhoeffer has exaggerated his historical importance, have suggested that historical attention should be focused elsewhere.[2] I prefer to think that the historian should be reconciled to the reality that Bonhoeffer

---

1. For the purposes of this chapter, what I mean by intellectual history is articulated by Quentin Skinner, who argues that the task of the intellectual historian is "to situate the texts we study within such intellectual contexts as enable us to make sense of what their authors were doing in writing them." To do intellectual history means "to grasp [the authors'] concepts, to follow their distinctions, to appreciate their beliefs and, so far as possible, to see things their way." Quentin Skinner, "Introduction: Seeing Things Their Way," in *Visions of Politics*, vol. 1 (Cambridge: Cambridge University Press, 2002), 3.

continues to attract a tremendous amount of interest from theologians and that he will likely be one of a select number of twentieth-century Christians who will continue to exert an influence on both life and thought in the twenty-first century. Bonhoeffer's perhaps exaggerated importance now is not a reason to direct historical inquiry away from him. Quite the opposite. It is fitting that a figure of such contemporary and perhaps enduring importance be integrated into the history of theology and intellectual history in general. In this way, the success of constructive thought about Bonhoeffer provides the opportunity and even necessity for historical work on Bonhoeffer. Historical work needs or depends on theological work.

On the other hand, constructive theological work on Bonhoeffer needs intellectual historical work. The very idea of entering into a dialogue with Bonhoeffer on contemporary issues presupposes treating Bonhoeffer, to the degree that it is possible, as an other. Bonhoeffer has something to say to us only if he is not us. And Bonhoeffer's otherness depends on a Bonhoeffer firmly rooted in history. For this reason, rigorous historical work on Bonhoeffer is a precondition for the continued vitality of constructive approaches. Theological work needs or depends on historical work.

Happily, such historical *and* theological work is facilitated by the German critical edition and now the English scholarly edition of Bonhoeffer's works. The translators, editors, publishers, and donors of these projects have provided current and future generations of Bonhoeffer scholars with tools and resources for historical *and* theological work unavailable to those who came before. This is because these editions allow us to read Bonhoeffer whole, to read his entire corpus, and to place his major and published works in conversation with his minor and previously unpublished works.

What I wish to do in this chapter is look at how the kind of reading facilitated by these editions has allowed us to progress in our understanding of Bonhoeffer's place in intellectual history or, more narrowly, the history of theology. My approach to situating Bonhoeffer in the history of theology will be to place Bonhoeffer in relationship to Karl Barth. Because it is generally recognized that Barth is the most important theologian of the twentieth century, relating Bonhoeffer to Barth is part of, though certainly not the whole of, the task of situating Bonhoeffer in the history of theology. Specifically, I want to show how, in conversation with Barth, the young Bonhoeffer develops some distinctive aspects of his own theology: an understanding of God as

2. I have in mind Andrew Chandler, "The Quest for the Historical Dietrich Bonhoeffer," *Journal of Ecclesiastical History* 54, no. 1 (2003): 92.

person, and a hermeneutical way of doing theology. These are in contrast to Barth's understanding of God as subject, and his dialectical way of doing theology.[3]

God Is Person

Traditionally, scholarship on Barth and Bonhoeffer has been heavily weighted toward Bonhoeffer's accusation in several of his late, prison letters, that Barth is guilty of something called "positivism of revelation."[4] It is understandable that the positivism-of-revelation charge has drawn so much theological attention, especially given the contingencies of Bonhoeffer reception in the decades following the Second World War, factors such as the popularity, availability, and perceived timeliness of Bonhoeffer's *Letters and Papers from Prison.*

But it could also be argued that starting with the "positivism of revelation" issue from *Letters and Papers* is not the best way to enter into a discussion of Bonhoeffer's relationship to Barth. Such a perspective might be distorting because it requires that we read Bonhoeffer backwards and quite selectively, beginning with an issue raised in a later writing before hunting for relevant material in the earlier writings.

For the reasons I mentioned earlier, we are in a better position now, on the other side of the German and English editions, to understand Bonhoeffer's relationship to Barth. We can add to our understanding of Bonhoeffer's late critique of Barth an account of Bonhoeffer's earlier critique, one developed in *Act and Being* and other early works. It is in these early works that we see Bonhoeffer developing his person-concept of God and hermeneutical form of thinking.

As a way into Bonhoeffer's early critique of Barth, let me take Barth's diagnosis that nineteenth- and early-twentieth-century theology suffers from what I will call the problem of transcendence. Barth thinks that, in ways subtle and not so subtle, theology has come to diminish the transcendence of God. One way that Barth talks about the problem of transcendence is with the language of subject and object. He faults theology for treating humans as the subjects in the story of theology, in the relationship between God and

---

3. A more detailed presentation of this paper's argument can be found in Michael P. DeJonge, *Bonhoeffer's Theological Formation: Berlin, Barth, and Protestant Theology* (Oxford: Oxford University Press, 2012).

4. As Clifford Green has noted, early Bonhoeffer scholarship had often operated with a "teleological bias," focusing on the prison letters at the expense of the "purpose and integrity of the early theology." Clifford J. Green, *Bonhoeffer: A Theology of Sociality*, rev. ed. (Grand Rapids: Eerdmans, 1999), 7ff.

humanity. If humans are the subjects, thinks Barth, it follows quite naturally that God is the object. The problem with treating God as an object is that, according to a basically Kantian epistemology, a known object is in important ways conditioned by the knowing subject. If God is an object of knowledge, then God becomes the opposite of what, according to Barth, God is supposed to be. God is not free and transcendent but rather comes under the power of the knowing subject. In short, if God is an object, then God becomes objectified, and we are left with the problem of transcendence.

Barth's solution to this problem of transcendence is to reorient theology's attention away from humanity and toward God. Now, in order for this reorientation of theology toward God to stick, Barth thinks it is necessary to work out precisely how theology should understand God. So, solving the problem of transcendence requires theology to think hard about the concept of God.

What concept of God, then, does Barth propose? He argues that God should be understood as subject. God is not an object to be known but a subject who reveals. God is a subject who, in a way analogous to Kant's transcendental subject, remains outside of space and time. So that God does not come under threat of objectification, Barth builds his theology on an understanding of God as subject.[5]

This sketch of Barth's theology as a response to the problem of transcendence through a subject-concept of God allows us to position Bonhoeffer's theology in relationship to Barth's. Bonhoeffer's early critique of Barth both affirms certain aspects of Barth's project while rejecting others.

First the affirmation. In the terms that I have outlined here, we can say specifically that Bonhoeffer follows Barth in recognizing that the problem of transcendence demonstrates the inadequacy of objective concepts of God, and requires theology to rethink the concept of God. Unless we recognize this Barthian background to Bonhoeffer's thinking—the conviction that the problem of transcendence requires a move away from objective concepts of God—it seems to me impossible to understand Bonhoeffer's thinking. On this count, Bonhoeffer is thoroughly Barthian.

But now the rejection. If Bonhoeffer agrees that the problem of transcendence requires a nonobjective concept of God, he disagrees about how to conceive of God's non-objectivity.[6] He resists Barth's subject-concept of

5. For more on Barth's theology as relevant for Bonhoeffer's early thinking, see DeJonge, *Bonhoeffer's Theological Formation*, ch. 3.

6. This is a good example of the kind of insight we gain through the Bonhoeffer Werke and their English translations. Bonhoeffer offers this succinct account of his divergence from Barth in lecture notes

God. If God is a subject, then God remains essentially outside of space and time. Bonhoeffer thinks this leads to a whole host of questions about the knowability and haveability of God's revelation. This in turn raises questions about the continuity of the Christian life that rests on knowledge of God. Bonhoeffer recognizes that Barth works to provide answers to these questions, but he is skeptical that such work will ever overcome the starting point of a theology that locates God's transcendence as transcendence outside of space and time. Ultimately, Bonhoeffer thinks a subject-concept of God is inadequate to reflect the God of the Bible, who is somehow haveable or graspable in the Christian life.

Essentially, then, Bonhoeffer wants to secure God's transcendence without removing God from history. Bonhoeffer wants to deal with the problem of transcendence in a way that nonetheless portrays that transcendence as transcendence in history. The difficulties facing this impulse are clear. How can theology portray God as somehow in space and time without delivering God up to objectification? According to the Kantian logic that drives both the problem of transcendence and Barth's solution to it, objects are liable to objectification precisely because they are conditioned by space and time; subjects are not liable to objectification precisely because they are not conditioned by space and time. So, it seems that either God is transcendent and outside of space and time or God's transcendence is diminished as God is in space and time. How can Bonhoeffer work his way through this dilemma to portray God as transcendent in history?

Bonhoeffer's solution hangs on the introduction of a third concept in addition to subject and object; this concept is person. According to Bonhoeffer, person is, like a subject, free from objectification, but, like an object, in space and time. For Bonhoeffer, person is a concept that captures the positive aspects of both subject and object without their negative features. For this reason, Bonhoeffer argues that God should be understood as person.[7]

I cannot deal in this context with the complexities of Bonhoeffer's notion of person. Nor can I demonstrate that the various implications following from it are so dramatic that it ought to be recognized as the central concept of Bonhoeffer's early thought. I can only hint at the importance of this concept by pointing out what it gains Bonhoeffer in relationship to the problem of transcendence. Namely, it allows Bonhoeffer to secure God's transcendence as

---

not published in his lifetime: Dietrich Bonhoeffer, "The History of Twentieth-Century Systematic Theology" in *Ecumenical, Academic and Pastoral Work: 1931–1932*, ed. Victoria J. Barnett, Mark S. Brocker, and Michael B. Lukens (Minneapolis: Fortress Press, 2012), DBWE 11:233–34.

7. See especially DeJonge, *Bonhoeffer's Theological Formation*, ch. 4.

transcendence in history. This in turn means the concept of person marks off Bonhoeffer's theology from Barth's, since it grounds his alternative solution to the shared problem of transcendence. Bonhoeffer argues that while Barth is correct to seek a nonobjective concept of God, God should be understood not as subject, but as person.

Thinking Hermeneutically

I said that I cannot discuss all the various implications that follow from Bonhoeffer's concept of person, but I do want to discuss one important implication. Bonhoeffer's understanding of God as person encourages a certain style of thinking that I call hermeneutical.[8] With "hermeneutical" I am not referring to theories of interpretation but rather, as I will explain in a moment, to the way of understanding the relationship of parts and wholes that stands behind such theories.

In order to bring Bonhoeffer's hermeneutical style of thinking into view, I need first to talk about the understanding of the incarnation that stands behind Bonhoeffer's person-concept of God. Bonhoeffer's person-concept of God presupposes an understanding of the incarnation in which God enters history without reserve. God does more than act in history; God's very being enters history. God enters the person of Christ in such a way that God's divinity fully enters humanity. So, standing behind Bonhoeffer's person-concept of God is a radical understanding of the incarnation in which otherwise irreconcilable oppositions, oppositions between history and eternity or divinity and humanity, are overcome. Add to this understanding of the incarnation Bonhoeffer's claims about what he calls Christ-reality; for Bonhoeffer, Christ, in some way, is reality. This means that, for Bonhoeffer, reality itself has the form of reconciled opposites.

Here is what all of this implies for Bonhoeffer's form of thought. To do theology with a person-concept of God is to take seriously the reality that, in the person of Christ, God has overcome the oppositions between eternity and time and between God and humanity. In fact, theology begins with, or thinks from, these reconciliations. For Bonhoeffer, there is no thinking about God except as the God who is reconciled to humanity, and there is no talk about humanity except as humanity that is reconciled to God. There is no thinking about history except as history sanctified by God's entry into history, and there is no talk about God except as the God who has entered history. To think from

8. See especially ibid., 97ff.

a person-concept of God means there can be no reference to the oppositions apart from their reconciliation. In other words, there can be no reference to the parts apart from the logically prior whole: a hermeneutic style of thinking.

Let me give just one of the many examples of Bonhoeffer's hermeneutic style of thinking in action.[9] In *Discipleship*, Bonhoeffer takes on the traditional Lutheran theme of the relationship between faith and works. Understanding this relationship properly means countering two errors. The first is works-righteousness, the idea that works logically precede faith. The second error is what Bonhoeffer calls cheap grace, the idea that faith precedes works, even making works unnecessary. Both of these errors, works-righteousness and cheap grace, share the same error of separating faith from works, and then privileging one over the other. Against these, Bonhoeffer argues that faith and works are inseparable as parts of a logically prior whole, the life of discipleship. So in this example Bonhoeffer thinks hermeneutically, countering two erroneous ways of thinking that establish as oppositions two aspects of a unified life in Christ.

This hermeneutical way of thinking again locates Bonhoeffer in relationship to Barth and thereby within the history of theology. A basic commitment of Barth's solution to the problem of transcendence, and of his theology in general, is the rigorous maintenance of the distinction between God and humanity. Even during revelation and in the incarnation, God remains God and humanity remains humanity. It is this understanding of revelation and incarnation that Barth's dialectical thinking is designed to respect. Barth thinks dialectically—both affirming and denying that God and humanity come together—in order to respect the not-yet-ness of the reconciliation of God and humanity.

The contrast between Bonhoeffer's hermeneutic thinking and Barth's dialectical thinking is noteworthy because Bonhoeffer is sometimes presented as an adherent of dialectical theology. But according to the meaning of dialectic just outlined—the thought form designed to respect the not-yet-ness of the reconciliation of God and creation—is the sense in which Bonhoeffer tends to use the term in his early critique of Barth. And when dialectic is understood in this way, Bonhoeffer offers a fundamental critique of dialectical theology.

---

9. For more examples, see DeJonge, *Bonhoeffer's Theological Formation*, ch. 8.

CONCLUSION

With the advantage of the critical and scholarly editions, Bonhoeffer scholarship can now read Bonhoeffer whole. To a greater degree than before, we can approach his thought on its own terms. I have suggested that the central category of Bonhoeffer's early theology is the concept of person. By virtue of God's entry into history in the person of Christ, thinks Bonhoeffer, God and revelation have the form of person; they are transcendent in history. From this core of Bonhoeffer's early theology, a number of important intellectual historical questions can begin to be addressed. The one I have discussed here is Bonhoeffer's relationship to Karl Barth.

Barth convinces Bonhoeffer that the problem of transcendence poses a fundamental challenge for theology that can be met only through a nonobjective concept of God. In this sense, Bonhoeffer is a Barthian. But on the basis of this shared agreement there is a basic disagreement about how to understand God's non-objectivity. Barth understands God as a subject whose being remains outside of history, while Bonhoeffer understands God as a person whose being is in history. Since the concept of God is a fundamental concept of a theology designed to address the problem of transcendence, this disagreement constitutes a basic opposition between Barth's and Bonhoeffer's theologies. Bonhoeffer's understanding of God as person means he sees the reconciliation of God and world as an accomplished fact in the historical person of Christ. Such an understanding of reconciliation requires not dialectical but hermeneutical thinking, a way of thinking that begins with the reconciliation of God and world in Christ. Because Barth is generally recognized as the most significant theologian of the twentieth century, positioning Bonhoeffer in relationship to him in this way brings us closer to integrating Dietrich Bonhoeffer into this history of theology and intellectual history in general.

20

Bonhoeffer's Contribution to a New Christian Paradigm

Clifford J. Green

The publication of the complete works of Dietrich Bonhoeffer, first in German and now in English, should prompt theologians to address the question: What is Bonhoeffer's theology *read as a whole* all about? Is there a coherence to it? Are his writings just fragments, or is there a unifying perspective? I will argue that there is a fundamental vision, namely, a worldly theology centered in Christ *for* the world and Christ *in* the world. Further, I contend that Bonhoeffer became increasingly clear about the necessity of a new Christian paradigm, and made essential contributions to it.

I make these assertions quite aware that Bonhoeffer the theologian has largely disappeared behind the dramatic narrative of Bonhoeffer the historical agent, not only among the general public but even among theologians. In fact this process began quite early, as John Macquarrie exemplified in a 1970 review of Bonhoeffer in the *New York Times Book Review*.[1]

One way to rebut this neglect of Bonhoeffer the thinker is to show that Bonhoeffer's theology is not an epiphenomenon of the church struggle and political resistance to National Socialism. Witness the foundations he had laid down before 1933. The theology of his two dissertations,[2] his new valorization of the Sermon on the Mount beginning in 1931, his reconfiguring the relation of faith and obedience as discipleship, his foundation for the book *Discipleship*[3]—all of this was completed in the five years *before* Hitler dominated

---

1. See Clifford Green, *Bonhoeffer: A Theology of Sociality*, rev. ed. (Grand Rapids: Eerdmans, 1999), 6, note 6.

2. See comments below. For *Sanctorum Communio*, see Green, *Bonhoeffer: A Theology of Sociality*, esp. ch. 2; for *Act and Being*, see Michael P. DeJonge, *Bonhoeffer's Theological Formation: Berlin, Barth, and Protestant Theology* (Oxford: Oxford University Press, 2012).

3. The 1932 address "Christ and Peace" (DBWE 12:258–62) presented central ideas of the 1937 publication *Nachfolge* (*Discipleship*).

the scene. Further, Bonhoeffer, who was both philosophical and a biblical theologian, was profoundly influenced by Luther and Barth. In addition, offering a theological alternative to Kant was an enduring effort of his writings from first to last. None of this can be reduced to, or deduced from, the struggle against Hitler and National Socialism. I do not wish in the least to abstract Bonhoeffer's thought from his life and history. But his theology must be understood in its own integrity and relative autonomy, and in relation to its intrinsic sources and traditions.

With respect to the paradigm issue, we should note that Bonhoeffer's theological work took place in the ferment of twentieth-century Christian theology about the very nature of the Christian paradigm in the modern world. (I will illustrate historically what I mean by "paradigm" in the next section of this chapter.) Barth championed a theology of revelation against what he called neo-Protestant cultural-anthropocentric theology. Very differently, Bultmann caused an uproar by proposing that the modern scientific method and mentality required demythologizing the biblical and traditional worldview. (Note well: before Bonhoeffer criticized Bultmann, he praised him.) Process theology tried a different tack in response to the scientific challenge. Tillich thought the transcendence problem could be resolved by a philosophy of being. In a different mode, various forms of liberation theology—Black theology, Latin American liberation theology, feminist theology—challenged the traditional paradigm, rebelling against historic oppressions and social injustices. Each of these very different theological movements simultaneously critiques the tradition and addresses contemporary concerns. They all pose fundamental questions to the inherited Christian paradigm. Bonhoeffer's thinking—he belonged to a younger generation than Barth, Bultmann, and Tillich—was part of this ferment in twentieth-century Protestant theology about an authentic Christian paradigm in the modern age.

PARADIGM SHIFTS: FROM ATHANASIUS TO ANSELM, FROM PAUL TO LUTHER

I want to situate Bonhoeffer's theology in the framework of the big picture of Christian history, exemplified by a comparison of the patristic Athanasius with the early medieval Anselm, and of the late medieval Luther with the Apostle Paul. Athanasius, Anselm, and Luther each exemplify different forms of the Christian paradigm, and they illustrate paradigm[4] shifts.

---

4. Briefly stated, I use the term "paradigm" here to mean a normative complex of beliefs, images, and practices that give a distinctive focus and pattern to Christian life. Central to each historical variation is a

For the Harvard historian George Hunston Williams, Athanasius (296–373) represents baptismal redemption.[5] His treatise on the incarnation[6] presents the triumph of *Christus Victor* over the devil, demonic powers, and death. Human beings, created *ex nihilo* by the power of the divine Word, were sustained in their creatureliness by the creative Word. But sin vitiated their bond to the Creator and put them in thrall to the devil, subjecting humanity to corruption in death, to the physical and spiritual entropy that regressed back to the *nihil* from which they had come. In the goodness and loving-kindness of God, the Word became flesh to reverse the corruption and redeem the creation. Taking a human body, Christ gave his body over to death on behalf of all, so that those who died in him through baptism would, first, be relieved of death as the consequence of sin, and second, by partaking of his resurrection in baptism, would be restored to incorruption. Christ is the *Christus Victor*. His cross, says Athanasius repeatedly, is "a monument of victory."[7] Baptism, administered decisively at Easter, is the once-in-a-lifetime event, the preeminent sacrament in which the faithful receive salvation by participating in the death and resurrection of Christ. With Athanasius we are still in a world that is not yet officially Christian, and "baptism remained preeminently an experiential sacrament of adult believers."[8]

The Christendom of Anselm (1033–1109) in the eleventh century is a different world. Now virtually everybody is Christian. Baptism was no longer the identity-changing transition from paganism, polytheism, and the rule of the devil; it was the normal childhood beginning of everyday Christian life. Now the monastic practice of penitential piety was the norm for a truly "religious" Christian life. Anselm, too, wrote a treatise on the incarnation, now in a changed spiritual context, and provided the atonement theory that informed the theology of the Catholic Mass and, later, the altar call of every Protestant revivalist preacher. Central now is the Christology of medieval penitential piety,[9] the *Christus patiens*, the suffering Christ whose sacrifice is

controlling image of Christ that correlates to a particular diagnosis of, and remedy for, the human condition. Stated theologically, this is a correlation of Christology and soteriology. My use of "paradigm" is not based on the theory of Thomas Kuhn in his *The Structure of Scientific Revolutions*, and differs from his usage in essential respects.

5. George Hunston Williams, *Anselm: Communion and Atonement* (St. Louis: Concordia, 1960).

6. *On the Incarnation of the Word of God*, ed. E. R. Hardy, Library of Christian Classics, vol. 3, (Philadelphia: Westminster, 1954), 55–110. Williams notes multiple patristic "baptismal" theories of salvation and remarks that they are not mutually exclusive (see *Anselm*, 13f., n. 15).

7. Ibid., 77, 79, 84.

8. Williams, *Anselm*, 18.

reiterated in the Mass. Baptism is no longer the preeminent sacrament, the singular, life-changing redemptive event that joins the believer to the death and resurrection of Christ. Now the Eucharist is the center of Christian piety and devotion, the supreme "means of grace." Day by day, nurtured by the practice of self-examination, confession, and penance,[10] and fed at the altar in the Mass, monks and ordinary Christians dealt with the sins of everyday life and grew in grace. Western iconography now portrayed not the *Christus Victor* but the *Christus Patiens*, the suffering Christ, the crucifix later found in every parish church,[11] the sacrificial "lamb of God who takes away the sins of the world." Williams summarizes Anselm's agenda thus: he was a devout monk for whom "Pauline Law [i.e., Torah], patristic death, and pagan fate were experientially remote." He had "left the Christian world to seek salvation in . . . a Benedictine monastery" whose sacramental life had evolved over a millennium. He needed "to reformulate for his age a scholastic answer to the question of how man is saved and also from what."[12] In short, he articulated a new paradigm, one that has endured among many Christians into our own time. The new paradigm, centered in a reformulated Christology and soteriology, reshaped the whole pattern and interpretation of life.

Luther represents a variant on the Anselmian paradigm with his reforming doctrine of grace and justification by faith, *sola fide*. He is a late-medieval example of the penitential piety just described, and he illustrates a paradigm shift in his exegesis of Paul in Romans.[13] Luther purports to leap right over Anselm and Athanasius and go straight back to Paul. That he was actually rereading Paul we see by asking: What do Paul and Luther respectively mean by "law" and "justification"? And what crucial issues in their different religious and historical-social contexts did these key terms engage?

According to Krister Stendahl, for Paul the law is Torah, and the crucial issue is whether the gospel of Jesus the Messiah is for Jews only, or for Gentiles too, i.e., for everyone. Paul's answer: Gentiles do not have to become Jews first,

---

9. For a concise comparison of baptism and Eucharist as "competitive" sacraments correlated to distinct theories of atonement, see Williams, *Anselm*, 10.

10. By this time penance is a sacrament interposed between baptism and Eucharist.

11. On the transition from the regal Romanesque crucifix to the Gothic Man of Sorrows, see Williams, *Anselm*, 25, citing Southern, *The Making of the Middle Ages* (London: Arrow Books, 1959); see the illustrations in ch. 5.

12. Williams, *Anselm*, 26.

13. See Krister Stendahl's groundbreaking article in Pauline studies, "The Apostle Paul and the Introspective Conscience of the West," *Harvard Theological Review* 56 (1963): 199–215; also 78–96 in Stendahl, *Paul among Jews and Gentiles* (Philadelphia: Fortress Press, 1976), the edition I cite here.

by circumcision and submitting to the laws of Torah. They are "justified by faith" in the Messiah, not by following the laws of Torah. Faith and justification, then, resolve a religious-social problem for Paul, the problem of incorporating Gentiles into the messianic community. This issue was settled already in the first century. Paul was not trying to resolve a timeless human problem of the conflicted conscience; he was not addressing an intra-psychic problem of individual conscience and guilt (e.g., "the good that I would I do not, and the evil I would not is what I do"[14]). That is to read a post-Augustine problematic back into Paul. On the contrary, according to Stendahl, the apostle had a quite robust conscience.[15]

But this is precisely the problem for Luther, as he reveals in his Galatians commentary and the Preface to his Latin Writings. He felt himself "a sinner before God with an extremely disturbed conscience." Indeed, he "raged with a fierce and troubled conscience"[16] against the wrath and punishment of the righteous God. *This* is the problem that Luther's paradigm addresses, what Erik Erikson calls "the hypertrophy of the negative conscience"[17] derived from Luther's monastic experience of the medieval penitential piety. In *this* context "law" is no longer Torah but the righteous demand and judgment of God. In *this* context, justification by faith apart from the law is the answer to the question "How do I find a gracious God?" It is not the answer to Paul's question about Jews, Gentiles, and the Messiah.[18] Luther's reading of Paul, in the radically different spiritual and social context of the sixteenth century, updated the Anselmian paradigm.[19] It was a saving and liberating message that spoke to the spiritual crises of the age. Luther's teaching gave rise to a theological architecture of traditional Lutheranism with four main pillars—the doctrine of law and gospel and the doctrine of two kingdoms—an architecture that continues to have personal and political traction in some quarters down to our own time.

---

14. Romans 7:19.

15. Stendahl, *Paul among Jews and Gentiles*, 80.

16. Luther, "Preface to the Complete Edition of Luther's Latin Writings," in *Luther's Works*, vol. 34, *Career of the Reformer IV*, ed. Lewis W. Spitz (Philadelphia: Fortress Press, 1960), 336–37.

17. Erikson, *Young Man Luther* (New York: Norton, 1962), 195.

18. Stendahl, *Paul among Jews and Gentiles*, 83.

19. By comparison with Paul, Luther represents a new paradigm; by comparison with Anselm, Luther represents a revision, especially in his interpretation of how Christ's sacrifice is appropriated by the faithful.

Bonhoeffer's Statements Bearing on the Paradigm Issue

Following these examples of major historical paradigm shifts, I will now present a number of representative statements characteristic of Bonhoeffer's theology, drawn from various stages of his work.[20] In retrospect there is a real coherence to this series of statements, until finally, in several paragraphs in his prison letters, he asserts the need for a new paradigm for the coming age—though without using the term "paradigm" of course. Most passages are familiar, though they have never been collected together previously. They critique common versions of an inherited Catholic-Reformation—predominantly Lutheran—paradigm, and they also reveal Bonhoeffer reaching for something new. I do not regard this list as a developmental sequence, but rather as a series of clues pointing to the paradigm issue. Later in the chapter I will offer a more systematic interpretation of key ideas.

1927: "*The concepts of person, community, and God* are inseparably and essentially interrelated."[21] This key statement expresses Bonhoeffer's conviction about "the social intention of all the basic Christian concepts,"[22] which is developed in what I call his "theology of sociality." It is intrinsically connected to the next quotation arguing that a social rather than an epistemological model is the proper framework for Christian theology. This refers to the Kantian impact on nineteenth- and early twentieth-century Protestant theology up to Barth and Bultmann, for example in Barth's appropriation of the terms "Subject" and "act" applied to God and revelation.[23] These statements signal a shift from an epistemological framework to a social model of theological thinking.

1927: "*The attempt to derive the social from the epistemological category must be rejected. . . .*" "Thus the basic problem [of *Sanctorum Communio*] can be defined as the problem of a specifically Christian social philosophy and sociology."[24]

1927: "Conscience can just as well be the ultimate prop of human self-justification as the site where Christ strikes home at one through the law."[25] Here the common view of conscience in the traditional Lutheran law-gospel

---

20. At the Union Seminary conference, the paragraphs in this section were provided in a handout and only briefly summarized in the presentation.

21. Bonhoeffer, *Sanctorum Communio* (DBWE 1) (Minneapolis: Fortress Press, 1998), 34, Bonhoeffer's italics.

22. Ibid., 21.

23. See DeJonge's analysis of Barth in *Bonhoeffer's Theological Formation*; see also Bultmann's neo-Kantianism.

24. DBWE 1:45, Bonhoeffer's italics, and 22, note 5. See also Green, *Bonhoeffer*, 23.

25. DBWE 1:108.

model is critiqued, while the critique of Gogarten in the next quotation attacks the common view of the state in the two-kingdoms model.

1933: "Gogarten ignores the ambiguity of the state. He proclaims a Christian conservatism. That is Lutheran, but [it is] not from the New Testament. The state can be seen as the order of evil."[26]

1934: "It is high time to bring the focus back to the Sermon on the Mount, to some degree on the basis of a restoration of Reformation theology, but in a way different from the Reformation understanding. . . . The new church that must come into being in Germany will look very different from the opposition church of today."[27] Such a different understanding would not regard of the Sermon on the Mount as a "mirror" to reveal sin, but as an encounter with the word and command of Jesus. Here the relation of "law" and "gospel" is reconfigured to display the coinherence of faith and ethics, belief and obedience, that Bonhoeffer called "discipleship." The following quotation exemplifies that coinherence in the chapters of *Discipleship* leading up to the exposition of the Sermon on the Mount.

1937: "*Only those who obey believe and only those who believe are obedient.*"[28]

1940: "It is a denial of God's revelation in Jesus Christ to wish to be 'Christian' without being 'worldly' or [to] wish to be worldly without seeing and recognizing the world in Christ. Hence there are not two realms but only the one realm of the Christ-reality, in which the reality of God and the reality of the world are united. Because this is so, the theme of two realms, which has dominated the history of the church again and again, is foreign to the New Testament."[29] This very wide-ranging critique involves not only the familiar Lutheran pairs law-gospel and two-kingdoms, but a host of others spelled out especially in *Ethics*. The issue of being "worldly" and "Christian" is part of a long list: natural-supernatural, profane-sacred, rational-revelational, good-evil, is-ought, knowing-doing, idea-reality, reason-instinct, necessity-freedom, universal-concrete, individual-collective. Because the "Christ-reality" (*Christuswirklichkeit*) is the reconciliation of God and world in Jesus Christ,

---

26. DBWE 12:203. Probably January 1933. See my comment on this passage in Green, *Bonhoeffer*, 205–6, n. 58.

27. Letter to Reinhold Niebuhr, July 13, 1934, DBWE 12:183–84. The editors read the reference to "Reformation theology" as referring to the "solus Christus" of the Barmen Declaration the previous May; "Opposition Church" refers to the Confessing Church movement. Distinctive is Bonhoeffer's reference to the Sermon on the Mount, which is not in the Barmen Declaration, and insisting that it needs to be understood differently from the "Reformation understanding."

28. Bonhoeffer, *Discipleship*, DBWE 4:63, Bonhoeffer's italics, my translation; see esp. n. 16.

29. *Ethics*, DBWE 6:58.

then a "worldly Christianity" is Bonhoeffer's alternative to the dualism worldly-otherworldly.

April 30, 1944: "What keeps gnawing at me is the question, what is Christianity, or who is Christ actually for us today?"[30] This statement launches the theological reflections in the prison letters. Bonhoeffer asks about the fundamental meaning of Christianity and Christ in relation to the modern age, the "world come of age." This is a succinct statement of the paradigm issue.

August 3, 1944: "Outdated controversies, especially the interconfessional ones; the differences between Lutheran and Reformed (and to some extent Roman Catholic) are no longer real."[31] If Christianity for a thousand years has been divided into Orthodox and Catholic, Catholic and Protestant, Lutheran and Reformed, these controversies are outdated because they do not address the decisive issues of faith and life in the emerging age. Even the confessionalism of the Confessing Church, necessary though it was, is critiqued in the following quotation because it does not exemplify a personal faith providing a compelling reason for following Jesus. Implication: a new paradigm is needed.

August 3, 1944: "Confessing Church: revelation theology. . . . Little personal faith in Christ. 'Jesus' disappears from view. Sociologically: no impact on the broader masses."[32]

June 27, 1944: "Christianity is always characterized as a religion of redemption. Isn't there a cardinal error here, through which Christ is separated from the OT and interpreted in the sense of redemption myths?"[33] In this and the following statement Bonhoeffer characterizes prevailing beliefs about redemption and personal salvation as otherworldly and individualistic, and therefore unbiblical. A new paradigm would reframe salvation in terms of "God's righteousness and kingdom on earth [as] the center of everything. . . . What matters is not the beyond but this world. . . ."[34]

May 5, 1944: "Hasn't the individualistic question about saving our personal souls almost faded away for most of us? Isn't it our impression that there are really more important things than this question (perhaps not more important than this *matter*, but certainly more important than the *question*!?)? I know it sounds outrageous to say that, but after all, is it not fundamentally biblical? Does the question of saving one's soul even come up in the Old Testament? Is God's righteousness and kingdom on earth not the center of everything? And

30. Bonhoeffer, *Letters and Papers from Prison*, DBWE 8:362.

31. DBWE 8:502.

32. DBWE 8:500.

33. DBWE 8:447.

34. DBWE 8:373.

is Romans 3:24ff not the culmination of the view that God alone is righteous, rather than an individualistic doctrine of salvation? What matters is not the beyond but this world, how it is created and preserved, is given laws, reconciled and renewed."[35] In this passage, "God's righteousness and kingdom on earth" is the alternative to a doctrine of saving one's personal soul construed as a redemption from this world into the "beyond" (*Jenseits*).

May, 1944: "But we too are being thrown back all the way to the beginnings of our understanding. What reconciliation and redemption mean, rebirth and Holy Spirit, love for one's enemies, cross and resurrection, what it means to live in Christ and follow Christ, all that is so difficult and remote that we hardly dare speak of it anymore. In these words and actions handed down to us, we sense something totally new and revolutionary, but we cannot yet grasp it and express it. . . . It is not for us to predict the day—but the day will come—when people will be once more called to speak the word of God in such a way that the world is changed and renewed. It will be in a new language, perhaps quite nonreligious language, but liberating and redeeming like Jesus's language, so that people will be alarmed and yet overcome by its power—the language of a new righteousness and truth, a language that proclaims that God makes peace with humankind and that God's kingdom is drawing near."[36] These words in the meditation for his godson's baptism are the most pregnant formulation of the paradigm problem that Bonhoeffer makes without explicitly using the concept.

In all the above quotations, then, and especially in the prison theology, the underlying issue is not just another hermeneutical proposal (like Bultmann's demythologizing, for example). Rather, it is a sustained effort to articulate a fundamental restatement of the Christian paradigm itself. I don't suggest that Bonhoeffer was fully aware of what he was trying to do, though he came close to it in the prison theology. This series of quotations from Bonhoeffer's earliest to his latest writings contains two main themes: critique of traditional Catholic-Reformation-Lutheran[37] ideas, and pointers toward a fundamental restatement of the Christian paradigm.

35. DBWE 8:372–73.

36. DBWE 8:389–90.

37. Bonhoeffer's critique of various formulations of the Lutheran tradition is relevant to the issue of a new Christian paradigm, and raises the complex question of his own relation to Luther's theology. I hold that in major theological points he differed from Luther, and yet on the central point of the real presence of Christ in the world he was Lutheran to the core. I have addressed the Bonhoeffer-Luther relationship at some length elsewhere: see the article, "Christus in Mundo, Christus pro Mundo: Bonhoeffer's Foundations for a New Christian Paradigm," in note 1 above. See also Green, *Bonhoeffer*, 122–25, 166–70, 287–91; also Green, "Bonhoeffer in the Context of Erikson's Luther Study," in *Psychohistory and*

Toward a New Christian Paradigm: Worldly, Nonreligious Christianity

My proposal is that the new Christian paradigm Bonhoeffer was beginning to articulate affirms the worldly presence of Christ and the worldly-social character of Christian existence. That is its positive affirmation. Negatively, the new paradigm is a polemic against any dualism of another world or reality behind and above the actual present world, a rejection of rooting Christ and Christian existence in such other reality. The logic of Bonhoeffer's thinking leads to the assertion: there is no "up."

Bonhoeffer's path to the worldly, nonreligious Christianity of his letters from prison was a complex twenty-year pilgrimage. Here I can only highlight three examples from this development: the worldliness of Christ and the church in *Sanctorum Communio*; the explicit critique of otherworldliness in the 1932 exposition of the Lord's Prayer; and the programmatic advocacy of a new worldly Christianity in the prison letters.

First example. *Sanctorum Communio* is already "worldly" theology. I have called it a "theology of sociality." It is more than ecclesiology—it is concerned with creation, sin, and redemption understood as social realities. The transcendence of God is encountered in the midst of human social and communal relations. Bonhoeffer boldly states this, in italics, of the I-You relationship: "*The You of the other person is the divine You.*"[38] The real presence of Christ in the Christian church-community means two things: first, it is Christ's presence that makes it church: the *sanctorum communio* is "Christ existing as church-community" (*Christus als Gemeinde existierend*); second, the church is the new humanity, that is, what is going on in the church goes on representatively for all humanity. The renewal of human life by the divine love creates the new community as a co-humanity of love.

Second example. If *Sanctorum Communio* represents a positive presentation of the worldly communal presence of Christ in historical-social life, its counterpart is the vigorous polemic against otherworldliness in the November 1932 address, "Thy Kingdom Come: The Prayer of the Church-Community for God's Kingdom on Earth."[39] Consistently Bonhoeffer states that God's

---

Religion: The Case of Young Man Luther, ed. Roger A. Johnson (Philadelphia: Fortress Press, 1977), 162–96.

38. *Sanctorum Communio*, DBWE 1:55.

39. DBWE 12:285–97.

world is dawning in *this* world, and that those who pray for the coming of God's kingdom do so only "as those who are wholly on the earth . . . [in] the most profound solidarity with the world."[40] Thus, even though secular Christians are roundly criticized by Bonhoeffer, it is the otherworldly Christians, lusting for an eternal hereafter, who come off worse in the polemics. Bonhoeffer advocates *Christian worldliness* as the alternative to both secularized Christianity and Christian otherworldliness.[41]

Third example: *Letters and Papers from Prison.* Here Bonhoeffer comes closest to explicitly stating what he was implicitly reaching for all along, namely, that the trajectory of his theology leads to a new Christian paradigm. In the prison letters he looks at the self-understanding of modern people, at the culture and psyche of modernity. And he lifts up his mind's eye from the minutiae of the church struggle, and the chess-like maneuvering of the resistance and conspiracy, to review the long history of Christianity. Then he asks: What form of Christianity is viable now? That is to say: What is the paradigm of the Christianity of the future? What are the problems with the inherited paradigm? What are the lineaments of a new paradigm? His name for the new paradigm is a "worldly nonreligious" Christianity.[42]

The prison theology carries forward and intensifies the polemic against otherworldliness in the address "Thy Kingdom Come . . . on Earth." There are several impressive examples in the list of quotations above. Two brief clarifications about Bonhoeffer's terminology in the prison theology are essential. First, the word "*weltlich*" in Bonhoeffer must be translated "worldly," not "secular." Second, all the debates and misunderstandings about "religion" and "religionlessness" in the prison letters have distracted from the main point of Bonhoeffer's new theological proposal: he explicitly says it is about "worldly"

---

40. DBWE 12:288–89.

41. Bonhoeffer is not rejecting Christian eschatology but replacing a dualistic eschatology with a biblically inspired, historical-messianic eschatology. Christians are pilgrims traveling "toward that foreign land that they love above all," namely God's kingdom. But "only pilgrims of this kind, who love the Earth and God as one, can believe in God's kingdom" (DBWE 12:286). One is reminded of the traveler Abraham "who looked forward to the city that has foundations, whose architect and builder is God" (Heb. 11:10), and also to the vision of "the new Jerusalem coming down out of heaven from God" (Rev. 21:2).

42. DBWE 8:490. Sometimes Bonhoeffer speaks of a *nonreligious* or *religionless* interpretation (DBWE 8:363, 367, 372, 429, 482) and other times simply of *worldly* interpretation (DBWE 8:364, 373, 457, 501). Especially significant are the occasions where he hyphenates the two words, showing that they are equivalent, as in "religionless-worldly Christians" (DBWE 8:364) and "worldly, non-religious interpretation" (DBWE 8:490). "Worldly" is the positive, affirmative partner of this pair, "religionless" the critical, polemical partner.

Christianity. If the adjectives "nonreligious" and "religionless" are the negative and polemical description of the project, the adjective "worldly" is its positive and affirmative description. What Bonhoeffer advocates as the alternative to religious and otherworldly Christianity is a Christianity that is radically intra-worldly, embedded in the social, historical, natural world.

I add my commentary here about the implications I see: Forget about "up"—popular Christian spirituality must give up its dualistic spatial cosmology, its spirit-body dualistic anthropology, and its immortality eschatology. It must recover instead the biblical and primitive-Christian eschatology, a temporal-historical eschatology, and really believe, with the creed, those counterintuitive words, "the resurrection of the body."

Now to sum up these three examples: from the first articulation of the theology of sociality in *Sanctorum Communio* to the radical worldliness of the letters, this result comes into focus: the theology of sociality and the affirmation of worldliness are two ways of making the same point. Worldliness is the explicit form and the implicit polemic in the theology of sociality. Sociality is about worldliness: God encountered in the world—not "beyond" it—in history, in human relationships and communities, especially in the community of the present Christ. In other words: the theology of sociality requires the polemic against otherworldliness; the polemic against otherworldliness protects the theology of sociality from evaporating into a dualistic, otherworldly spirituality.[43]

CONCLUDING SKETCH OF A WORLDLY CHRISTIANITY PARADIGM

I conclude by sketching a few main lines of Bonhoeffer's new worldly Christianity paradigm. The central theme is Christ *in* the world, Christ *for* the world.[44] As in the cases of Athanasius, Anselm, and Luther, there are two interrelated poles, Christology (b) and soteriology (c), situated in a specific historical-cultural field (a).

a) Social-historical theology. Bonhoeffer's new paradigm is situated in the midst of life in the social-historical-bodily world. It is neither the world of Luther, nor of Anselm's monastery, nor of Augustine. Born a child of the modern world nearly a millennium after Anselm and four hundred years after Luther, Bonhoeffer's paradigm marks a shift from the intra-subjective

---

43. Here individualistic interiority is just the subjective expression of a spiritual *Hinterweltlichkeit*; they are two sides of the same orientation or mentality.

44. Following earlier descriptions of patristic and medieval Christology with the terms *Christus Victor* and *Christus Patiens*, we could here employ the phrases *Christus in Mundo*, *Christus pro Mundo*.

orientation of the late medieval-Reformation paradigm to the social, public, and political world of the current age. Like his predecessors, Bonhoeffer's theology is contextual, engaging the characteristic human-cultural-ethical issues of the present era.

b) Christology. Bonhoeffer's distinctive and core Christological note first sounds clearly in *Act and Being* where he speaks of the freedom of God. "Christ is the word of God's freedom." "The freedom of God . . . finds its strongest evidence precisely in that God freely chose to be bound to historical human beings. . . . God is free not from human beings but for them. . . ."[45] This is enriched by the Jesus of the Sermon on the Mount in *Discipleship*, and further developed in the *Menschgewordene* of the *Ethics*, "the God who became human." God's freedom for the world in becoming human both reconciles God and humanity-in-the-world, and sets loose a transforming process of humanization in history.[46] Indeed, compared to Anselm, and also to Athanasius, Bonhoeffer's soteriology appears to shift the emphasis from the cross to the incarnation.[47] God's freedom for humanity in becoming human in the world leads directly to soteriology, the church, and ethics. Central to each of these is the theme "freedom for others," which is enabled and sustained by the freedom of God for the world.

c) Soteriology and Ethics. Unlike Luther's anxiety about the guilty conscience,[48] Anselm's awe at the slightest glance in a direction forbidden by God, or Athanasius' fight with the devil, Bonhoeffer's soteriology engages the modern world. I believe it is in the field of social relations—from the most personal to the most political—that we find him locating the crucial and characteristic soteriological problem of our age, namely the issue of power.[49]

45. *Act and Being*, DBWE 2:90–91.

46. See DBWE 8:361–62 on being "caught up into . . . the Messianic event" and 370 on "becoming human and Christian" in this way.

47. See my Editor's Introduction to Bonhoeffer, *Ethics*, DBWE 6:6–9, esp. 7–8, where I propose that the litany of incarnation, crucifixion, and resurrection found repeatedly in *Ethics* concentrates on human historical transformation and is the anthropological-existential effect of the ontological reconciliation effected by God's becoming human in Jesus Christ. The relationship of incarnation and crucifixion in Bonhoeffer, compared to Anselm's satisfaction theory, is an important research topic.

48. It is worth recalling here Bonhoeffer's question about whether modern people even understand sin anymore; cf. DBWE 8:366.

49. By focusing on corrupt power as a crucial soteriological problem of the current age, I presuppose an understanding of sin as *corruptio boni*, the corruption of the good. Genuine power is a necessary good for life—see, for example, the "power of being" as essential in Tillich's ontology. Therefore, the denial of power to people on grounds of race, religion, gender, etc. is as problematic as tyrannical and exploitative power. Bonhoeffer's meditation on "The View from Below," DBWE 8:52, about seeing "the great events

In the public realm, Bonhoeffer's opposition to war and his work for peace are obvious. Already in 1930, the sin of racism, in its American form, was a central preoccupation, as was anti-Semitism in Germany, especially after 1933. But that is not all. He identifies various forms of exploitation such as the Indian caste system, and colonialism, and writes that "Christianity stands or falls with its revolutionary protest against violence, arbitrariness, and pride of power, and with its apologia for the weak."[50] This is the same point that is stated more existentially in "The View from Below." Similarly he highlights—in 1932, again prior to Hitler—various forms of power struggle, including life-and-death economic competition, class struggle, nationalism, and the exploitation of the weak by the strong.[51] The common denominator in all of these sociopolitical pathologies is corrupt power. These social pathologies are typical of the modern era—certainty in scale and scope, if not in novelty.

In the personal realm, Bonhoeffer documents a more existential mode of power as a soteriological problem. An autobiographical fragment reveals that, in contrast to Luther, Bonhoeffer is troubled by a characteristically modern syndrome: "Bonhoeffer is troubled by dominance, not guilt; power, not self-doubt; success, not defeat; narcissistic isolation, not heavenly disapproval; Promethean posing as God's self-appointed champion, not hatred and fear of the demanding heavenly Father."[52]

The preceding paragraphs can only suggest how Bonhoeffer might have spelled out in systematic form the key points of a new Christian paradigm for the current age. His writings provide ample material for filling out what can only be a suggestive sketch here. What is not conjectural, however, is that reading him whole discloses that Bonhoeffer the theologian was from beginning to end, with ever-increasing self-consciousness and force, working at a new Christian paradigm, at the center of which is the vision of Christ-for-the-world, Christ-in-the-world, for the humanization of all people into a life of worldly sociality.

---

of world history from the perspective of . . . the powerless, the oppressed and reviled, in short from the perspective of the suffering," revealed his sensitivity to this.

50. DBWE 13:402.

51. DBWE 11:363, in the address on the theological foundation of the ecumenical movement.

52. Green, "Bonhoeffer in the Context of Erikson's Luther Study," 190. On power as a soteriological problem, including consideration of the autobiographical dimension of Bonhoeffer's theology, see Green, *Bonhoeffer*, esp. ch. 4.

21

Epilogue

Bonhoeffer: Theologian, Activist, Educator: Challenges for the Church of the Coming Generations

Samuel Wells

On July 21, 1944, the day after a turning point in German history, Dietrich Bonhoeffer wrote from prison to his friend Eberhard Bethge,

> If one has completely renounced making something of oneself . . .—then one throws oneself completely into the arms of God, and this is what I call this-worldliness: living fully in the midst of life's tasks, questions, successes and failures, experiences, and perplexities—then one takes seriously no longer one's own sufferings but rather the suffering of God in the world. Then one stays awake with Christ in Gethsemane. And I think this is faith; this is *metanoia*. And this is how one becomes a human being, a Christian.[1]

Three weeks earlier he had written these words to Bethge: "Christians do not have an ultimate escape route out of their earthly tasks and difficulties into eternity. Like Christ . . . , they have to drink the cup of earthly life to the last drop, and only when they do this is the Crucified and Risen One with them, and they are crucified and resurrected with Christ."[2]

Everyone is familiar with the Bonhoeffer of a wardrobe of conventional guises: the pacifist who discovered responsibility, the humanist who proclaimed a world come of age, the uncompromising radical who heard Christ calling each disciple to come and die, the prodigy who had published two doctorates

---

1. Bonhoeffer, *Letters and Papers from Prison*, DBWE 8:486 (Minneapolis: Fortress Press, 2010).
2. Ibid., 447–48.

before the age anyone here today had even embarked on one, and the scornful European who dismissed American Christianity as Protestantism without reformation. These are the personae that place Bonhoeffer along with Dorothy Day, Martin Luther King Jr., Clarence Jordan, Flannery O'Connor, Mother Teresa, and Oscar Romero in the communion of overcited saints in twentieth-century North American liberal Protestant sermons. I would like to suggest that we cherish Dietrich Bonhoeffer not so much in these conventional guises, but more because, in his own words, he "drank the cup of earthly life to the last drop," because he "lived fully in the midst of life's tasks, questions, successes and failures, experiences, and perplexities," because when he did this "the Crucified and Risen One was with him," and because "this is how he became a human being, a Christian." And most of all because, walking in his steps, this is how we may do the same.

More precisely, I want to distinguish between two important small words, "for" and "with." Dietrich Bonhoeffer has been, I suggest, remembered mostly as a man "for" others. He wrote theology *for* the academy, he stood up *for* the Jews, he spoke up and established a seminary *for* the Confessing Church, he joined the bomb plot *for* Germany's salvation. But I believe he should be perhaps even more remembered as a man "with" others. At three defining moments in his life, he resolved that to be a faithful disciple meant to be *with* God by being *with* God's church, by being *with* his people and by being *with* his family, friends, trusted companions, and fellow conspirators.

I'm going to start by discerning in John chapter 11 a narrative shape that defines the arc of Jesus' life, and highlighting how a measure of Dietrich Bonhoeffer's faithfulness is that his life has a corresponding narrative shape. In the process I want to identify three moments in Bonhoeffer's life that disclose his deepest commitments, and to comment on ways in which those commitments were ones that I have already begun to describe as an embodiment of an incarnate ethic of being *with*. In conclusion I want to look briefly at some of the challenges for the church in the coming generations and to draw out how Bonhoeffer's discipleship and witness may inspire us in rather different times. So I begin with the story of Jesus, Mary, Martha, and Lazarus in John 11.

Jesus' words in John 11:4 resonate deeply with the story of Dietrich Bonhoeffer: "This illness does not lead to death; rather, it is for God's glory, so that the Son of God may be glorified through it." This was Bonhoeffer's prayer for the crisis of the German churches and of Germany and Europe as a whole: that this crisis, for all its horror and terror, and for all its slaughter, speaks not, finally, of death but of the glory of God. This is also our prayer for Bonhoeffer's life and legacy: that they speak to us not of death, of war, genocide, oppression, and oblivion, but that they speak to us of the glory of the Son of God.

I want to look with you at how Jesus crosses three key thresholds in John chapter 11. First, he crosses the threshold into Judea. The message comes from Martha and Mary that Lazarus is ill. Curiously, Jesus stays two days longer in the place where he is. It's not entirely clear why. There follows an intense and illuminating interchange. Jesus announces it's time to return to Judea. The disciples say "But they were all ready to stone you when you were last there." Jesus is not to be deterred. He discloses the true reason for his journey: "So that you may believe." And Thomas gets the message, proclaiming: "Let us also go, that we may die with him."

Here lies the first defining moment of Bonhoeffer's life. It is June 1939. He is in New York. The Executive Secretary of the Federal Council of Churches has made an offer to employ him for three years coordinating work among German refugees in the city. He ponders his situation for two weeks, echoing Jesus' delay after receiving Martha and Mary's message. When he meets with the Executive Secretary on June 20, he declines the offer, to the consternation and bemusement of those making it. His motives are partly a mystery to himself: in his journal he writes, "We are acting in a plane that is hidden from us, and we can only ask that God may judge and forgive us."[3] But with Reinhold Niebuhr he is less equivocal, explaining,

> I have made a mistake in coming to America. I must live through this difficult period of our national history with the Christian people of Germany. I will have no right to participate in the reconstruction of Christian life in Germany after the war if I do not share the trials of this time with my people. Christians in Germany will face the terrible alternative of either willing the defeat of their nation in order that Christian civilisation may survive, or willing the victory of their nation and thereby destroying our civilisation. I know which of these alternatives I must choose; but I cannot make the choice in security![4]

One can almost hear resonances of the First Book of Kings, and Elijah's flight to Horeb, and the penetrating and searching question the Lord asks of his prophet, "What are you doing here, Elijah?"[5]

---

3. Edwin Robertson, *The Shame and the Sacrifice: The Life and Preaching of Dietrich Bonhoeffer* (London: Hodder & Stoughton, 1987), 172.

4. Ibid.

5. 1 Kings 19:9.

Of all the dimensions of Bonhoeffer's momentous decision to return to Germany in 1939, I would like to highlight one in particular. And that is his conversation with George Bell, the bishop of Chichester. The conversation took place in early April 1939. In a letter dated March 25 to Bell before the meeting, Bonhoeffer expressed his anxiety about the prospect of being called up to military service and his reluctance to take the military oath.[6] He also communicated his recognition that very few of his Confessing Church companions would approve of his attitude. He acknowledged, "I should have to do violence to my Christian conviction, if I would take up arms 'here and now'"; but he admitted, "I have not made up my mind what I should do."[7] The meeting took place a few days later. Bethge describes it vividly. Bonhoeffer, he says, sought out Bell, "the man who stood in another world, but could listen to him calmly and yet realize the force of the alternatives: Confessing Church and family, pacifism and theology, political conspiracy and ecumenism. Within his family he could expect no close commitment to church theology and among his friends on the Council of Brethren no freedom toward the political realm. Bell understood both. . . . [Bonhoeffer] confided in the older man who, as he knew, understood how to pray and how to demand what was necessary."[8]

Bethge comments that Bell "probably eased Bonhoeffer's conscience about temporarily leaving Germany."[9] Keith Clements captures the spirit of the meeting by saying that Bell, "as a good counsellor, simply let him talk and talk, and listened." Citing Bonhoeffer's subsequent letter of April 13, in which he expresses gratitude to Bell and says "it means much to me to realize that you see the great conscientious difficulties with which we are faced,"[10] Clements describes the meeting as "a classic case of a good pastoral conversation."[11]

The reason I regard this conversation as so significant is that I believe in his compassionate concern and listening spirit toward Bonhoeffer, George Bell modeled the attitude Bonhoeffer would come to adopt toward Germany. Bell was profoundly "with" Bonhoeffer, in much the same way that Bonhoeffer came to understand himself as called to be profoundly "with" Germany. Only Bell truly comprehended the diverse commitments and characteristics of

---

6. Bonhoeffer was subject to the draft because he had been born in 1906.

7. Eberhard Bethge, *Dietrich Bonhoeffer: A Biography*, rev. ed. Victoria J. Barnett (Minneapolis: Fortress Press, 2000), 637.

8. Ibid., 638.

9. Ibid., 639.

10. Ibid., 996 n. 105.

11. Keith Clements, *Bonhoeffer and Britain* (London: Churches Together in Britain and Ireland, 2006), 100.

Bonhoeffer's personality, and perhaps only Bonhoeffer truly recognized the pathos and yet abiding possibility of Germany's situation. What Bell was helping Bonhoeffer to see was that there was no solution to his predicament, either in an appointment outside Germany or in simply consenting to being called up. Instead he was going to have to live without a solution. He was called to find a way to be "with" his people, not in a dramatic and conclusive decision, but in an extended series of daily discernments. Only thus was he going to imitate how God is "with" us. Let me repeat Bonhoeffer's letter to Bethge with which I began: "If one has completely renounced making something of oneself . . .—then one throws oneself completely into the arms of God, and this is what I call this-worldliness: living fully in the midst of life's tasks, questions, successes and failures, experiences, and perplexities—then one takes seriously no longer one's own sufferings but rather the suffering of God in the world. Then one stays awake with Christ in Gethsemane. This is faith." That is exactly how Bonhoeffer lived with the German people in the years after 1939.

It's time to move to our second moment. The second threshold Jesus crosses in John chapter 11 is into Bethany. Why does Jesus come to Bethany? Because, we are told in 11:5, "Jesus loved Martha and her sister and Lazarus." Bethany becomes a synecdoche for the world that Jesus enters because God so loves it. Martha and her sister and Lazarus become a synecdoche for the people of God with whom Jesus identifies. This is the threshold where the profound conversation takes place. The conversation about discipleship took place before crossing into Judea. But the conversation about the resurrection and the life takes place on this threshold, the threshold of Bethany. Mary says to Jesus, reproachfully but in words full of faith, "Lord, if you had been here, my brother would not have died" (11:32). These words sum up the quandary of the Confessing Church. Had Christians in Germany been more faithful, would the soul of Germany have descended to the point where Hitler captivated the national imagination? There is no certainty that it would not. Jesus doesn't affirm Mary's statement. He never says that if he had been there, Lazarus would not have died. God's action, it seems, is not to make bad things not happen. God's glory is revealed in that God does not leave us alone when they do.

Here lies the second defining moment of Bonhoeffer's life—a moment that came only a year after the first. Bethge describes sitting in the sun at a café in Memel, a small town in East Prussia, now a part of Lithuania, on June 17, 1940. Over the café's loudspeaker came an announcement that France had surrendered. Everyone stood up, sang *Deutschland über alles*, and saluted Hitler. Edwin Robertson sums up the significance of the moment like this: "Since the rise of Prussia almost a century earlier, the two contenders for the dominance of Europe were Germany and France. . . . The harsh terms of the Versailles treaty were thought to be the work of France." Thus the capitulation of France meant the erasure of Versailles and the undisputed supremacy of Germany in Europe. Bethge describes the scene in the café in withering terms. "The crowd jumped onto the chairs and forgot, in the jubilant tumult, both the means and the end of the victory. [Bonhoeffer] felt only shame at the success of the crime."[12] What the moment really meant for Bonhoeffer was that he and his circle were confronted with the horrifying truth that no one was going to get rid of Hitler for them. If they wanted Hitler gone, they would have to do it themselves. As Bethge puts it, "The expectation that the first military difficulties would topple the hated regime had proven false, and all dreams of its removal had vanished. The victory in France sealed an immense miscalculation by Bonhoeffer's informants and friends in the resistance movement. The professionals . . . were wrong, and Hitler the amateur was right."[13]

This moment was a turning point. As Bethge puts it, momentously, "It was then that Bonhoeffer's double life began. . . . He was acting out of an inner necessity for which his church as yet had no formulas. By normal standards everything had been turned upside down."[14] It's interesting and important to note that June 1940, rather than, for example, January 1933, is the date Bethge identifies in such shuddering terms. What it meant is expressed vividly by Mary Bosanquet. "As Bonhoeffer became more and more deeply enmeshed in the evil of his time, he was driven quietly to accept the loss of that particular personal treasure which he had many times struggled to abandon, but which had yet clung to him, wrapping its powerful tentacles round his inmost being; the sense of his own righteousness."[15] One can hear resonances of this moment in Bonhoeffer's *Ethics*, written four years later. Here Bonhoeffer maintains that responsible action involves "the willingness to become guilty," just as Christ entered into human guilt and took it upon himself out of selfless love for his brothers and sisters.[16]

As Edwin Robertson puts it, "Little by little this Christian man became completely a man of his time. His involvement in the conspiracy would require the abandoning of much that Christian life demands—expert lying built up gradually into closely woven deception, and ultimately the willingness to kill."[17]

---

12. Robertson, *The Shame and the Sacrifice*, 187.

13. Bethge, *Dietrich Bonhoeffer*, 682.

14. Ibid.

15. Quoted in Robertson, *The Shame and the Sacrifice*, 174.

16. Bonhoeffer, *Ethics*, DBWE 6:275 (Minneapolis: Fortress Press, 2005), 275.

Here Robertson points out the connection between these painful transformations and Bonhoeffer's words from Tegel Prison four years later: "We have been silent witnesses of evil deeds. We have become cunning and learned the arts of obfuscation and equivocal speech. Experience has rendered us suspicious of human beings, and often we have failed to speak to them a true and open word. Unbearable conflicts have worn us down or even made us cynical. Are we still of any use? Will our inner strength to resist what has been forced on us have remained strong enough, and our honesty with ourselves blunt enough, to find our way back to simplicity and honesty?"[18]

The key point I want to reiterate is that Bonhoeffer's participation in the plot to kill Hitler was not a lonely hero's quest to save Germany even at the risk of his own soul; it was his much humbler participation in the communion of saints. It was not something Bonhoeffer did "for"; it was something he did "with." In this lies its profound continuity with the previous threshold, the return to Germany a year earlier. The return to Germany was an incarnate expression of "with": to have remained aloof and beyond Germany would still have permitted Bonhoeffer to work and be "for" a new Germany. Yet it would not have permitted him truly to work and be "with" Germany in its most benighted hour. Having committed himself to "being with" Germany in 1939, it was not an incomprehensible step to begin to "work with" those who sought to remove the single force that was propelling Germany deeper and deeper into the mire. Bonhoeffer was under no illusion that the death of Hitler would be the salvation of Germany: that would have been the fantasy of "working for," the presumption that he could have the fate of a nation in his own hands. What Bonhoeffer was seeking to do was to help Germany get to a place from which it could begin to row back from catastrophe, to prevent things continuing to get worse, to bring about circumstances in which sanity could begin to break through the storm clouds of demonic fanaticism. In this he saw himself in solidarity with a diverse group of people whom he regarded as representing the best in German character and spirit. For that reason, it is appropriate to see his efforts in the resistance as a humble identification "with" Germany, rather than a high-handed action "for" his nation.

Bonhoeffer's being "with" Germany extended to his willingness to share the guilt for what Germany, collectively, had done. In a poem written in Tegel Prison, he speaks of the "we," rather than the "they," who had brought about Germany's descent into apostasy, in words reminiscent of Romans 1:

---

17. Robertson, *The Shame and the Sacrifice*, 175.

18. Bonhoeffer, *Letters and Papers from Prison*, DBWE 8:52. This quotation is longer than the one Robertson cites, which concludes at "Are we still of any use?"

We the offspring of devout generations,
once the defenders of justice and truth,
became despisers of God and humanity,
as Hell looked on, laughing. . . .
Only before thee, Fathomer of all Being,
before thee we are sinners.
Afraid of suffering and lacking good deeds,
we have betrayed you before humankind.
We saw the Lie raise its head
and failed to pay homage to Truth.
We saw others in direst need
and our own death was all we feared.[19]

The fact that Bonhoeffer was not an advocate of his nation's fall did not mean he thought he could avoid its cost. Like Jesus, he bore in his own body the sins of his people. He lived the logic of Christ's incarnation.

George Bell highlighted his friend's commitment to "be with" in his sermon at Bonhoeffer's memorial service in London in July 1945. For Bell, Bonhoeffer was "with" not just his family and his country and the Confessing Church, but with the saints and martyrs everywhere and always. "As one of a noble company of martyrs of differing traditions, he represents both the resistance of the believing soul, in the name of God, to the assault of evil, and also the moral and political revolt of the human conscience against injustice and cruelty. He and his fellows are indeed built upon the foundation of the Apostles and the Prophets. And it was this passion for justice that brought him, and so many others . . . into such a close partnership with other resisters, who, though outside the Church, shared the same humanitarian and liberal ideals."[20]

And that brings us to the third threshold Jesus crosses in John chapter 11: in verse 38 he comes to Lazarus' tomb. It takes thirty-eight verses of a forty-four-verse story for Jesus to reach Lazarus' tomb. Just as Bethany, in the persons of Mary and Martha, corresponds to Israel, so the tomb, the place of horror and of transformation, represents Jerusalem. This is the place where Jesus performs the seventh miracle in John's Gospel, the miracle that perfectly anticipates the definitive miracle upon which all the others converge, the miracle of his

19. Bonhoeffer, *Letters and Papers from Prison*, DBWE 8:467–68; see also Robertson, *Bonhoeffer's Heritage: The Christian Way in a World Without Religion* (London: Hodder & Stoughton, 1989), 178.

20. Eberhard Bethge, *Bonhoeffer Gedenkheft* (Berlin: Haus und Schule, 1947), 9.

own resurrection. And it's the place where we witness the confrontation that epitomizes the scandal of the cross. Jesus says, "Take away the stone." Martha responds, "Lord, already there is a stench because he has been dead four days." Jesus insists, "Did I not tell you that if you believed, you would see the glory of God?" So they took away the stone (11:39–41). Martha wants there to be a way to redeem her brother that does not involve the stench. Jesus asks if she is serious about wanting to see the glory of God.

This abiding presence of faith in the face of horror characterizes the third defining moment in Bonhoeffer's life. Bonhoeffer was kept in Tegel Prison in the northwest of Berlin from the day of his arrest, April 5, 1943, until his transfer to Central Security Office in central Berlin on October 8, 1944. In the summer of 1944 he had the opportunity to escape. But he didn't take it. That was his moment of facing the stench of the tomb, out of a deeper desire to see the glory of God.

The unexpected, absurdly unlucky, but nonetheless devastating failure of the plot to kill Hitler at his Wolf's Lair headquarters near Rastenburg in East Prussia (modern northeast Poland), on July 20, 1944, was described by one observer as "perhaps the most tragic day in modern German history."[21] It marks a turning point at least as significant as the fall of France. After the fall of Paris, it was clear no one could get rid of Hitler but the Germans themselves. After the failure of Claus von Stauffenberg's attempt on Hitler's life, it seemed that all who had plotted Hitler's downfall were set to be eliminated. Any hope for a solution to the demonic possession of Germany seemed at an end. Bonhoeffer's extended prison stay and delayed trial was predicated on the case against his brother-in-law Hans von Dohnanyi, and beyond him Admiral Wilhelm Canaris and the whole spider's web of officers grouped around the *Abwehr* office that shielded the resistance under the pretext of military intelligence. But after July 20, 1944, their exposure was no more than a matter of time. Thus Bonhoeffer began seriously to plan for escape, and persuaded his prison guard, Sergeant Knobloch, to disappear with him while Bonhoeffer would don a mechanic's uniform procured by his family. The clothing was transferred on September 24 and the chaplain to the Swedish embassy was put on standby.[22]

But on October 1, 1944, just days before the planned escape, Klaus Bonhoeffer, Dietrich's brother, was arrested, along with several others whose involvement in the plot had been hidden until this point. Dietrich perceived that his window for escape had closed. Any adventure now would cast a shadow

---

21. Robertson, *The Shame and the Sacrifice*, 261.

22. Bethge, *Dietrich Bonhoeffer*, 827–28.

of guilt upon his brother and expose his parents and his young fiancée Maria to significant danger. Within twenty-four hours he informed Sgt. Knobloch and, through him, his family, that there was to be no escape. Yet again "with" had conquered "for." In this case "with" meant his brother and his family and his fellow conspirators. We may look back and imagine what it could have meant if this great theologian and visionary German intellectual had escaped the demise of the German war effort, and what by this stage had become his almost inevitable death. The stench, to us, may seem unbearable. But Bonhoeffer withstood the stench. He was concerned to see the glory of God. He knew that when he would stand before the divine judgment seat he would face the question "Where are the others?" If he was going to spend eternity with them, he had to be prepared to remain with those others now.

To enter the mystery of this solidarity, a solidarity that finally took him to his own death, we can only draw on Bonhoeffer's own words. In "An Account at the Turn of the Year 1942-1943," he says, prophetically, "We must learn to regard human beings less in terms of what they do and neglect to do and more in terms of what they suffer. The only fruitful relation to human beings—particularly to the weak among them—is love, that is, the will to enter into and to keep community with them."[23] Keeping community was exactly what inhibited him from escaping. He goes on to say,

> Christ withdrew from suffering until his hour had come; then he walked toward it in freedom, took hold, and overcame it. Christ . . . experienced in his own body the whole suffering of all humanity as his own. . . . We are not Christ, but if we want to be Christians it means that we are to take part in Christ's greatness of heart, in the responsible action that in freedom lays hold of the hour and faces the danger, and in the true sympathy that springs forth not from fear but from Christ's freeing and redeeming love for all who suffer.[24]

If one were to choose a title for a biography of Bonhoeffer, one could do worse than call it "taking part in Christ's greatness of heart." Here again the emphasis is profoundly on being "with." In the same vein he writes to Bethge on July 28, 1944:

> . . . not only action but suffering, too, is a way to freedom. In suffering, liberation consists in being allowed to let the matter out

---

23. Bonhoeffer, *Letters and Papers from Prison*, DBWE 8:45.
24. Ibid., 49.

of one's own hands into the hands of God. In this sense death is the epitome of human freedom.[25]

These sentiments crystallize what it means for God to be with us in Christ and for us to imitate Christ in being with one another. In this spirit the poignancy of these words of Bonhoeffer's *Ethics*, written in prison, becomes piercingly clear:

> In Christ the reconciliation of the world with God took place. The world will be overcome not by destruction but by reconciliation. Not ideals or programs, not conscience, duty, responsibility, or virtue, but only the consummate love of God can meet and overcome reality. Again, this is accomplished not by a general idea of love, but by the love of God really lived in Jesus Christ. This love of God for the world does not withdraw from reality into noble souls detached from the world, but experiences and suffers the reality of the world at its worst. The world exhausts its rage on the body of Jesus Christ. But the martyred one forgives the world its sins. Thus reconciliation takes place. Ecce homo.[26]

Here he is clearly speaking of his own imitation of Christ in being with Germany.

It is important to look back to how Bonhoeffer had anticipated these commitments in his words in *Life Together*, as follows:

> The first service one owes to others in the community involves listening to them. Just as our love for God begins with listening to God's Word, the beginning of love for other Christians is learning to listen to them. . . . The other service one should perform for another person in a Christian community is active helpfulness. . . . Those who worry about the loss of time entailed by such small, external acts of helpfulness are usually taking their own work too seriously. . . . Third, we speak of the service involved in bearing with others. . . . The law of Christ is a law of forbearance. Forbearance means endurance and suffering. . . . In suffering and enduring human beings, God maintained community with them. It is the law of Christ that was fulfilled in the cross. Christians share in this law.[27]

25. Ibid., 493.

26. Bonhoeffer, *Ethics*, DBWE 6:82–83.

27. Bonhoeffer, *Life Together*, DBWE 5:98, 99, 100, 101.

Finally, in his *Ethics*, Bonhoeffer brings together the first, second, and third defining moments of his life in the following section. Listen to the resonances in this short passage of how the resolutions he made in June 1939, June 1940, and October 1944 coalesce in a Christological formulation:

> [Love] is the reality of being drawn and drawing others into an event, namely, into God's community with the world, which has already been accomplished in Jesus Christ. [Love] does not exist as an abstract attribute of God but only in God's actual loving of human beings and the world. Again, "love" does not exist as a human attribute but only as a real belonging-together and being-together of people with other human beings and with the world, based on God's love that is extended to me and to them.[28]

It is because love "does not exist as an abstract attribute of God" but *existed* as the "belonging-together and being-together" of Dietrich Bonhoeffer "with other human beings and with the world" that we are gathered together here tonight. The three key moments of his life are the places where the veil between heaven and earth is especially thin, and God's divinity is most evidently shown in Bonhoeffer's humanity. They are moments when Bonhoeffer's "with" most aptly reflects Christ's "with," a "with" that embodies God's being "with" the world.

In the rest of this chapter I want to distill what we have discerned about Bonhoeffer and explore its significance for the church of the coming generations. I'm going to do so under the three headings of theologian, activist, and educator. Let me start with theologian.

What we have seen is that the key moments of Bonhoeffer's story are episodes where he most keenly identifies with Jesus' birth and death. They are moments of embodying Christ's incarnation and crucifixion. Bonhoeffer embodies Christ's incarnation in the way he realizes he has to be with Germany, be with the conspirators, and be with his brother and brother-in-law, however flawed and fallen and fragile this fellowship might be. Jesus' incarnation united his divine and human nature: it did not, at a stroke, redeem human nature, but it identified human nature and destiny definitively and permanently with the nature of God. This is the most evident outcome of God's decision never to be except to be with us in Christ. Despite the damaged character of human nature, the incarnation did not besmirch the divine nature of Jesus: but it certainly exposed Jesus to the distress of the thousand natural shocks that flesh is heir to;

---

28. Bonhoeffer, *Ethics*, DBWE 6:241.

most extremely, crucifixion. Bonhoeffer was committed to be with his nation, with his family, and with those who, like him, discerned they could not look to others for an end to governmental insanity. These commitments led him into danger, into detention, and into death. This is how he embodied Christ's crucifixion. He took on the sins of his people, and the pathos of a pacifist joining the plot against Hitler is that it raised the fear for him that being with, and being faithful to, his people might make him somehow less with, and less faithful to, God.

What the incarnation and the crucifixion show us—and this is the central theological conclusion we can draw from Christ's life, as reflected and illustrated in Bonhoeffer's—is that the most important word in theology is "with." The Holy Trinity is the perfect epitome of "with": God being with God. The incarnation of Jesus is the embodiment of "with": God being with us, being among us. The crucifixion is the greatest test of God's being with us, because, in the cry of dereliction, we hear the question, "Does Jesus' being with us finally jeopardize his being with the Father and the Spirit?" The resurrection is the vindication of God's being both with us, and with God, and the ultimate and perpetual compatibility, and unity, of the two. Pentecost is the embodiment of that resurrection breakthrough, because in Pentecost the Holy Spirit becomes the guarantee and gift of our union with God in Christ and our union with one another in Christ's body. Perhaps the most tangible sense of Pentecost in Bonhoeffer's biography is his experience with the international ecumenical movement, and the depth of the relationships he made there. The fact that his final message before his execution was directed to George Bell expresses that debt, and its significance, succinctly. Being with, for Bonhoeffer, was not just a sober matter of incarnate humanity, or the inevitability of crucified sacrifice; it was also the Pentecostal joy of wondrous companionship across time and space.

In his epiphany in New York—in his realization that he had made a mistake in coming to America, and needed to live through this difficult period of their national history with the Christian people of Germany—Bonhoeffer displays the kind of epiphany that has appeared repeatedly in the new developments in theology in recent generations. Theologians have realized more and more kinds of people that they are called to be with, because God has always been with. James Cone, for example, articulates how God is with the experience of the African American not in an accidental but in a definitive way; Rosemary Radford Ruether makes an analogous point in relation to how God is with women, and Jean Vanier expresses beautifully how God is with those with multiple disabilities in ways God is not to be found anywhere else. Increasingly, theologians are describing how God is with the created ecological order and how Christians are called to be with the creation in a corresponding way. This being with is not simply incarnate—it is subject to the experience of crucifixion, resurrection, and Pentecost too.

The challenge this theological insight constitutes is thrown into relief when we turn to consider Bonhoeffer as an activist. Activists are not associated with "being"; they are spoken of as "working." They are not identified with the word "with": they are tied to the word "for." If Bonhoeffer is described as an activist, that designation belongs most obviously to his willingness to speak publicly about the plight of the Jews. It may be said that Bonhoeffer spoke up for the Jews. But I would suggest that, in the light of the argument I have been making, Bonhoeffer didn't so much speak up for the Jews as perceive the Jews as part of the Germany with whom he was called to abide.[29] The failure of the church in Germany in the Nazi era was obviously an activist failure, a failure to *do*. But prior to that it was much more fundamentally a failure to *see*—to see the Jews as those with whom Christians were called to be. The parable of the Last Judgment[30] is often interpreted as a call to activism; but it is more fundamentally an identification of those the church is called to be with. In the same spirit, Jesus' words in John 12 that "the poor will always be with you" presuppose that the majority of church members throughout its history have always *been* poor.[31] They are words that identify the poor as those the church is always called to be, or at least to be with.

---

29. This is trespassing on complex and disputed territory. Stephen R. Haynes, *The Bonhoeffer Legacy: Post-Holocaust Perspectives* (Minneapolis: Fortress Press, 2006) argues that Bonhoeffer always had a paradoxical view of the Jews, as both God's chosen people and the people who uniquely rejected God and murdered Jesus (106–7). Thus: "Nowhere does Bonhoeffer encourage Christians to view Jews simply as human beings whose rights must be respected. For Bonhoeffer, the Jew is always the other who is also Christ's brother; the other with whom is tied up the fate of the West; the other whose suffering reflects God's providence and whose treatment discloses the moral condition of church and society. Bonhoeffer's commitment to defend Jews may have formed the basis for a theology of solidarity with others more generally, but he never conflated the two categories" (142). According to Haynes, Bethge tries to make the point of Bonhoeffer's "deep solidarity" with the Jewish people, but Haynes remains skeptical. Haynes complains: "Bonhoeffer's use of this highly charged term [Jewish Question], coupled with his claim that the church exists wherever *Jew* and *German* 'stand together under the Word of God,' gave unwitting credence to a conviction . . . that 'Jews' were an alien people whose very existence posed a threat to ethnic Germans" (67; italics Haynes—Ed.).

30. Matthew 25:31-46.

31. Stanley Hauerwas, "The Appeal of Judas," in *A Cross-Shattered Church* (Grand Rapids: Brazos, 2009), 95. Hauerwas writes, "The one who said 'You always have the poor with you' was poor himself . . . . Christianity is determinatively the faith of the poor. That is why we, the moderately well off, are puzzled by the undeniable reality that the church across time and space has been constituted by the poor" (95).

One of the best-known activists of the twentieth century was Saul Alinsky. His iron rule, repeatedly expressed by his successor Ernie Cortès, was, "Never do for others what they can do for themselves."[32] Bonhoeffer's return to Germany, his joining the plot to kill Hitler, and his renunciation of escape from prison—the three defining moments of his life—were not actions for others. They were actions of solidarity empowering others to act for themselves. This is a profound challenge to conventional notions of activism, in the churches and elsewhere. Take the Millennium Development Goals[33] as an example. These are ambitious targets, largely identified by western experts, almost entirely to be realized in developing world contexts. They are not based on indigenous practical wisdom, on small, reversible steps, or on nuanced understandings of local histories, climate, rites of passage, conflicts, or health maps.[34] They are the thinking of what William Easterly calls "planners" rather than "searchers"—in other words, they are concerned with a superimposed blueprint rather than an engaged, listening presence.[35] In my language they are about achieving outcomes "for" people without the extensive and time-consuming commitment to be "with" them. By contrast, Bonhoeffer had no plan when he returned to Germany. He had no plan when he renounced escape from prison. William Easterly, reflecting on years of failure in world development, insists, "The right plan is to have no plan."[36] He would be proud of Bonhoeffer.

In this sense, Bonhoeffer's most radical activist step was to become an educator. In setting up the seminary at Finkenwalde, Bonhoeffer trained students, as Alinsky and Cortès would have advised, to learn to do what they

32. Jeffrey Stout, *Blessed Are the Organized: Grassroots Democracy in America* (Princeton: Princeton University Press, 2010), 136. See also Saul D. Alinsky, *Rules for Radicals: A Practical Primer for Realistic Radicals* (New York: Random House, 1971).

33. 1. End poverty and hunger. 2. Universal education. 3. Gender equality. 4. Child health. 5. Maternal health. 6. Combat HIV/AIDS. 7. Environmental sustainability. 8. Global partnership. See http://www .un.org/millenniumgoals/.

34. The most articulate advocate of such approaches is James C. Scott. For his notion of *métis*, see his *Seeing Like a State: How Certain Schemes to Improve the Human Condition Have Failed* (New Haven: Yale University Press 1999).

35. William Easterly, *The White Man's Burden: Why the West's Efforts to Aid the Rest Have Done So Much Ill and So Little Good* (New York: Penguin, 2006), 3–32. I acknowledge this is a generous reading of Easterly. In Easterly's eyes, Searchers are still trying to "solve problems" and thus continue to embody a "working for" model: "Planners fail to search for what does work to help the poor. . . . Yet Searchers in aid are already finding things that help the poor" (12). The commitment to "being with" on Easterly's terms is valid to the extent that it leads to a more effective working for and/or working with. The goal is still to help the poor. The key point, for Easterly, is that one goes in with no *preconceived* plan.

36. Ibid., 5.

could do for themselves. In *Life Together*, Bonhoeffer's whole attention is upon the challenge, gift, imperative, and grace of learning and "being with" one another. In that sense, and in the light of my argument here, we can see *Life Together* as the book that sums up Bonhoeffer's theology as well as his own life. We can find life, so long as we do so, together. We have come away as a mini-seminary these forty-eight hours to be with one another and to attend to the being with humanity and with God that was the life of Bonhoeffer, the better to discern and to practice that same being with in relation to those whose lives today are like the lives of Germans in 1939—those where the incarnation is most focused and transparent.

Let the last word go to our brother Dietrich himself, from his dissertation *Sanctorum Communio*. Commenting on Gal. 6:2 ("Bear one another's burdens"), he says, "The possibility of this 'being-with-one-another' does not rest on human will. It exists only in the community of saints, and goes beyond the ordinary sense of 'being-with-one-another.' It belongs to the sociological structure of the church-community."[37]

The challenge Dietrich Bonhoeffer presents to us in the coming generations is to change the sociological structure of the church into one of "being with."

---

37. Dietrich Bonhoeffer, *Sanctorum Communio*, DBWE 1:180. In fact, Bonhoeffer writes about the inseparability of being-with and being-for, when he discusses "the social acts that constitute the community of love" (i.e., the church): "(1) Church-community and church member being structurally 'with-each-other' [*miteinander*] as appointed by God and (2) the members' active 'being-for-each-other' [*füreinander*] and the principle of vicarious representative action [*Stellvertretung*]. In reality, however, one is possible only through the other; they depend on each other" (ibid., 178). "This being-for-each-other must now be actualized through acts of love" (ibid., 184), i.e., through being and acting for one another. I don't regard this as a convincing argument for the complementarity of being with and being for—I believe it invites an expanded notion of being with, which is what I offer in this chapter.

Afterword

Busso von Alvensleben

It is an honor and great pleasure for me to speak to you here at Union Theological Seminary. Before I first came to Union—it was in the 1990s—I was made to understand that Union was sort of an equivalent to the Vatican and—though being very much a Protestant—I approached this place with a considerable amount of awe. Today, with great joy and undiminished respect, I have come as the local representative of the German state to greet all of you and to express our immense appreciation at the finalization of the Dietrich Bonhoeffer Works English Edition. It is good to see that the strong bonds that exist between German institutions and individuals and Union have proven so helpful in this great endeavor—let me only mention the Goethe-Institut and the sponsors of the Dietrich Bonhoeffer Chair and the Bonhoeffer Lectures here at Union.

Public Ethics was the subject of your conference, "Bonhoeffer for the coming generations." I could hardly think of a more timely theme. The crises we are going through in Europe, and not only there, put the fundamentals of our societies into question. Where are the moral authorities that could lead the way? Rome faces its own challenges. Does the Protestant world have a clear guideline? Bonhoeffer's works, no doubt, can help on our way to find answers. This again is a reason to warmly thank all those who participated in this opus magnum.

Bonhoeffer distinguished last from penultimate things. How to deal with them and where to draw the line is a broad subject and I would not want to spark off a discussion right now, especially speaking in front of luminaries in this field from all over the world. But, again, there is a dire need for spiritual leadership that is sometimes being hijacked by fundamentalists of various backgrounds. There is not only a chance, there is a duty to engage more strongly than ever in public affairs, not necessarily as a member of the clergy but as a citizen and, if so, as a Christian.

In the German House here in New York that houses the German Consulate General, the German Mission to the UN, and other German institutions, we are going to name our Auditorium after a former German Consul General to New York, Otto Carl Kiep, who was also killed as an opponent to the Nazi regime. You might ask, why so late, almost seventy years after his death? I think, today, perhaps even more than in years before, we are called upon to recall our individual responsibility for what is happening in our societies. Bonhoeffer's works are a most valuable guideline for those seeking to engage. In this sense I congratulate the International Bonhoeffer Society on its great achievement and wish the new English edition of Bonhoeffer's works the wide acclaim it should have.

Contributors

Busso von Alvensleben

Consul General of the Federal Republic of Germany, New York. 1977 Assessor jur., Faculty of Law, Free University Berlin. 1977 Deutsche Bank AG. 1978 Federal Foreign Office, Bonn. 1982 First Secretary, German Embassy Nairobi. 1985 Counselor, German Embassy Tel Aviv. 1987 Counselor, Permanent Mission of the Federal Republic of Germany to the UN, Geneva. 1990 Protocol Division, Federal Foreign Office. 1994 Private Secretary to the Federal President. 1994 Head of former Federal President von Weizsäcker's office. 1998 Deputy Chief of Protocol, Federal Foreign Office. 2000 Ambassador, Chief of Protocol. 2003 Ambassador to Sweden. 2006 Ambassador, Commissioner for Global Issues: Civilian Crisis Prevention, Human Rights, Humanitarian Aid and International Terrorism, Federal Foreign Office. 2009 Ambassador to Ireland. 2011 Consul General of the Federal Republic of Germany, New York.

Victoria J. Barnett

Staff Director of Church Relations at the U.S. Holocaust Memorial Museum, Washington, DC (USHMM). MDiv Union Theological Seminary, New York. PhD George Mason University. Author: *For the Soul of the People: Protestant Protest Against Hitler* (Oxford University Press, 1992) and *Bystanders: Conscience and Complicity during the Holocaust* (Greenwood Press, 1999). Editor and translator: *Dietrich Bonhoeffer: A Biography*, by Eberhard Bethge (Fortress, 2000) and *And the Witnesses Were Silent: The Confessing Church and the Jews*, by Wolfgang Gerlach (University of Nebraska, 2000). General Editor, Dietrich Bonhoeffer Works English Edition.

Doris L. Bergen

Chancellor Rose and Ray Wolfe Professor of Holocaust Studies, University of Toronto. PhD University of North Carolina, Chapel Hill. Member Academic USHMM Advisory Committee of the Center for Advanced Holocaust Studies (CAHS). Author: *Twisted Cross: The German Christian Movement in the Third Reich* (Chapel Hill: University of North Carolina, 1996) and *War and Genocide:*

A Concise History of the Holocaust (Lanham, MD: Rowman & Littlefield, 2003). Editor: *The Sword of the Lord: Military Chaplains from the First to the Twenty-First Centuries* (Notre Dame: University of Notre Dame, 2004), *The Holocaust: A New History* (Stroud: Tempus, 2008), *Lessons and Legacies VIII* (Evanston, IL: Northwestern University, 2008), and, with Rafał Witkowski and Miłosz Sosnowski, *Wojna i ludobójstwo: krótka historia Holokaustu* (Poznań: Wydawnictwo Poznańskie, 2011).

Carlos Ribeiro Caldas, Filho

PhD São Paulo Methodist University, Brazil. Main academic appointment: Assemblies of God Biblical Institute, Pindamonhangaba (Brazil). Author: *Fé e café* (Didaquê, 1999); *O ultimo missionário* (Mundo Cristiao, 2001); *Orlando Costas: sua contribuição na história da teologia latino-americana* (Vida: 2007); *Fundamentos da teologia da igreja* (Mundo Cristiao, 2007; *O Evangelho da Terra-média* (Mackenzie, 2012) and *Aragem do sagrado: Deus na literatura brasileira contemporânea* (Loyola, 2012). Current research: theology of Dietrich Bonhoeffer from perspective of Latin American theology.

Guy C. Carter

PhD Marquette University with doctoral dissertation on the so-called "Bethel Confession." Arthur J. Schmitt Fellow of Marquette University. Fellow, Institute for European History, Division for Western History of Religion, Mainz. Main teaching appointment: assistant professor of historical theology, Saint Peter's University, Jersey City, NJ. Conference Coordinator and Registrar, "Bonhoeffer for the Coming Generations" Conference on Bonhoeffer and Public Ethics, Union Theological Seminary, New York, November 2011. Scientific Secretary, 5th IBS Congress, Amsterdam. With René van Eyden, Hans-Dirk van Hoogstraten, and Jurjen Wiersma, co-editor of *Bonhoeffer's Ethics: Old Europe and New Frontiers. Papers of the 5th International Bonhoeffer Society Conference, Amsterdam, 1988* (Kampen: Kok Pharos, 1991). Past IBS International Corresponding Secretary and board member, IBS-ELS. Since 2008 active retirement including work in German interpreting and translation.

Keith Clements

PhD University of Bristol, England. British scholar and ecumenist; graduate of Cambridge and Oxford Universities; doctorate from Bristol University. Main teaching appointments: tutor, Bristol Baptist College, lecturer theology and religious studies, Bristol University. Secretary for International Affairs in the Council of Churches for Britain and Ireland. General Secretary of the Conference of European Churches, Geneva. Author: *Henry Lamb: The Artist and His Friends* (Intl. Specialized Book Service, 1986), *The Churches in Europe as Witnesses to Healing* (WCC, 2003), *Moot Papers: Faith, Freedom and Society 1938–1944* (T. & T. Clark, 2010), *The SPCK Introduction to Bonhoeffer* (SPCK, 2010). Current research: history of modern Christian life and thought, and relation between church and society from the vantage point of the life and thought of Dietrich Bonhoeffer. Editor DBWE 13, *London, 1933–1935.*

Lisa E. Dahill

Associate Professor of Worship and Christian Spirituality at Trinity Lutheran Seminary, Columbus, OH. She is author of *Reading from the Underside of Selfhood: Bonhoeffer and Spiritual Formation,* Princeton Theological Monograph Series (Wipf & Stock, 2009) and past chair of the Bonhoeffer: Theology and Social Analysis Group of the American Academy of Religion. In addition, she is translator of DBWE 16 (*Conspiracy and Imprisonment: 1940–1945,* Fortress Press, 2006) and part of the translation team for DBWE 8 (*Letters and Papers from Prison,* Fortress Press, 2010). She is a frequent teacher and presenter on Bonhoeffer's spirituality and is an ordained and rostered leader in the ELCA.

Michael DeJonge

Associate Professor of Religious Studies, University of South Florida. PhD Emory University. Fulbright scholar and doctoral research fellow, Berlin Program for Advanced German and European Studies, Freie Universität Berlin. Author: *Bonhoeffer's Theological Formation: Barth, Berlin, and Protestant Theology* (Oxford, 2012).

Gary Dorrien

Reinhold Niebuhr Professor of Social Ethics, Union Theological Seminary, Professor of Religion, Columbia University, Paul E. Raither Distinguished

Scholar, Trinity College. PhD Union Theological Seminary. Main teaching appointments: Parfet Distinguished Professor and Dean of Stetson Chapel, Kalamazoo College. Author: *Kantian Reason and Hegelian Spirit: The Idealistic Logic of Modern Theology* (Chichester, UK: Wiley-Blackwell, 2012) and *Obama in Question: A Progressive Perspective* (Lanham, MD: Rowman & Littlefield, 2012).

Robert P. Ericksen

Kurt Mayer Professor of Holocaust Studies, Pacific Lutheran University. PhD University of London. Member Church Relations Committee USHMM. Author: *Theologians under Hitler: Georg Kittel, Paul Althaus and Emanuel Hirsch* (Yale, 1985). *Complicity in the Holocaust: Churches and Universities in Nazi Germany* (Cambridge, 2012). Editor with Susanne Heschel, *Betrayal: German Churches and the Holocaust* (Fortress, 1999). Co-editor: *Kirchliche Zeitgeschichte.* Current research: Christian teachings about Jews; Göttingen University during the Nazi period.

Clifford J. Green

Executive Director, Dietrich Bonhoeffer Works English Edition. Professor of Theology Emeritus, Hartford Seminary, Connecticut. ThD (distinction) Union Theological Seminary, New York. Main teaching appointments: Wellesley College; Goucher College; Hartford Seminary. Author: *Bonhoeffer: A Theology of Sociality* (1975, 2nd ed. Eerdmans, 1999). Co-editor, DBW 6, *Ethik*, and DBW 9, *Jugend und Studium.* Co-editor DBWE 9, *The Young Bonhoeffer.* Editor, DBWE 1, *Sanctorum Communio*, DBWE 6, *Ethics*, DBWE 7, *Fiction from Tegel Prison*, and DBWE 10, *Barcelona, Berlin, New York: 1928-1931.*

John W. de Gruchy

Professor Emeritus, University of Cape Town and extraordinary professor, University of Stellenbosch. ThD Chicago Theological Seminary, PhD (social sciences) University of Chicago and University of South Africa. Main teaching appointment: Robert Selby Taylor Professor of Christian Studies, University of Cape Town. Director of Communications and Studies, South African Council of Churches. Head of Research Institute on Christianity in South Africa. Host-convenor, 7th International Bonhoeffer Congress, Cape Town 1996. Author: *Bonhoeffer and South Africa* (Eerdmans, 1984) and *Dietrich Bonhoeffer: Witness to*

Jesus Christ (Fortress, 1991). Editor DBWE 3, *Creation and Fall*, and DBWE 8, *Letters and Papers from Prison.*

Matthew Hockenos

Associate Professor and Chair, Department of History, Skidmore College. PhD New York University. Author, *A Church Divided: German Protestants Confront the Nazi Past* (2004) and articles on "The Church Struggle and the Confessing Church: An Introduction to Bonhoeffer's Context"; "Proselytizing Jews after the Holocaust: The German Protestant Church and Its *Judenmission,* 1945–1950." 2008–2009 Charles H. Revson Foundation Fellow of the Center for Advanced Holocaust Studies of the United States Holocaust Memorial Museum for research on "Converting the Jews: Antisemitism and the Berlin *Judenmission,* 1933-1950s."

Wolfgang Huber

Studied Protestant theology from 1960 to 1966 at the Universities of Heidelberg, Göttingen, and Tübingen. Served the church as minister (1966–68), later as deputy director of the Protestant Institute for Interdisciplinary Research (FEST) in Heidelberg (1968–80). Professor of Social Ethics, Marburg (1980–84), Systematic Theology, Heidelberg (1984–94). Bishop of the Evangelical Church in Berlin-Brandenburg from 1994 to 2009; chairperson, National Council of the Evangelical Church in Germany 2003–2009. Leader in the Kirchentag, and member of the Executive Council of the World Council of Churches. Member of the editorial board, Dietrich Bonhoeffer Werke (DBW), editor-in-chief from 1990. Author of popular and scholarly works, including issues of peace, conflict and violence, justice and human rights, bioethics and ecological issues, the nature and witness of the church, education, public values and policy.

Brigitte Kahl

Professor of New Testament at Union Seminary specializing in Pauline studies. A native of East Germany, she took her doctorate at Humboldt University, East Berlin, teaching there and at Paderborn University before joining the faculty at Union in 1998. Her first major publication in German was *The Gospel for the Poor and the Gospel for the Gentiles in Luke-Acts* (1986). Her *Galatians Re-Imagined: Reading with the Eyes of the Vanquished* (2010) was published by Fortress Press. Dr. Kahl was also a translator and editor of the German Protestant inclusive-language Bible, *Die Bibel in gerechter Sprache* (2006).

Reinhard Krauss

A native of Germany, studied at Tübingen and Bonn, PhD in theology, University of St. Andrews. A Presbyterian pastor in California, he also lectures at the Center for the Study of Religion at UCLA, and serves on the Board of the Academy for Judaic, Christian, and Islamic Studies at UCLA. His doctoral research on Karl Barth's concept of religion and its indebtedness to nineteenth-century liberal theology was published by Edwin Mellen in 1992. Member of the Dietrich Bonhoeffer Works Editorial Board and a translator of DBWE 1, *Sanctorum Communio*, DBWE 6, *Ethics*, and DBWE 8, *Letters and Papers from Prison*.

Hans Pfeifer

Theological studies at Heidelberg, Basel, Göttingen, and Princeton, where Paul Lehmann encouraged him to research Bonhoeffer's theological legacy. Doctoral dissertation: *Das Kirchenverständnis Dietrich Bonhoeffer, ein Beitrag zur theologischen Prinzipienlehre* ("Dietrich Bonhoeffer's Understanding of the Church: A Contribution to Theological Prolegomena"). Student chaplaincy University of Hamburg; service at Diaconal Institution Kaiserswerth. School pastor teaching religious education and later parish pastor in Freiburg im Breisgau. Co-founder, International Bonhoeffer Society; sometime secretary for the German Section. Editor, DBW 9, *Jugend und Studium*. Member DBW Editorial Board; Liaison between Editorial Boards DBW and DBWE. Co-editor, *Dietrich Bonhoeffer Yearbook*.

Larry Rasmussen

Reinhold Niebuhr Professor of Social Ethics Emeritus, Union Theological Seminary, New York City. Author: *Dietrich Bonhoeffer: Reality and Resistance* (Abingdon, 1972), *Dietrich Bonhoeffer: His Significance for North Americans* (Fortress, 1990), *Earth Community, Earth Ethics* (Maryknoll, NY: Orbis, 1996). Host-convenor, 6th International Bonhoeffer Society Congress, New York, 1992. Member, Editorial Board, Dietrich Bonhoeffer Works English Edition. Member, steering committee, Bonhoeffer Lectures in Public Ethics. Editor DBWE: 12, *Berlin: 1932-1933*.

Florian Schmitz

Postdoctoral assistant, Department of Protestant Theology, Johannes Gutenberg University, Mainz, under Professor Christiane Tietz. PhD Mainz. Current research: Habilitation research on "Discipleship" and the theology of the Church Struggle, on Bonhoeffer's theological development, and on the interpretation and understanding of Bonhoeffer's essay "The Church and the Jewish Question," especially on the phrase "to put a spoke in the wheel itself."

Christiane Tietz

Professor of Systematic Theology at the University of Zurich, Switzerland, President of the German Section of the International Bonhoeffer Society, Dr. theol., Dr. theol. habil., University of Tübingen. Visiting Teaching Scholar at Union Seminary, Fall 2004, Member in Residence, Center of Theological Inquiry, Princeton, 2007/08. Author: books, articles, and public addresses spanning various aspects of theological reflection and Christian life in Germany and the world today.

Samuel Wells

Rector, Church of Saint Martin in the Fields, London. Author: *Transforming Fate into Destiny* (Paternoster, 1998), *Improvisation* (Brazos, 2004), *God's Companions* (Blackwell, 2006), *Introducing Christian Ethics* (with Ben Quash, Wiley-Blackwell, 2010), and *Power and Passion: Six Characters in Search of Resurrection* (Zondervan, 2007); co-editor, with Stanley Hauerwas, *The Blackwell Companion to Christian Ethics* (2004; 2nd edition, 2011), *Be Not Afraid: Facing Fear with Faith* (Brazos, 2011), and, with Marcia A. Owen, *Living Without Enemies: Ministry in the Wake of Violence* (IVP, 2011).

Reggie Williams

Assistant Professor of Christian ethics, McCormick Theological Seminary, Chicago. PhD Fuller Theological Seminary, Pasadena, California. Current research: Dietrich Bonhoeffer within the global transformation of international identity on the unfavorable side of what W. E. B. Du Bois described as "The Color Line." Bonhoeffer's exposure to Harlem Renaissance literature and theology, while studying at Union Theological Seminary in New York,

1930–31, friendship and correspondence between Dietrich Bonhoeffer with his Union Seminary friend, Frank Fisher, during those years.

Kazuaki Yamasaki

Professor of Political Science in department of sociology, Shikoku-Gakuin University on the Island of Shikoku, Japan. Undergraduate and graduate study, City University of Osaka. Postgraduate study in Germany with Professors Ernst Feil (Munich), Karl Dietrich Bracher and Eberhard Bethge (Bonn), and Heinz-Eduard Tödt (Heidelberg). LLD University of Tohoku. Co-translator: *Brennpunkte in Kirche und Theologie Japans. Beiträge und Dokumente*, ed. Yoshiki Terazono and Heyo E. Hamer (Neukirchner, 1988). Author: chapter on Bonhoeffer reception in East Asia for *Dietrich Bonhoeffer Handbuch*, ed. Christiane Tietz, and lecture "Dietrich Bonhoeffer in Japan, Wahrnehmungen und Wirkungen" ("Dietrich Bonhoeffer in Japan, Perceptions and Effects") under the theme *For God's Sake for the World* at Berlin 2006, on the occasion of the 100th anniversary of Dietrich Bonhoeffer's birth.

Index